Books by Carlos Castaneda

Published by POCKET BOOKS/WASHINGTON SQUARE PRESS

CARLOS CASTANEDA

THE POWER OF SILENCE

Further Lessons of don Juan

POCKET BOOKS

New York   London   Toronto   Sydney   Tokyo

POCKET BOOKS, a division of Simon & Schuster Inc.
1230 Avenue of the Americas, New York, NY 10020

ISBN: 0-671-67323-8

First Pocket Books printing October 1988

10 9 8 7 6 5 4 3 2

POCKET and colophon are trademarks of
Simon & Schuster Inc.

Cover design and illustration by Bob Giusti

Printed in the U.S.A.

Contents

CONTENTS

Foreword

My books are a true account of a teaching method that don Juan Matus, a Mexican Indian sorcerer, used in order to help me understand the sorcerers' world. In this sense, my books are the account of an on-going process which becomes more clear to me as time goes by.

It takes years of training to teach us to deal intelligently with the world of everyday life. Our schooling—whether in plain reasoning or formal topics—is rigorous, because the knowledge we are trying to impart is very complex. The same criteria apply to the sorcerers' world: their schooling, which relies on oral instruction and the manipulation of awareness, although different from ours, is just as rigorous, because their knowledge is as, or perhaps *more,* complex.

Introduction

At various times don Juan attempted to name his knowledge for my benefit. He felt that the most appropriate name was *nagualism,* but that the term was too obscure. Calling it simply "knowledge" made it too vague, and to call it "witchcraft" was debasing. "The mastery of *intent*" was too abstract, and "the search for total freedom" too long and metaphorical. Finally, because he was unable to find a more appropriate name, he called it "sorcery," although he admitted it was not really accurate.

Over the years, he had given me different definitions of sorcery, but he had always maintained that definitions change as knowledge increases. Toward the end of my apprenticeship, I felt I was in a position to appreciate a clearer definition, so I asked him once more.

"From where the average man stands," don Juan said, "sorcery is nonsense or an ominous mystery beyond his reach. And he is right—not because this is an absolute fact, but because the average man lacks the energy to deal with sorcery.''

He stopped for a moment before he continued. ''Human beings are born with a finite amount of energy,'' don Juan said, ''an energy that is systematically deployed, beginning at the moment of birth, in order that it may be used most advantageously by the modality of the time.''

''What do you mean by the modality of the time?'' I asked.

''The modality of the time is the precise bundle of energy fields being perceived,'' he answered. ''I believe man's perception has changed through the ages. The actual time decides the mode; the time decides which precise bundle of energy fields, out of an incalculable number, are to be used. And handling the modality of the time—those few, selected energy fields—takes all our available energy, leaving us nothing that would help us use any of the other energy fields.''

He urged me with a subtle movement of his eyebrows to consider all this.

''This is what I mean when I say that the average man lacks the energy needed to deal with sorcery,'' he went on. ''If he uses only the energy he has, he can't perceive the worlds sorcerers do. To perceive them, sorcerers need to use a cluster of energy fields not ordinarily used. Naturally, if the average man is to perceive those worlds and understand sorcerers' perception he must use the same cluster they have used. And this is just not possible, because all his energy is already deployed.''

He paused as if searching for the appropriate words to make his point.

''Think of it this way,'' he proceeded. ''It isn't that as time goes by you're learning sorcery; rather, what you're learning is to save energy. And this energy will enable you to handle some of the energy fields which are inaccessible to you now. And that is sorcery: the ability to use energy fields that are not employed in perceiving the ordinary world we know. Sorcery is a state of awareness. Sorcery is the ability to perceive something which ordinary perception cannot.

"Everything I've put you through," don Juan went on, "each of the things I've shown you was only a device to convince you that there's more to us than meets the eye. We don't need anyone to teach us sorcery, because there is really nothing to learn. What we need is a teacher to convince us that there is incalculable power at our fingertips. What a strange paradox! Every warrior on the path of knowledge thinks, at one time or another, that he's learning sorcery, but all he's doing is allowing himself to be convinced of the power hidden in his being, and that he can reach it."

"Is that what you're doing, don Juan—convincing me?"

"Exactly. I'm trying to convince you that you can reach that power. I went through the same thing. And I was as hard to convince as you are."

"Once we have reached it, what exactly do we do with it, don Juan?"

"Nothing. Once we have reached it, it will, by itself, make use of energy fields which are available to us but inaccessible. And that, as I have said, is sorcery. We begin then to *see*—that is, to perceive—something else; not as imagination, but as real and concrete. And then we begin to know without having to use words. And what any of us does with that increased perception, with that silent knowledge, depends on our own temperament."

On another occasion, he gave me another kind of explanation. We were discussing an unrelated topic when he abruptly changed the subject and began to tell me a joke. He laughed and, very gently, patted my back between the shoulder blades, as if he were shy and it was too forward of him to touch me. He chuckled at my nervous reaction.

"You're skittish," he said teasingly, and slapped my back with greater force.

My ears buzzed. For an instant I lost my breath. It felt as though he had hurt my lungs. Every breath brought me great discomfort. Yet, after I had coughed and choked a few times, my nasal passages opened and I found myself taking deep, soothing breaths. I had such a feeling of well-being that I was not even annoyed at him for his blow, which had been hard as well as unexpected.

Then don Juan began a most remarkable explanation. Clearly and concisely, he gave me a different and more precise definition of sorcery.

I had entered into a wondrous state of awareness! I had such clarity of mind that I was able to comprehend and assimilate everything don Juan was saying. He said that in the universe there is an unmeasurable, indescribable force which sorcerers call *intent*, and that absolutely everything that exists in the entire cosmos is attached to *intent* by a connecting link. Sorcerers, or warriors, as he called them, were concerned with discussing, understanding, and employing that connecting link. They were especially concerned with cleaning it of the numbing effects brought about by the ordinary concerns of their everyday lives. Sorcery at this level could be defined as the procedure of cleaning one's connecting link to *intent*. Don Juan stressed that this "cleaning procedure" was extremely difficult to understand, or to learn to perform. Sorcerers, therefore, divided their instruction into two categories. One was instruction for the everyday-life state of awareness, in which the cleaning process was presented in a disguised fashion. The other was instruction for the states of heightened awareness, such as the one I was presently experiencing, in which sorcerers obtained knowledge directly from *intent,* without the distracting intervention of spoken language.

Don Juan explained that by using heightened awareness over thousands of years of painful struggle, sorcerers had gained specific insights into *intent;* and that they had passed these nuggets of direct knowledge on from generation to generation to the present. He said that the task of sorcery is to take this seemingly incomprehensible knowledge and make it understandable by the standards of awareness of everyday life.

Then he explained the role of the guide in the lives of sorcerers. He said that a guide is called "the nagual," and that the nagual is a man or a woman with extraordinary energy, a teacher who has sobriety, endurance, stability; someone seers *see* as a luminous sphere having four compartments, as if four luminous balls have been compressed together. Because of their extraordinary energy, naguals are intermediaries. Their energy allows them to channel peace, harmony, laughter, and knowledge directly from the source, from *intent,* and transmit them to their companions. Naguals are responsible for supplying what sorcerers call "the minimal chance": the awareness of one's connection with *intent.*

I told him that my mind was grasping everything he was telling me, that the only part of his explanation still unclear to me was why two sets of teachings were needed. I could understand everything he was saying about his world easily, and yet he had described the process of understanding as very difficult.

"You will need a lifetime to remember the insights you've had today," he said, "because most of them were silent knowledge. A few moments from now you will have forgotten them. That's one of the unfathomable mysteries of awareness."

Don Juan then made me shift levels of consciousness by striking me on my left side, at the edge of my ribcage.

Instantly I lost my extraordinary clarity of mind and could not remember having ever had it. . . .

Don Juan himself set me the task of writing about the premises of sorcery. Once, very casually in the early stages of my apprenticeship, he suggested that I write a book in order to make use of the notes I had always taken. I had accumulated reams of notes and never considered what to do with them.

I argued that the suggestion was absurd because I was not a writer.

"Of course, you're not a writer," he said, "so you will have to use sorcery. First, you must visualize your experiences as if you were reliving them, and then you must *see* the text in your *dreaming*. For you, writing should not be a literary exercise, but rather an exercise in sorcery."

I have written in that manner about the premises of sorcery just as don Juan explained them to me, within the context of his teaching.

In his teaching scheme, which was developed by sorcerers of ancient times, there were two categories of instruction. One was called "teachings for the right side," carried out in the ordinary state of awareness. The other was called "teachings for the left side," put into practice solely in states of heightened awareness.

These two categories allowed teachers to school

their apprentices toward three areas of expertise: the mastery of *awareness*, the art of *stalking*, and the mastery of *intent*.

These three areas of expertise are the three riddles sorcerers encounter in their search for knowledge.

The mastery of awareness is the riddle of the mind; the perplexity sorcerers experience when they recognize the astounding mystery and scope of awareness and perception.

The art of *stalking* is the riddle of the heart; the puzzlement sorcerers feel upon becoming aware of two things: first that the world appears to us to be unalterably objective and factual, because of peculiarities of our awareness and perception; second, that if different peculiarities of perception come into play, the very things about the world that seem so unalterably objective and factual change.

The mastery of *intent* is the riddle of the spirit, or the paradox of the abstract—sorcerers' thoughts and actions projected beyond our human condition.

Don Juan's instruction on the art of *stalking* and the mastery of *intent* depended upon his instruction on the mastery of awareness, which was the cornerstone of his teachings, and which consist of the following basic premises:

1. The universe is an infinite agglomeration of energy fields, resembling threads of light.

2. These energy fields, called the Eagle's emanations, radiate from a source of inconceivable proportions metaphorically called the Eagle.

3. Human beings are also composed of an incalculable number of the same threadlike energy fields. These Eagle's emanations form an encased agglomeration that manifests itself as a ball of light the size of the person's body with the arms extended laterally, like a giant luminous egg.

4. Only a very small group of the energy fields inside this luminous ball are lit up by a point of intense brilliance located on the ball's surface.

5. Perception occurs when the energy fields in that small group immediately surrounding the point of brilliance extend their light to illuminate identical energy fields outside the ball. Since the only energy fields perceivable are those lit by the point of brilliance, that point is named "the point where perception is assembled" or simply "the assemblage point."

6. The assemblage point can be moved from its usual position on the surface of the luminous ball to another position on the surface, or into the interior. Since the brilliance of the assemblage point can light up whatever energy field it comes in contact with, when it moves to a new position it immediately brightens up new energy fields, making them perceivable. This perception is known as *seeing*.

7. When the assemblage point shifts, it makes possible the perception of an entirely different world—as objective and factual as the one we normally perceive. Sorcerers go into that other world to get energy, power, solutions to general and particular problems, or to face the unimaginable.

8. *Intent* is the pervasive force that causes us to perceive. We do not become aware because we perceive; rather, we perceive as a result of the pressure and intrusion of *intent*.

9. The aim of sorcerers is to reach a state of total awareness in order to experience all the possibilities of perception available to man. This state of awareness even implies an alternative way of dying.

A level of practical knowledge was included as part of teaching the mastery of awareness. On that practical level don Juan taught the procedures necessary to move the assemblage point. The two great systems devised by the sorcerer seers of ancient times to accomplish this were: *dreaming,* the control and utilization of dreams; and *stalking,* the control of behavior.

Moving one's assemblage point was an essential maneuver that every sorcerer had to learn. Some of them, the naguals, also learned to perform it for others. They were able to dislodge the assemblage point from its customary position by delivering a hard slap directly to the assemblage point. This blow, which was experienced as a smack on the right shoulder blade—although the body was never touched—resulted in a state of heightened awareness.

In compliance with his tradition, it was exclusively in these states of heightened awareness that don Juan carried out the most important and dramatic part of his teachings: the instructions for the left side. Because of the extraordinary quality of these states, don Juan demanded that I not discuss them with others until we had concluded everything in the sorcerers' teaching scheme. That demand was not difficult for me to accept. In those unique states of awareness my capabilities for understanding the instruction were unbelievably enhanced, but at the same time my capabilities for describing or even remembering it were impaired. I could function in those states with proficiency and assuredness, but I could not recollect anything about them once I returned to my normal consciousness.

It took me years to be able to make the crucial conversion of my enhanced awareness into plain memory. My reason and common sense delayed this moment because they were colliding head-on with the preposterous, unthinkable reality of heightened awareness and direct knowledge. For years the resulting cognitive disarrangement forced me to avoid the issue by not thinking about it.

Whatever I have written about my sorcery apprenticeship, up to now, has been a recounting of how don Juan taught me the mastery of awareness. I have not yet described the art of *stalking* or the mastery of *intent*.

Don Juan taught me their principles and applications with the help of two of his companions: a sorcerer named Vicente Medrano and another named Silvio Manuel, but whatever I learned from them still remains clouded in what don Juan called the intricacies of heightened awareness. Until now it has been impossible for me to write or even to think coherently about the art of *stalking* and the mastery of *intent*. My mistake has been to regard them as subjects for normal memory and recollection. They are, but at the same time they are not. In order to resolve this contradiction, I have not pursued the subjects directly —a virtual impossibility—but have dealt with them indirectly through the concluding topic of don Juan's instruction: the stories of the sorcerers of the past.

He recounted these stories to make evident what he called the abstract cores of his lessons. But I was incapable of grasping the nature of the abstract cores despite his comprehensive explanations, which, I know now, were intended more to open my mind than to explain anything in a rational manner. His way of talking made me believe for many years that his explanations of the abstract cores were like academic dissertations; and all I was able to do, under these circumstances, was to take his explanations as given. They became part of my tacit acceptance of his teachings, but without the thorough assessment on my part that was essential to understanding them.

Don Juan presented three sets of six abstract cores

each, arranged in an increasing level of complexity. I have dealt here with the first set, which is composed of the following: the manifestations of the spirit, the knock of the spirit, the trickery of the spirit, the descent of the spirit, the requirements of *intent,* and handling *intent.*

THE POWER
OF SILENCE

1

The Manifestations of the Spirit

THE FIRST ABSTRACT CORE

Don Juan, whenever it was pertinent, used to tell me brief stories about the sorcerers of his lineage, especially his teacher, the nagual Julian. They were not really stories, but rather descriptions of the way those sorcerers behaved and of aspects of their personalities. These accounts were each designed to shed light on a specific topic in my apprenticeship.

I had heard the same stories from the other fifteen members of don Juan's group of sorcerers, but none of these accounts had been able to give me a clear picture of the people they described. Since I had no way of persuading don Juan to give me more details about those sorcerers, I had resigned myself to the idea of never knowing about them in any depth.

One afternoon, in the mountains of southern Mexico, don Juan, after having explained to me more about the intricacies of the mastery of awareness, made a statement that completely baffled me.

"I think it's time for us to talk about the sorcerers of our past," he said.

Don Juan explained that it was necessary that I begin drawing conclusions based on a systematic view of the past, conclusions about both the world of daily affairs and the sorcerers' world.

"Sorcerers are vitally concerned with their past," he said. "But I don't mean their personal past. For sorcerers their past is what other sorcerers in bygone days have done. And what we are now going to do is examine that past.

"The average man also examines the past. But it's mostly his personal past he examines, and he does so for personal reasons. Sorcerers do quite the opposite; they consult their past in order to obtain a point of reference."

"But isn't that what everyone does? Look at the past to get a point of reference?"

"No!" he answered emphatically. "The average man measures himself against the past, whether his personal past or the past knowledge of his time, in order to find justifications for his present or future behavior, or to establish a model for himself. Only sorcerers genuinely seek a point of reference in their past."

"Perhaps, don Juan, things would be clear to me if you tell me what a point of reference for a sorcerer is."

"For sorcerers, establishing a point of reference means getting a chance to examine *intent*," he replied. "Which is exactly the aim of this final topic of instruction. And nothing can give sorcerers a better view of *intent* than examining stories of other sorcerers battling to understand the same force."

He explained that as they examined their past, the sorcerers of his lineage took careful notice of the basic abstract order of their knowledge.

"In sorcery there are twenty-one abstract cores,"

don Juan went on. "And then, based on those abstract cores, there are scores of sorcery stories about the naguals of our lineage battling to understand the spirit. It's time to tell you the abstract cores and the sorcery stories."

I waited for don Juan to begin telling me the stories, but he changed the subject and went back to explaining awareness.

"Wait a minute," I protested. "What about the sorcery stories? Aren't you going to tell them to me?"

"Of course I am," he said. "But they are not stories that one can tell as if they were tales. You've got to think your way through them and then rethink them—relive them, so to speak."

There was a long silence. I became very cautious and was afraid that if I persisted in asking him again to tell me the stories, I could be committing myself to something I might later regret. But my curiosity was greater than my good sense.

"Well, let's get on with them," I croaked.

Don Juan, obviously catching the gist of my thoughts, smiled maliciously. He stood and signaled me to follow. We had been sitting on some dry rocks at the bottom of a gully. It was midafternoon. The sky was dark and cloudy. Low, almost-black rain clouds hovered above the peaks to the east. In comparison, the high clouds made the sky seem clear to the south. Earlier it had rained heavily, but then the rain seemed to have retreated to a hiding place, leaving behind only a threat.

I should have been chilled to the bone, for it was very cold. But I was warm. As I clutched a rock don Juan had given me to hold, I realized that this sensation of being warm in nearly freezing weather was familiar to me, yet it amazed me each time. Whenever I seemed about to freeze, don Juan would give me a branch to hold, or a stone, or he would put a bunch of leaves under my shirt, on the tip of my sternum, and that would be sufficient to raise my body temperature.

I had tried unsuccessfully to recreate, by myself, the effect of his ministrations. He told me it was not the ministrations but his inner silence that kept me warm, and the branches or stones or leaves were merely devices to trap my attention and maintain it in focus.

Moving quickly, we climbed the steep west side of a mountain until we reached a rock ledge at the very top. We were in the foothills of a higher range of mountains. From the rock ledge I could see that fog had begun to move onto the south end of the valley floor below us. Low, wispy clouds seemed to be closing in on us, too, sliding down from the black-green, high mountain peaks to the west. After the rain, under the dark cloudy sky the valley and the mountains to the east and south appeared covered in a mantle of black-green silence.

"This is the ideal place to have a talk," don Juan said, sitting on the rock floor of a concealed shallow cave.

The cave was perfect for the two of us to sit side by side. Our heads were nearly touching the roof and our backs fitted snugly against the curved surface of the rock wall. It was as if the cave had been carved deliberately to accommodate two persons of our size.

I noticed another strange feature of the cave: when I stood on the ledge, I could see the entire valley and the mountain ranges to the east and south, but when I sat down, I was boxed in by the rocks. Yet the ledge was at the level of the cave floor, and flat.

I was about to point this strange effect out to don Juan, but he anticipated me.

"This cave is man-made," he said. "The ledge is slanted but the eye doesn't register the incline."

"Who made this cave, don Juan?"

"The ancient sorcerers. Perhaps thousands of years ago. And one of the peculiarities of this cave is that animals and insects and even people stay away from it. The ancient sorcerers seem to have infused it with an ominous charge that makes every living thing feel ill at ease."

But strangely I felt irrationally secure and happy there. A sensation of physical contentment made my entire body tingle. I actually felt the most agreeable, the most delectable, sensation in my stomach. It was as if my nerves were being tickled.

"I don't feel ill at ease," I commented.

"Neither do I," he said. "Which only means that you and I aren't that far temperamentally from those old sorcerers of the past; something which worries me no end."

I was afraid to pursue that subject any further, so I waited for him to talk.

"The first sorcery story I am going to tell you is called 'The Manifestations of the Spirit,' " don Juan began, "but don't let the title mystify you. The manifestations of the spirit is only the first abstract core around which the first sorcery story is built.

"That first abstract core is a story in itself," he went on. "The story says that once upon a time there was a man, an average man without any special attributes. He was, like everyone else, a conduit for the spirit. And by virtue of that, like everyone else, he was part of the spirit, part of the abstract. But he didn't know it. The world kept him so busy that he had neither the time nor the inclination really to examine the matter.

"The spirit tried, uselessly, to reveal their connection. Using an inner voice, the spirit disclosed its secrets, but the man was incapable of understanding the revelations. Naturally, he heard the inner voice, but he believed it to be his own feelings he was feeling and his own thoughts he was thinking.

"The spirit, in order to shake him out of his slumber, gave him three signs, three successive manifestations. The spirit physically crossed the man's path in the most obvious manner. But the man was oblivious to anything but his self-concern."

Don Juan stopped and looked at me as he did whenever he was waiting for my comments and questions. I had nothing to say. I did not understand the point he was trying to make.

"I've just told you the first abstract core," he continued. "The only other thing I could add is that because of the man's absolute unwillingness to understand, the spirit was forced to use trickery. And trickery became the essence of the sorcerers' path. But that is another story."

Don Juan explained that sorcerers understood this abstract core to be a blueprint for events, or a recurrent pattern that appeared every time *intent* was giving an indication of something meaningful. Abstract cores, then, were blueprints of complete chains of events.

He assured me that by means beyond comprehension, every detail of every abstract core reoccurred to every apprentice nagual. He further assured me that he had helped *intent* to involve me in all the abstract cores of sorcery in the same manner that his benefactor, the nagual Julian and all the naguals before him, had involved their apprentices. The process by which each apprentice nagual encountered the abstract cores created a series of accounts woven around those abstract cores incorporating the particular details of each apprentice's personality and circumstances.

He said, for example, that I had my own story about the manifestations of the spirit, he had his, his benefactor had his own, so had the nagual that preceded him, and so on, and so forth.

"What is my story about the manifestations of the spirit?" I asked, somewhat mystified.

"If any warrior is aware of his stories it's you," he replied. "After all, you've been writing about them for years. But you didn't notice the abstract cores because you are a practical man. You do everything only for the purpose of enhancing your practicality. Although you handled your stories to exhaustion you had no idea that there was an abstract core in them. Everything I've done appears to you, therefore, as an often-whimsical practical activity: teaching sorcery to a reluctant and, most of the time, stupid, apprentice. As long as you see it in those terms, the abstract cores will elude you."

"You must forgive me, don Juan," I said, "but your statements are very confusing. What are you saying?"

"I'm trying to introduce the sorcery stories as a subject," he replied. "I've never talked to you specifically about this topic because traditionally it's left hidden. It is the spirit's last artifice. It is said that when the apprentice understands the abstract cores it's like the placing of the stone that caps and seals a pyramid."

It was getting dark and it looked as though it was about to rain again. I worried that if the wind blew from east to west while it was raining, we were going to get soaked in that cave. I was sure don Juan was aware of that, but he seemed to ignore it.

"It won't rain again until tomorrow morning," he said.

Hearing my inner thoughts being answered made me jump involuntarily and hit the top of my head on the cave roof. It was a thud that sounded worse than it felt.

Don Juan held his sides laughing. After a while my head really began to hurt and I had to massage it.

"Your company is as enjoyable to me as mine must

7

have been to my benefactor," he said and began to laugh again.

We were quiet for a few minutes. The silence around me was ominous. I fancied that I could hear the rustling of the low clouds as they descended on us from the higher mountains. Then I realized that what I was hearing was the soft wind. From my position in the shallow cave, it sounded like the whispering of human voices.

"I had the incredible good luck to be taught by two naguals," don Juan said and broke the mesmeric grip the wind had on me at that moment. "One was, of course, my benefactor, the nagual Julian, and the other was his benefactor, the nagual Elías. My case was unique."

"Why was your case unique?" I asked.

"Because for generations naguals have gathered their apprentices years after their own teachers have left the world," he explained. "Except my benefactor. I became the nagual Julian's apprentice eight years before his benefactor left the world. I had eight years' grace. It was the luckiest thing that could have happened to me, for I had the opportunity to be taught by two opposite temperaments. It was like being reared by a powerful father and an even more powerful grandfather who don't see eye to eye. In such a contest, the grandfather always wins. So I'm properly the product of the nagual Elías's teachings. I was closer to him not only in temperament but also in looks. I'd say that I owe him my fine tuning. However, the bulk of the work that went into turning me from a miserable being into an impeccable warrior I owe to my benefactor, the nagual Julian."

"What was the nagual Julian like physically?" I asked.

"Do you know that to this day it's hard for me to visualize him?" don Juan said. "I know that sounds absurd, but depending on his needs or the circumstances, he could be either young or old, handsome or homely, effete and weak or strong and virile, fat or slender, of medium height or extremely short.''

"Do you mean he was an actor acting out different roles with the aid of props?"

"No, there were no props involved and he was not merely an actor. He was, of course, a great actor in his own right, but that is different. The point is that he was capable of transforming himself and becoming all those diametrically opposed persons. Being a great actor enabled him to portray all the minute peculiarities of behavior that made each specific being real. Let us say that he was at ease in every change of being. As you are at ease in every change of clothes.''

Eagerly, I asked don Juan to tell me more about his benefactor's transformations. He said that someone taught him how to elicit those transformations, but that to explain any further would force him to overlap into different stories.

"What did the nagual Julian look like when he wasn't transforming himself?'' I asked.

"Let's say that before he became a nagual he was very slim and muscular,'' don Juan said. "His hair was black, thick, and wavy. He had a long, fine nose, strong big white teeth, an oval face, strong jaw, and shiny dark-brown eyes. He was about five feet eight inches tall. He was not Indian or even a brown Mexican, but he was not Anglo white either. In fact, his complexion seemed to be like no one else's, especially in his later years when his ever-changing complexion shifted constantly from dark to very light and back again to dark. When I first met him he was a light-brown old man, then as time went by, he became a light-skinned young man, perhaps only a few years older than me. I was twenty at that time.

"But if the changes of his outer appearance were

astonishing," don Juan went on, "the changes of mood and behavior that accompanied each transformation were even more astonishing. For example, when he was a fat young man, he was jolly and sensual. When he was a skinny old man, he was petty and vindictive. When he was a fat old man, he was the greatest imbecile there was."

"Was he ever himself?" I asked.

"Not the way I am myself," he replied. "Since I'm not interested in transformation I am always the same. But he was not like me at all."

Don Juan looked at me as if he were assessing my inner strength. He smiled, shook his head from side to side and broke into a belly laugh.

"What's so funny, don Juan?" I asked.

"The fact is that you're still too prudish and stiff to appreciate fully the nature of my benefactor's transformations and their total scope," he said. "I only hope that when I tell you about them you don't become morbidly obsessed."

For some reason I suddenly became quite uncomfortable and had to change the subject.

"Why are the naguals called 'benefactors' and not simply teachers?" I asked nervously.

"Calling a nagual a benefactor is a gesture his apprentices make," don Juan said. "A nagual creates an overwhelming feeling of gratitude in his disciples. After all, a nagual molds them and guides them through unimaginable areas."

I remarked that to teach was in my opinion the greatest, most altruistic act anyone could perform for another.

"For you, teaching is talking about patterns," he said. "For a sorcerer, to teach is what a nagual does for his apprentices. For them he taps the prevailing force in the universe: *intent*—the force that changes and reorders things or keeps them as they are. The nagual formulates, then guides the consequences that that force can have on his disciples. Without the nagual's molding *intent* there would be no awe, no wonder for them. And his apprentices, instead of embarking on a magical journey of discovery, would only be learning a trade: healer, sorcerer, diviner, charlatan, or whatever."

"Can you explain *intent* to me?" I asked.

"The only way to know *intent*," he replied, "is to know it directly through a living connection that exists between *intent* and all sentient beings. Sorcerers call *intent* the indescribable, the spirit, the abstract, the nagual. I would prefer to call it nagual, but it overlaps with the name for the leader, the benefactor, who is also called nagual, so I have opted for calling it the spirit, *intent*, the abstract."

Don Juan stopped abruptly and recommended that I keep quiet and think about what he had told me. By then it was very dark. The silence was so profound that instead of lulling me into a restful state, it agitated me. I could not maintain order in my thoughts. I tried to focus my attention on the story he had told me, but instead I thought of everything else, until finally I fell asleep.

THE IMPECCABILITY OF THE NAGUAL ELIAS

I had no way of telling how long I slept in that cave. Don Juan's voice startled me and I awoke. He was saying that the first sorcery story concerning the manifestations of the spirit was an account of the relationship between *intent* and the nagual. It was the story of how the spirit set up a lure for the nagual, a prospective disciple, and of how the nagual had to evaluate the lure before making his decision either to accept or reject it.

It was very dark in the cave, and the small space was confining. Ordinarily an area of that size would have made me claustrophobic, but the cave kept soothing me, dispelling my feelings of annoyance. Also, something in the configuration of the cave absorbed the echoes of don Juan's words.

Don Juan explained that every act performed by sorcerers, especially by the naguals, was either performed as a way to strengthen their link with *intent* or as a response triggered by the link itself. Sorcerers, and specifically the naguals, therefore had to be actively and permanently on the lookout for manifestations of the spirit. Such manifestations were called gestures of the spirit or, more simply, indications or omens.

He repeated a story he had already told me; the story of how he had met his benefactor, the nagual Julian.

Don Juan had been cajoled by two crooked men to take a job on an isolated hacienda. One of the men, the foreman of the hacienda, simply took possession of don Juan and in effect made him a slave.

Desperate and with no other course of action, don Juan escaped. The violent foreman chased him and caught him on a country road where he shot don Juan in the chest and left him for dead.

Don Juan was lying unconscious in the road, bleeding to death, when the nagual Julian came along. Using his healer's knowledge, he stopped the bleeding, took don Juan, who was still unconscious, home and cured him.

The indications the spirit gave the nagual Julian about don Juan were, first, a small cyclone that lifted a cone of dust on the road a couple of yards from where he lay. The second omen was the thought which had crossed the nagual Julian's mind an instant before he had heard the report of the gun a few yards away: that it was time to have an apprentice nagual. Moments later, the spirit gave him the third omen, when he ran to take cover and instead collided with the gunman, putting him to flight, perhaps preventing him from shooting don Juan a second time. A collision with someone was the type of blunder which no sorcerer, much less a nagual, should ever make.

The nagual Julian immediately evaluated the opportunity. When he *saw* don Juan he understood the reason for the spirit's manifestation: here was a double man, a perfect candidate to be his apprentice nagual.

This brought up a nagging rational concern for me. I wanted to know if sorcerers could interpret an omen erroneously. Don Juan replied that although my question sounded perfectly legitimate, it was inapplicable, like the majority of my questions, because I asked them based on my experiences in the world of everyday life. Thus they were always about tested procedures, steps to be followed, and rules of meticulousness, but had nothing to do with the premises of sorcery. He pointed out that the flaw in my reasoning was that I always failed to include my experiences in the sorcerers' world.

I argued that very few of my experiences in the sorcerers' world had continuity, and therefore I could not make use of those experiences in my present day-to-day life. Very few times, and only when I was in states of profound heightened awareness, had I remembered everything. At the level of heightened awareness I usually reached, the only experience that had continuity between past and present was that of knowing him.

He responded cuttingly that I was perfectly capable of engaging in sorcerers' reasonings because I had experienced the sorcery premises in my normal state of awareness. In a more mellow tone he added that heightened awareness did not reveal everything until the whole edifice of sorcery knowledge was completed.

Then he answered my question about whether or not sorcerers could misinterpret omens. He explained that when a sorcerer interpreted an omen he knew its exact meaning without having any notion of how he knew it. This was one of the bewildering effects of the connecting link with *intent*. Sorcerers had a sense of knowing things directly. How sure they were depended on the strength and clarity of their connecting link.

He said that the feeling everyone knows as "intuition" is the activation of our link with *intent*. And since sorcerers deliberately pursue the understanding and strengthening of that link, it could be said that they intuit everything unerringly and accurately. Reading omens is commonplace for sorcerers—mistakes happen only when personal feelings intervene and cloud the sorcerers' connecting link with *intent*. Otherwise their direct knowledge is totally accurate and functional.

We remained quiet for a while.

All of a sudden he said, "I am going to tell you a story about the nagual Elías and the manifestation of the spirit. The spirit manifests itself to a sorcerer, especially to a nagual, at every turn. However, this is not the entire truth. The entire truth is that the spirit reveals itself to everyone with the same intensity and consistency, but only sorcerers, and naguals in particular, are attuned to such revelations."

Don Juan began his story. He said that the nagual Elías had been riding his horse to the city one day, taking him through a shortcut by some cornfields when suddenly his horse shied, frightened by the low, fast sweep of a falcon that missed the nagual's straw hat by only a few inches. The nagual immediately dismounted and began to look around. He saw a strange young man among the tall, dry cornstalks. The man was dressed in an expensive dark suit and appeared alien there. The nagual Elías was used to the sight of peasants or landowners in the fields, but he had never seen an elegantly dressed city man moving through the fields with apparent disregard for his expensive shoes and clothes.

The nagual tethered his horse and walked toward the young man. He recognized the flight of the falcon, as well as the man's apparel, as obvious manifestations of the spirit which he could not disregard. He got very close to the young man and saw what was going on. The man was chasing a peasant woman who was running a few yards ahead of him, dodging and laughing with him.

The contradiction was quite apparent to the nagual. The two people cavorting in the cornfield did not belong together. The nagual thought that the man must be the landowner's son and the woman a servant in the house. He felt embarrassed to be observing them and was about to turn and leave when the falcon again swept over the cornfield and this time brushed the young man's head. The falcon alarmed the couple and they stopped and looked up, trying to anticipate another sweep. The nagual noticed that the man was thin and handsome, and had haunting, restless eyes.

Then the couple became bored watching for the falcon, and returned to their play. The man caught the woman, embraced her and gently laid her on the ground. But instead of trying to make love to her, as

15

the nagual assumed he would do next, he removed his own clothes and paraded naked in front of the woman.

She did not shyly close her eyes or scream with embarrassment or fright. She giggled, mesmerized by the prancing naked man, who moved around her like a satyr, making lewd gestures and laughing. Finally, apparently overpowered by the sight, she uttered a wild cry, rose, and threw herself into the young man's arms.

Don Juan said that the nagual Elías confessed to him that the indications of the spirit on that occasion had been most baffling. It was clearly evident that the man was insane. Otherwise, knowing how protective peasants were of their women, he would not have considered seducing a young peasant woman in broad daylight a few yards from the road—and naked to boot.

Don Juan broke into a laugh and told me that in those days to take off one's clothes and engage in a sexual act in broad daylight in such a place meant one had to be either insane or blessed by the spirit. He added that what the man had done might not seem remarkable nowadays. But then, nearly a hundred years ago, people were infinitely more inhibited.

All of this convinced the nagual Elías from the moment he laid eyes on the man that he was both insane and blessed by the spirit. He worried that peasants might happen by, become enraged and lynch the man on the spot. But no one did. It felt to the nagual as if time had been suspended.

When the man finished making love, he put on his clothes, took out a handkerchief, meticulously dusted his shoes and, all the while making wild promises to the girl, went on his way. The nagual Elías followed him. In fact, he followed him for several days and found out that his name was Julian and that he was an actor.

Subsequently the nagual saw him on the stage often enough to realize that the actor had a great deal of charisma. The audience, especially the women, loved him. And he had no scruples about making use of his charismatic gifts to seduce female admirers. As the nagual followed the actor, he was able to witness his seduction technique more than once. It entailed showing himself naked to his adoring fans as soon as he got them alone, then waiting until the women, stunned by his display, surrendered. The technique seemed extremely effective for him. The nagual had to admit that the actor was a great success, except on one count. He was mortally ill. The nagual had *seen* the black shadow of death that followed him everywhere.

Don Juan explained again something he had told me years before—that our death was a black spot right behind the left shoulder. He said that sorcerers knew when a person was close to dying because they could *see* the dark spot, which became a moving shadow the exact size and shape of the person to whom it belonged.

As he recognized the imminent presence of death the nagual was plunged into a numbing perplexity. He wondered why the spirit was singling out such a sick person. He had been taught that in a natural state replacement, not repair, prevailed. And the nagual doubted that he had the ability or the strength to heal this young man, or resist the black shadow of his death. He even doubted if he would be able to discover why the spirit had involved him in a display of such obvious waste.

The nagual could do nothing but stay with the actor, follow him around, and wait for the opportunity to *see* in greater depth. Don Juan explained that a nagual's first reaction, upon being faced with the manifestations of the spirit, is to *see* the persons involved. The nagual Elías had been meticulous about *seeing* the man the moment he laid eyes on him. He had also *seen* the peasant woman who was part of the spirit's manifestation, but he had *seen* nothing that, in his judgment, could have warranted the spirit's display.

In the course of witnessing another seduction, however, the nagual's ability to *see* took on a new depth. This time the actor's adoring fan was the daughter of a rich landowner. And from the start she was in complete control. The nagual found out about their rendezvous because he overheard her daring the actor to meet her the next day. The nagual was hiding across the street at dawn when the young woman left her house, and instead of going to early mass she went to join the actor. The actor was waiting for her and she coaxed him into following her to the open fields. He appeared to hesitate, but she taunted him and would not allow him to withdraw.

As the nagual watched them sneaking away, he had an absolute conviction that something was going to happen on that day which neither of the players was anticipating. He *saw* that the actor's black shadow had grown to almost twice his height. The nagual deduced from the mysterious hard look in the young woman's eyes that she too had felt the black shadow of death at an intuitive level. The actor seemed preoccupied. He did not laugh as he had on other occasions.

They walked quite a distance. At one point, they spotted the nagual following them, but he instantly pretended to be working the land, a peasant who belonged there. That made the couple relax and allowed the nagual to come closer.

Then the moment came when the actor tossed off his clothes and showed himself to the girl. But instead of swooning and falling into his arms as his other conquests had, this girl began to hit him. She kicked and punched him mercilessly and stepped on his bare toes, making him cry out with pain.

The nagual knew the man had not threatened or harmed the young woman. He had not laid a finger on her. She was the only one fighting. He was merely trying to parry the blows, and persistently, but without enthusiasm, trying to entice her by showing her his genitals.

The nagual was filled with both revulsion and admiration. He could perceive that the actor was an irredeemable libertine, but he could also perceive equally easily that there was something unique, although revolting, about him. It baffled the nagual to *see* that the man's connecting link with the spirit was extraordinarily clear.

Finally the attack ended. The woman stopped beating the actor. But then, instead of running away, she surrendered, lay down and told the actor he could now have his way with her.

The nagual observed that the man was so exhausted he was practically unconscious. Yet despite his fatigue he went right ahead and consummated his seduction.

The nagual was laughing and pondering that useless man's great stamina and determination when the woman screamed and the actor began to gasp. The nagual *saw* how the black shadow struck the actor. It went like a dagger, with pinpoint accuracy into his gap.

Don Juan made a digression at this point to elaborate on something he had explained before: he had described the gap, an opening in our luminous shell at the height of the navel, where the force of death ceaselessly struck. What don Juan now explained was that when death hit healthy beings it was with a ball-like blow—like the punch of a fist. But when beings were dying, death struck them with a dagger-like thrust.

Thus the nagual Elías knew without any question that the actor was as good as dead, and his death automatically finished his own interest in the spirit's designs. There were no designs left; death had leveled everything.

He rose from his hiding place and started to leave when something made him hesitate. It was the young woman's calmness. She was nonchalantly putting on the few pieces of clothing she had taken off and was whistling tunelessly as if nothing had happened.

And then the nagual *saw* that in relaxing to accept the presence of death, the man's body had released a protecting veil and revealed his true nature. He was a double man of tremendous resources, capable of creating a screen for protection or disguise—a natural sorcerer and a perfect candidate for a nagual apprentice, had it not been for the black shadow of death.

The nagual was completely taken aback by that sight. He now understood the designs of the spirit, but failed to comprehend how such a useless man could fit in the sorcerers' scheme of things.

The woman in the meantime had stood up and without so much as a glance at the man, whose body was contorting with death spasms, walked away.

The nagual then *saw* her luminosity and realized that her extreme aggressiveness was the result of an enormous flow of superfluous energy. He became convinced that if she did not put that energy to sober use, it would get the best of her and there was no telling what misfortunes it would cause her.

As the nagual watched the unconcern with which she walked away, he realized that the spirit had given him another manifestation. He needed to be calm, nonchalant. He needed to act as if he had nothing to lose and intervene for the hell of it. In true nagual fashion he decided to tackle the impossible, with no one except the spirit as witness.

Don Juan commented that it took incidents like this to test whether a nagual is the real thing or a fake. Naguals make decisions. With no regard for the consequences they take action or choose not to. Imposters ponder and become paralyzed. The nagual Elías, having made his decision, walked calmly to the side of the dying man and did the first thing his body, not his mind, compelled him to do: he struck the man's assemblage point to cause him to enter into heightened awareness. He struck him frantically again and again until his assemblage point moved. Aided by the force of death itself, the nagual's blows sent the man's assemblage point to a place where death no longer mattered, and there he stopped dying.

By the time the actor was breathing again, the nagual had become aware of the magnitude of his responsibility. If the man was to fend off the force of his death, it would be necessary for him to remain in deep heightened awareness until death had been repelled. The man's advanced physical deterioration meant he could not be moved from the spot or he would instantly die. The nagual did the only thing possible under the circumstances: he built a shack around the body. There, for three months he nursed the totally immobilized man.

My rational thoughts took over, and instead of just listening, I wanted to know how the nagual Elías could build a shack on someone else's land. I was aware of the rural peoples' passion about land ownership and its accompanying feelings of territoriality.

Don Juan admitted that he had asked the same question himself. And the nagual Elías had said that the spirit itself had made it possible. This was the case with everything a nagual undertook, providing he followed the spirit's manifestations.

The first thing the nagual Elías did, when the actor was breathing again, was to run after the young woman. She was an important part of the spirit's manifestation. He caught up with her not too far from the spot where the actor lay barely alive. Rather than talking to her about the man's plight and trying to convince her to help him, he again assumed total responsibility for his actions and jumped on her like a lion, striking her assemblage point a mighty blow. Both she and the actor were capable of sustaining life or death blows. Her assemblage point moved, but began to shift erratically once it was loose.

The nagual carried the young woman to where the actor lay. Then he spent the entire day trying to keep her from losing her mind and the man from losing his life.

When he was fairly certain he had a degree of control he went to the woman's father and told him that lightning must have struck his daughter and made her temporarily mad. He took the father to where she lay and said that the young man, whoever he was, had taken the whole charge of the lightning with his body, thus saving the girl from certain death, but injuring himself to the point that he could not be moved.

The grateful father helped the nagual build the shack for the man who had saved his daughter. And in three months the nagual accomplished the impossible. He healed the young man.

When the time came for the nagual to leave, his sense of responsibility and his duty required him both to warn the young woman about her excess energy and the injurious consequences it would have on her life and well being, and to ask her to join the sorcerers' world, as that would be the only defense against her self-destructive strength.

The woman did not respond. And the nagual Elías was obliged to tell her what every nagual has said to a prospective apprentice throughout the ages: that sorcerers speak of sorcery as a magical, mysterious bird which has paused in its flight for a moment in order to give man hope and purpose; that sorcerers live under the wing of that bird, which they call the bird of wisdom, the bird of freedom; that they nourish it with their dedication and impeccability. He told her that sorcerers knew the flight of the bird of freedom was always a straight line, since it had no way of making a loop, no way of circling back and returning; and that the bird of freedom could do only two things, take sorcerers along, or leave them behind.

The nagual Elías could not talk to the young actor, who was still mortally ill, in the same way. The young man did not have much of a choice. Still, the nagual told him that if he wanted to be cured, he would have to follow the nagual unconditionally. The actor accepted the terms instantly.

The day the nagual Elías and the actor started back home, the young woman was waiting silently at the edge of town. She carried no suitcases, not even a basket. She seemed to have come merely to see them off. The nagual kept walking without looking at her, but the actor, being carried on a stretcher, strained to say goodbye to her. She laughed and wordlessly merged into the nagual's party. She had no doubts and no problem about leaving everything behind. She had understood perfectly that there was no second chance for her, that the bird of freedom either took sorcerers along or left them behind.

Don Juan commented that that was not surprising. The force of the nagual's personality was always so overwhelming that he was practically irresistible, and the nagual Elías had affected those two people deeply. He had had three months of daily interaction to accustom them to his consistency, his detachment, his objectivity. They had become enchanted by his sobriety and, above all, by his total dedication to them. Through his example and his actions, the nagual Elías had given them a sustained view of the sorcerers' world: supportive and nurturing, yet utterly demanding. It was a world that admitted very few mistakes.

Don Juan reminded me then of something he had repeated to me often but which I had always managed not to think about. He said that I should not forget, even for an instant, that the bird of freedom had very little patience with indecision, and when it flew away, it never returned.

The chilling resonance of his voice made the surroundings, which only a second before had been peacefully dark, burst with immediacy.

Don Juan summoned the peaceful darkness back as fast as he had summoned urgency. He punched me lightly on the arm.

"That woman was so powerful that she could dance circles around anyone," he said. "Her name was Talía."

2

The Knock of the Spirit

THE ABSTRACT

We returned to don Juan's house in the early hours of the morning. It took us a long time to climb down the mountain, mainly because I was afraid of stumbling into a precipice in the dark, and don Juan had to keep stopping to catch the breath he lost laughing at me.

I was dead tired, but I could not fall asleep. Before noon, it began to rain. The sound of the heavy downpour on the tile roof, instead of making me feel drowsy, removed every trace of sleepiness.

I got up and went to look for don Juan. I found him dozing in a chair. The moment I approached him he was wide-awake. I said good morning.

"You seem to be having no trouble falling asleep," I commented.

"When you have been afraid or upset, don't lie down to sleep," he said without looking at me. "Sleep sitting up on a soft chair as I'm doing."

He had suggested once that if I wanted to give my

body healing rest I should take long naps, lying on my stomach with my face turned to the left and my feet over the foot of the bed. In order to avoid being cold, he recommended I put a soft pillow over my shoulders, away from my neck, and wear heavy socks, or just leave my shoes on.

When I first heard his suggestion, I thought he was being funny, but later changed my mind. Sleeping in that position helped me rest extraordinarily well. When I commented on the surprising results, he advised that I follow his suggestions to the letter without bothering to believe or disbelieve him.

I suggested to don Juan that he might have told me the night before about the sleeping in a sitting position. I explained to him that the cause of my sleeplessness, besides my extreme fatigue, was a strange concern about what he had told me in the sorcerer's cave.

"Cut it out!" he exclaimed. "You've seen and heard infinitely more distressing things without losing a moment's sleep. Something else is bothering you."

For a moment I thought he meant I was not being truthful with him about my real preoccupation. I began to explain, but he kept talking as if I had not spoken.

"You stated categorically last night that the cave didn't make you feel ill at ease," he said. "Well, it obviously did. Last night I didn't pursue the subject of the cave any further because I was waiting to observe your reaction."

Don Juan explained that the cave had been designed by sorcerers in ancient times to serve as a catalyst. Its shape had been carefully constructed to accommodate two people as two fields of energy. The theory of the sorcerers was that the nature of the rock and the manner in which it had been carved allowed the two bodies, the two luminous balls, to intertwine their energy.

"I took you to that cave on purpose," he continued, "not because I like the place—I don't—but because it was created as an instrument to push the apprentice deep into heightened awareness. But unfortunately, as it helps, it also obscures issues. The ancient sorcerers were not given to thought. They leaned toward action."

"You always say that your benefactor was like that," I said.

"That's my own exaggeration," he answered, "very much like when I say you're a fool. My benefactor was a modern nagual, involved in the pursuit of freedom, but he leaned toward action instead of thoughts. You're a modern nagual, involved in the same quest, but you lean heavily toward the aberrations of reason."

He must have thought his comparison was very funny; his laughter echoed in the empty room.

When I brought the conversation back to the subject of the cave, he pretended not to hear me. I knew he was pretending because of the glint in his eyes and the way he smiled.

"Last night, I deliberately told you the first abstract core," he said, "in the hope that by reflecting on the way I have acted with you over the years you'll get an idea about the other cores. You've been with me for a long time so you know me very well. During every minute of our association I have tried to adjust my actions and thoughts to the patterns of the abstract cores.

"The nagual Elías's story is another matter. Although it seems to be a story about people, it is really a story about *intent*. *Intent* creates edifices before us and invites us to enter them. This is the way sorcerers understand what is happening around them."

Don Juan reminded me that I had always insisted on trying to discover the underlying order in everything he said to me. I thought he was criticizing me for my attempt to turn whatever he was teaching me into a social science problem. I began to tell him that my outlook had changed under his influence. He stopped me and smiled.

"You really don't think too well," he said and sighed. "I want you to understand the underlying order of what I teach you. My objection is to what you think is the underlying order. To you, it means secret procedures or a hidden consistency. To me, it means two things: both the edifice that *intent* manufactures in the blink of an eye and places in front of us to enter, and the signs it gives us so we won't get lost once we are inside.

"As you can see, the story of the nagual Elías was more than merely an account of the sequential details that made up the event," he went on. "Underneath all that was the edifice of *intent*. And the story was meant to give you an idea of what the naguals of the past were like, so that you would recognize how they acted in order to adjust their thoughts and actions to the edifices of *intent*."

There was a prolonged silence. I did not have anything to say. Rather than let the conversation die, I said the first thing that came into my mind. I said that from the stories I had heard about the nagual Elías I had formed a very positive opinion of him. I liked the nagual Elías, but for unknown reasons, everything don Juan had told me about the nagual Julian bothered me.

The mere mention of my discomfort delighted don Juan beyond measure. He had to stand up from his chair lest he choke on his laughter. He put his arm on my shoulder and said that we either loved or hated those who were reflections of ourselves.

Again a silly self-consciousness prevented me from asking him what he meant. Don Juan kept on laughing, obviously aware of my mood. He finally commented that the nagual Julian was like a child whose sobriety and moderation came always from without. He had no inner discipline beyond his training as an apprentice in sorcery.

I had an irrational urge to defend myself. I told don Juan that my discipline came from within me.

"Of course," he said patronizingly. "You just can't expect to be exactly like him." And began to laugh again.

Sometimes don Juan exasperated me so that I was ready to yell. But my mood did not last. It dissipated so rapidly that another concern began to loom. I asked don Juan if it was possible that I had entered into heightened awareness without being conscious of it? Or maybe I had remained in it for days?

"At this stage you enter into heightened awareness all by yourself," he said. "Heightened awareness is a mystery only for our reason. In practice, it's very simple. As with everything else, we complicate matters by trying to make the immensity that surrounds us reasonable."

He remarked that I should be thinking about the abstract core he had given me instead of arguing uselessly about my person.

I told him that I had been thinking about it all morning and had come to realize that the metaphorical theme of the story was the manifestations of the spirit. What I could not discern, however, was the abstract core he was talking about. It had to be something unstated.

"I repeat," he said, as if he were a schoolteacher drilling his students, "the Manifestations of the Spirit is the name for the first abstract core in the sorcery stories. Obviously, what sorcerers recognize as an abstract core is something that bypasses you at this moment. That part which escapes you sorcerers know as

29

the edifice of *intent,* or the silent voice of the spirit, or the ulterior arrangement of the abstract."

I said I understood ulterior to mean something not overtly revealed, as in "ulterior motive." And he replied that in this case ulterior meant more; it meant knowledge without words, outside our immediate comprehension—especially mine. He allowed that the comprehension he was referring to was merely beyond my aptitudes of the moment, not beyond my ultimate possibilities for understanding.

"If the abstract cores are beyond my comprehension what's the point of talking about them?" I asked.

"The rule says that the abstract cores and the sorcery stories must be told at this point," he replied. "And some day the ulterior arrangement of the abstract, which is knowledge without words or the edifice of *intent* inherent in the stories, will be revealed to you by the stories themselves."

I still did not understand.

"The ulterior arrangement of the abstract is not merely the order in which the abstract cores were presented to you," he explained, "or what they have in common either, nor even the web that joins them. Rather it's to know the abstract directly, without the intervention of language."

He scrutinized me in silence from head to toe with the obvious purpose of *seeing* me.

"It's not evident to you yet," he declared.

He made a gesture of impatience, even short temper, as though he were annoyed at my slowness. And that worried me. Don Juan was not given to expressions of psychological displeasure.

"It has nothing to do with you or your actions," he said when I asked if he was angry or disappointed with me. "It was a thought that crossed my mind the moment I *saw* you. There is a feature in your luminous being that the old sorcerers would have given anything to have."

"Tell me what it is," I demanded.

"I'll remind you of this some other time," he said. "Meanwhile, let's continue with the element that propels us: the abstract. The element without which there could be no warrior's path, nor any warriors in search of knowledge."

He said that the difficulties I was experiencing were nothing new to him. He himself had gone through agonies in order to understand the ulterior order of the abstract. And had it not been for the helping hand of the nagual Elías, he would have wound up just like his benefactor, all action and very little understanding.

"What was the nagual Elías like?" I asked, to change the subject.

"He was not like his disciple at all," don Juan said. "He was an Indian. Very dark and massive. He had rough features, big mouth, strong nose, small black eyes, thick black hair with no gray in it. He was shorter than the nagual Julian and had big hands and feet. He was very humble and very wise, but he had no flare. Compared with my benefactor, he was dull. Always all by himself, pondering questions. The nagual Julian used to joke that his teacher imparted wisdom by the ton. Behind his back he used to call him the nagual Tonnage.

"I never saw the reason for his jokes," don Juan went on. "To me the nagual Elías was like a breath of fresh air. He would patiently explain everything to me. Very much as I explain things to you, but perhaps with a bit more of something. I wouldn't call it compassion, but rather, empathy. Warriors are incapable of feeling compassion because they no longer feel sorry for themselves. Without the driving force of self-pity, compassion is meaningless."

"Are you saying, don Juan, that a warrior is all for himself?"

"In a way, yes. For a warrior everything begins and ends with himself. However, his contact with the abstract causes him to overcome his feeling of self-importance. Then the self becomes abstract and impersonal.

"The nagual Elías felt that our lives and our personalities were quite similar," don Juan continued. "For this reason, he felt obliged to help me. I don't feel that similarity with you, so I suppose I regard you very much the way the nagual Julian used to regard me."

Don Juan said that the nagual Elías took him under his wing from the very first day he arrived at his benefactor's house to start his apprenticeship and began to explain what was taking place in his training, regardless of whether don Juan was capable of understanding. His urge to help don Juan was so intense that he practically held him prisoner. He protected him in this manner from the nagual Julian's harsh onslaughts.

"At the beginning, I used to stay at the nagual Elías's house all the time," don Juan continued. "And I loved it. In my benefactor's house I was always on the lookout, on guard, afraid of what he was going to do to me next. But in the nagual Elías's home I felt confident, at ease.

"My benefactor used to press me mercilessly. And I couldn't figure out why he was pressuring me so hard. I thought that the man was plain crazy."

Don Juan said that the nagual Elías was an Indian from the state of Oaxaca, who had been taught by another nagual named Rosendo, who came from the same area. Don Juan described the nagual Elías as being a very conservative man who cherished his privacy. And yet he was a famous healer and sorcerer, not only in Oaxaca, but in all of southern Mexico.

Nonetheless, in spite of his occupation and notoriety, he lived in complete isolation at the opposite end of the country, in northern Mexico.

Don Juan stopped talking. Raising his eyebrows, he fixed me with a questioning look. But all I wanted was for him to continue his story.

"Every single time I think you should ask questions, you don't," he said. "I'm sure you heard me say that the nagual Elías was a famous sorcerer who dealt with people daily in southern Mexico, and at the same time he was a hermit in northern Mexico. Doesn't that arouse your curiosity?"

I felt abysmally stupid. I told him that the thought had crossed my mind, as he was telling me those facts, that the man must have had terrible difficulty commuting.

Don Juan laughed, and, since he had made me aware of the question, I asked how it had been possible for the nagual Elías to be in two places at once.

"*Dreaming* is a sorcerer's jet plane," he said. "The nagual Elías was a *dreamer* as my benefactor was a *stalker*. He was able to create and project what sorcerers know as the *dreaming body,* or the Other, and to be in two distant places at the same time. With his *dreaming body,* he could carry on his business as a sorcerer, and with his natural self be a recluse."

I remarked that it amazed me that I could accept so easily the premise that the nagual Elías had the ability to project a solid three-dimensional image of himself, and yet could not for the life of me understand the explanations about the abstract cores.

Don Juan said that I could accept the idea of the nagual Elías's dual life because the spirit was making final adjustments in my capacity for awareness. And I exploded into a barrage of protests at the obscurity of his statement.

"It isn't obscure," he said. "It's a statement of fact.

You could say that it's an incomprehensible fact for the moment, but the moment will change."

Before I could reply, he began to talk again about the nagual Elías. He said that the nagual Elías had a very inquisitive mind and could work well with his hands. In his journeys as a *dreamer* he saw many objects, which he copied in wood and forged iron. Don Juan assured me that some of those models were of a haunting, exquisite beauty.

"What kind of objects were the originals?" I asked.

"There's no way of knowing," don Juan said. "You've got to consider that because he was an Indian the nagual Elías went into his *dreaming* journeys the way a wild animal prowls for food. An animal never shows up at a site when there are signs of activity. He comes only when no one is around. The nagual Elías, as a solitary *dreamer,* visited, let's say, the junkyard of infinity, when no one was around—and copied whatever he saw, but never knew what those things were used for, or their source."

Again, I had no trouble accepting what he was saying. The idea did not appear to me farfetched in any way. I was about to comment when he interrupted me with a gesture of his eyebrows. He then continued his account about the nagual Elías.

"Visiting him was for me the ultimate treat," he said, "and simultaneously, a source of strange guilt. I used to get bored to death there. Not because the nagual Elías was boring, but because the nagual Julian had no peers and he spoiled anyone for life."

"But I thought you were confident and at ease in the nagual Elías's house," I said.

"I was, and that was the source of my guilt and my imagined problem. Like you, I loved to torment myself. I think at the very beginning I found peace in the nagual Elías's company, but later on, when I understood the nagual Julian better, I went his way."

He told me that the nagual Elías's house had an open, roofed section in the front, where he had a forge and a carpentry bench and tools. The tiled-roof adobe house consisted of a huge room with a dirt floor where he lived with five women seers, who were actually his wives. There were also four men, sorcerer-seers of his party who lived in small houses around the nagual's house. They were all Indians from different parts of the country who had migrated to northern Mexico.

"The nagual Elías had great respect for sexual energy," don Juan said. "He believed it has been given to us so we can use it in *dreaming*. He believed *dreaming* had fallen into disuse because it can upset the precarious mental balance of susceptible people.

"I've taught you *dreaming* the same way he taught me," he continued. "He taught me that while we dream the assemblage point moves very gently and naturally. Mental balance is nothing but the fixing of the assemblage point on one spot we're accustomed to. If dreams make that point move, and *dreaming* is used to control that natural movement, and sexual energy is needed for *dreaming,* the result is sometimes disastrous when sexual energy is dissipated in sex instead of *dreaming*. Then *dreamers* move their assemblage point erratically and lose their minds."

"What are you trying to tell me, don Juan?" I asked because I felt that the subject of *dreaming* had not been a natural drift in the conversation.

"You are a *dreamer*," he said. "If you're not careful with your sexual energy, you might as well get used to the idea of erratic shifts of your assemblage point. A moment ago you were bewildered by your reactions. Well, your assemblage point moves almost erratically, because your sexual energy is not in balance."

I made a stupid and inappropriate comment about the sex life of adult males.

"Our sexual energy is what governs *dreaming*," he explained. "The nagual Elías taught me—and I taught you—that you either make love with your sexual energy or you *dream* with it. There is no other way. The reason I mention it at all is because you are having great difficulty shifting your assemblage point to grasp our last topic: the abstract.

"The same thing happened to me," don Juan went. on. "It was only when my sexual energy was freed from the world that everything fit into place. That is the rule for *dreamers*. *Stalkers* are the opposite. My benefactor was, you could say, a sexual libertine both as an average man and as a nagual."

Don Juan seemed to be on the verge of revealing his benefactor's doings, but he obviously changed his mind. He shook his head and said that I was way too stiff for such revelations. I did not insist.

He said that the nagual Elías had the sobriety that only *dreamers* acquired after inconceivable battles with themselves. He used his sobriety to plunge himself into the task of answering don Juan's questions.

"The nagual Elías explained that my difficulty in understanding the spirit was the same as his own," don Juan continued. "He thought there were two different issues. One, the need to understand indirectly what the spirit is, and the other, to understand the spirit directly.

"You're having problems with the first. Once you understand what the spirit is, the second issue will be resolved automatically, and vice versa. If the spirit speaks to you, using its silent words, you will certainly know immediately what the spirit is."

He said that the nagual Elías believed that the difficulty was our reluctance to accept the idea that knowledge could exist without words to explain it.

"But I have no difficulty accepting that," I said.

"Accepting this proposition is not as easy as saying

36

you accept it," don Juan said. "The nagual Elías used to tell me that the whole of humanity has moved away from the abstract, although at one time we must have been close to it. It must have been our sustaining force. And then something happened and pulled us away from the abstract. Now we can't get back to it. He used to say that it takes years for an apprentice to be able to go back to the abstract, that is, to know that knowledge and language can exist independent of each other."

Don Juan repeated that the crux of our difficulty in going back to the abstract was our refusal to accept that we could know without words or even without thoughts.

I was going to argue that he was talking nonsense when I got the strong feeling I was missing something and that his point was of crucial importance to me. He was really trying to tell me something, something I either could not grasp or which could not be told completely.

"Knowledge and language are separate," he repeated softly.

And I was just about to say, "I know it," as if indeed I knew it, when I caught myself.

"I told you there is no way to talk about the spirit," he continued, "because the spirit can only be experienced. Sorcerers try to explain this condition when they say that the spirit is nothing you can see or feel. But it's there looming over us always. Sometimes it comes to some of us. Most of the time it seems indifferent."

I kept quiet. And he continued to explain. He said that the spirit in many ways was a sort of wild animal. It kept its distance from us until a moment when something enticed it forward. It was then that the spirit manifested itself.

I raised the point that if the spirit wasn't an entity,

or a presence, and had no essence, how could anyone entice it?

"Your problem," he said, "is that you consider only your own idea of what's abstract. For instance, the inner essence of man, or the fundamental principle, are abstracts for you. Or perhaps something a bit less vague, such as character, volition, courage, dignity, honor. The spirit, of course, can be described in terms of all of these. And that's what's so confusing —that it's all these and none of them."

He added that what I considered abstractions were either the opposites of all the practicalities I could think of or things I had decided did not have concrete existence.

"Whereas for a sorcerer an abstract is something with no parallel in the human condition," he said.

"But they're the same thing," I shouted. "Don't you see that we're both talking about the same thing?"

"We are not," he insisted. "For a sorcerer, the spirit is an abstract simply because he knows it without words or even thoughts. It's an abstract because he can't conceive what the spirit is. Yet without the slightest chance or desire to understand it, a sorcerer handles the spirit. He recognizes it, beckons it, entices it, becomes familiar with it, and expresses it with his acts."

I shook my head in despair. I could not see the difference.

"The root of your misconception is that I have used the term 'abstract' to describe the spirit," he said. "For you, abstracts are words which describe states of intuition. An example is the word 'spirit,' which doesn't describe reason or pragmatic experience, and which, of course, is of no use to you other than to tickle your fancy."

I was furious with don Juan. I called him obstinate and he laughed at me. He suggested that if I would think about the proposition that knowledge might be independent of language, without bothering to understand it, perhaps I could see the light.

"Consider this," he said. "It was not the act of meeting me that mattered to you. The day I met you, you met the abstract. But since you couldn't talk about it, you didn't notice it. Sorcerers meet the abstract without thinking about it or seeing it or touching it or feeling its presence."

I remained quiet because I did not enjoy arguing with him. At times I considered him to be quite willfully abstruse. But don Juan seemed to be enjoying himself immensely.

THE LAST SEDUCTION OF THE NAGUAL JULIAN

It was as cool and quiet in the patio of don Juan's house as in the cloister of a convent. There were a number of large fruit trees planted extremely close together, which seemed to regulate the temperature and absorb all noises. When I first came to his house, I had made critical remarks about the illogical way the fruit trees had been planted. I would have given them more space. His answer was that those trees were not his property, they were free and independent warrior trees that had joined his party of warriors, and that my comments—which applied to regular trees—were not relevant.

His reply sounded metaphorical to me. What I

didn't know then was that don Juan meant everything he said literally.

Don Juan and I were sitting in cane armchairs facing the fruit trees now. The trees were all bearing fruit. I commented that it was not only a beautiful sight but an extremely intriguing one, for it was not the fruit season.

"There is an interesting story about it," he admitted. "As you know, these trees are warriors of my party. They are bearing now because all the members of my party have been talking and expressing feelings about our definitive journey, here in front of them. And the trees know now that when we embark on our definitive journey, they will accompany us."

I looked at him, astonished.

"I can't leave them behind," he explained. "They are warriors too. They have thrown their lot in with the nagual's party. And they know how I feel about them. The assemblage point of trees is located very low in their enormous luminous shell, and that permits them to know our feelings, for instance, the feelings we are having now as we discuss my definitive journey."

I remained quiet, for I did not want to dwell on the subject. Don Juan spoke and dispelled my mood.

"The second abstract core of the sorcery stories is called the Knock of the Spirit," he said. "The first core, the Manifestations of the Spirit, is the edifice that *intent* builds and places before a sorcerer, then invites him to enter. It is the edifice of *intent seen* by a sorcerer. The Knock of the Spirit is the same edifice seen by the beginner who is invited—or rather forced —to enter.

"This second abstract core could be a story in itself. The story says that after the spirit had manifested itself to that man we have talked about and had gotten no response, the spirit laid a trap for the man. It was a final subterfuge, not because the man was special, but because the incomprehensible chain of events of the spirit made that man available at the very moment that the spirit knocked on the door.

"It goes without saying that whatever the spirit revealed to that man made no sense to him. In fact, it went against everything the man knew, everything he was. The man, of course, refused on the spot, and in no uncertain terms, to have anything to do with the spirit. He wasn't going to fall for such preposterous nonsense. He knew better. The result was a total stalemate.

"I can say that this is an idiotic story," he continued. "I can say that what I've given you is the pacifier for those who are uncomfortable with the silence of the abstract."

He peered at me for a moment and then smiled.

"You like words," he said accusingly. "The mere idea of silent knowledge scares you. But stories, no matter how stupid, delight you and make you feel secure."

His smile was so mischievous that I couldn't help laughing.

Then he reminded me that I had already heard his detailed account of the first time the spirit had knocked on his door. For a moment I could not figure out what he was talking about.

"It was not just my benefactor who stumbled upon me as I was dying from the gunshot," he explained. "The spirit also found me and knocked on my door that day. My benefactor understood that he was there to be a conduit for the spirit. Without the spirit's intervention, meeting my benefactor would have meant nothing."

He said that a nagual can be a conduit only after the spirit has manifested its willingness to be used—either almost imperceptibly or with outright commands. It was therefore not possible for a nagual to choose his apprentices according to his own volition, or his own calculations. But once the willingness of the spirit was revealed through omens, the nagual spared no effort to satisfy it.

"After a lifetime of practice," he continued, "sorcerers, naguals in particular, know if the spirit is inviting them to enter the edifice being flaunted before them. They have learned to discipline their connecting links to *intent*. So they are always forewarned, always know what the spirit has in store for them."

Don Juan said that progress along the sorcerers' path was, in general, a drastic process the purpose of which was to bring this connecting link to order. The average man's connecting link with *intent* is practically dead, and sorcerers begin with a link that is useless, because it does not respond voluntarily.

He stressed that in order to revive that link sorcerers needed a rigorous, fierce purpose—a special state of mind called *unbending intent*. Accepting that the nagual was the only being capable of supplying *unbending intent* was the most difficult part of the sorcerer's apprenticeship.

I argued that I could not see the difficulty.

"An apprentice is someone who is striving to clear and revive his connecting link with the spirit," he explained. "Once the link is revived, he is no longer an apprentice, but until that time, in order to keep going he needs a fierce purpose, which, of course, he doesn't have. So he allows the nagual to provide the purpose and to do that he has to relinquish his individuality. That's the difficult part."

He reminded me of something he had told me often: that volunteers were not welcome in the sorcerers' world, because they already had a purpose of their own, which made it particularly hard for them to relinquish their individuality. If the sorcerers' world demanded ideas and actions contrary to the volunteers' purpose, the volunteers simply refused to change.

"Reviving an apprentice's link is a nagual's most challenging and intriguing work," don Juan continued, "and one of his biggest headaches too. Depending, of course, on the apprentice's personality, the designs of the spirit are either sublimely simple or the most complex labyrinths."

Don Juan assured me that, although I might have had notions to the contrary, my apprenticeship had not been as onerous to him as his must have been to his benefactor. He admitted that I had a modicum of self-discipline that came in very handy, while he had had none whatever. And his benefactor, in turn, had had even less.

"The difference is discernible in the manifestations of the spirit," he continued. "In some cases, they are barely noticeable; in my case, they were commands. I had been shot. Blood was pouring out of a hole in my chest. My benefactor had to act with speed and sureness, just as his own benefactor had for him. Sorcerers know that the more difficult the command is, the more difficult the disciple turns out to be."

Don Juan explained that one of the most advantageous aspects of his association with two naguals was that he could hear the same stories from two opposite points of view. For instance, the story about the nagual Elías and the manifestations of the spirit, from the apprentice's perspective, was the story of the spirit's difficult knock on his benefactor's door.

"Everything connected with my benefactor was very difficult," he said and began to laugh. "When he was twenty-four years old, the spirit didn't just knock on his door, it nearly banged it down."

He said that the story had really begun years earlier, when his benefactor had been a handsome adolescent from a good family in Mexico City. He was wealthy, educated, charming, and had a charismatic personality. Women fell in love with him at first sight. But he was already self-indulgent and undisciplined, lazy about anything that did not give him immediate gratification.

Don Juan said that with that personality and his type of upbringing—he was the only son of a wealthy widow who, together with his four adoring sisters, doted on him—he could only behave one way. He indulged in every impropriety he could think of. Even among his equally self-indulgent friends, he was seen as a moral delinquent who lived to do anything that the world considered morally wrong.

In the long run, his excesses weakened him physically and he fell mortally ill with tuberculosis—the dreaded disease of the time. But his illness, instead of restraining him, created a physical condition in which he felt more sensual than ever. Since he did not have one iota of self-control, he gave himself over fully to debauchery, and his health deteriorated until there was no hope.

The saying that it never rains but it pours was certainly true for don Juan's benefactor then. As his health declined, his mother, who was his only source of support and the only restraint on him, died. She left him a sizable inheritance, which should have supported him adequately for life, but undisciplined as he was, in a few months he had spent every cent. With no profession or trade to fall back on, he was left to scrounge for a living.

Without money he no longer had friends; and even the women who once loved him turned their backs. For the first time in his life, he found himself confronting a harsh reality. Considering the state of his health, it should have been the end. But he was resilient. He decided to work for a living.

His sensual habits, however, could not be changed,

and they forced him to seek work in the only place he felt comfortable: the theater. His qualifications were that he was a born ham and had spent most of his adult life in the company of actresses. He joined a theatrical troupe in the provinces, away from his familiar circle of friends and acquaintances, and became a very intense actor, the consumptive hero in religious and morality plays.

Don Juan commented on the strange irony that had always marked his benefactor's life. There he was, a perfect reprobate, dying as a result of his dissolute ways and playing the roles of saints and mystics. He even played Jesus in the Passion Play during Holy Week.

His health lasted through one theatrical tour of the northern states. Then two things happened in the city of Durango: his life came to an end and the spirit knocked on his door.

Both his death and the spirit's knock came at the same time—in broad daylight in the bushes. His death caught him in the act of seducing a young woman. He was already extremely weak, and that day he overexerted himself. The young woman, who was vivacious and strong and madly infatuated, had by promising to make love induced him to walk to a secluded spot miles from nowhere. And there she had fought him off for hours. When she finally submitted, he was completely worn out, and coughing so badly that he could hardly breathe.

During his last passionate outburst he felt a searing pain in his shoulder. His chest felt as if it were being ripped apart and a coughing spell made him retch uncontrollably. But his compulsion to seek pleasure kept him going until his death came in the form of a hemorrhage. It was then that the spirit made its entry, borne by an Indian who came to his aid. Earlier he had noticed the Indian following them around, but had not given him a second thought, absorbed as he was in the seduction.

He saw, as in a dream, the girl. She was not scared nor did she lose her composure. Quietly and efficiently she put her clothes back on and took off as fast as a rabbit chased by hounds.

He also saw the Indian rushing to him trying to make him sit up. He heard him saying idiotic things. He heard him pledging himself to the spirit and mumbling incomprehensible words in a foreign language. Then the Indian acted very quickly. Standing behind him, he gave him a smacking blow on the back.

Very rationally, the dying man deduced that the Indian was trying either to dislodge the blood clot or to kill him.

As the Indian struck him repeatedly on the back, the dying man became convinced that the Indian was the woman's lover or husband and was murdering him. But seeing the intensely brilliant eyes of that Indian, he changed his mind. He knew that the Indian was simply crazy and was not connected with the woman. With his last bit of consciousness, he focused his attention on the man's mumblings. What he was saying was that the power of man was incalculable, that death existed only because we had *intended* it since the moment of our birth, that the *intent* of death could be suspended by making the assemblage point change positions.

He then knew that the Indian was totally insane. His situation was so theatrical—dying at the hands of a crazy Indian mumbling gibberish—that he vowed he would be a ham actor to the bitter end, and he promised himself not to die of either the hemorrhaging or the blows, but to die of laughter. And he laughed until he was dead.

Don Juan remarked that naturally his benefactor could not possibly have taken the Indian seriously. No one could take such a person seriously, especially not a prospective apprentice who was not supposed to be volunteering for the sorcery task.

Don Juan then said that he had given me different versions of what that sorcery task consisted. He said it would not be presumptuous of him to disclose that, from the spirit's point of view, the task consisted of clearing our connecting link with it. The edifice that *intent* flaunts before us is, then, a clearinghouse, within which we find not so much the procedures to clear our connecting link as the silent knowledge that allows the clearing process to take place. Without that silent knowledge no process could work, and all we would have would be an indefinite sense of needing something.

He explained that the events unleashed by sorcerers as a result of silent knowledge were so simple and yet so abstract that sorcerers had decided long ago to speak of those events only in symbolic terms. The manifestations and the knock of the spirit were examples.

Don Juan said that, for instance, a description of what took place during the initial meeting between a nagual and a prospective apprentice from the sorcerers' point of view, would be absolutely incomprehensible. It would be nonsense to explain that the nagual, by virtue of his lifelong experience, was focusing something we couldn't imagine, his second attention —the increased awareness gained through sorcery training—on his invisible connection with some indefinable abstract. He was doing this to emphasize and clarify someone else's invisible connection with that indefinable abstract.

He remarked that each of us was barred from silent knowledge by natural barriers, specific to each individual; and that the most impregnable of my barriers was the drive to disguise my complacency as independence.

I challenged him to give me a concrete example. I reminded him that he had once warned me that a favorite debating ploy was to raise general criticisms that could not be supported by concrete examples.

Don Juan looked at me and beamed.

"In the past, I used to give you power plants," he said. "At first, you went to extremes to convince yourself that what you were experiencing were hallucinations. Then you wanted them to be special hallucinations. I remember I made fun of your insistence on calling them didactic hallucinatory experiences."

He said that my need to prove my illusory independence forced me into a position where I could not accept what he had told me was happening, although it was what I silently knew for myself. I knew he was employing power plants, as the very limited tools they were, to make me enter partial or temporary states of heightened awareness by moving my assemblage point away from its habitual location.

"You used your barrier of independence to get you over that obstruction," he went on. "The same barrier has continued to work to this day, so you still retain that sense of indefinite anguish, perhaps not so pronounced. Now the question is, how are you arranging your conclusions so that your current experiences fit into your scheme of complacency?"

I confessed that the only way I could maintain my independence was not to think about my experiences at all.

Don Juan's hearty laugh nearly made him fall out of his cane chair. He stood and walked around to catch his breath. He sat down again and composed himself. He pushed his chair back and crossed his legs.

He said that we, as average men did not know, nor

would we ever know, that it was something utterly real and functional—our connecting link with *intent*—which gave us our hereditary preoccupation with fate. He asserted that during our active lives we never have the chance to go beyond the level of mere preoccupation, because since time immemorial the lull of daily affairs has made us drowsy. It is only when our lives are nearly over that our hereditary preoccupation with fate begins to take on a different character. It begins to make us see through the fog of daily affairs. Unfortunately, this awakening always comes hand in hand with loss of energy caused by aging, when we have no more strength left to turn our preoccupation into a pragmatic and positive discovery. At this point, all there is left is an amorphous, piercing anguish, a longing for something indescribable, and simple anger at having missed out.

"I like poems for many reasons," he said. "One reason is that they catch the mood of warriors and explain what can hardly be explained."

He conceded that poets were keenly aware of our connecting link with the spirit, but that they were aware of it intuitively, not in the deliberate, pragmatic way of sorcerers.

"Poets have no firsthand knowledge of the spirit," he went on. "That is why their poems cannot really hit the center of true gestures for the spirit. They hit pretty close to it, though."

He picked up one of my poetry books from a chair next to him, a collection by Juan Ramón Jiménez. He opened it to where he had placed a marker, handed it to me and signaled me to read.

> *Is it I who walks tonight*
> *in my room or is it the beggar*
> *who was prowling in my garden*
> *at nightfall?*

I look around
and find that everything
is the same and it is not the same . . .
Was the window open?
Had I not already fallen asleep?

Was not the garden pale green? . . .
The sky was clear and blue . . .
And there are clouds
and it is windy
and the garden is dark and gloomy.

I think that my hair was black . . .
I was dressed in grey . . .
And my hair is grey
and I am wearing black . . .
Is this my gait?
Does this voice, which now resounds in me,
have the rhythms of the voice I used to have?
Am I myself or am I the beggar
who was prowling in my garden
at nightfall?

I look around . . .
There are clouds and it is windy . . .
The garden is dark and gloomy . . .

I come and go . . . Is it not true
that I had already fallen asleep?
My hair is grey . . . And everything
is the same and it is not the same . . .

I reread the poem to myself and I caught the poet's mood of impotence and bewilderment. I asked don Juan if he felt the same.

"I think the poet senses the pressure of aging and the anxiety that that realization produces," don Juan said. "But that is only one part of it. The other part, which interests me, is that the poet, although he never moves his assemblage point, intuits that something extraordinary is at stake. He intuits with great certainty that there is some unnamed factor, awesome because of its simplicity, that is determining our fate."

3

The Trickery of the Spirit

DUSTING THE LINK WITH THE SPIRIT

The sun had not yet risen from behind the eastern peaks, but the day was already hot. As we reached the first steep slope, a couple of miles along the road from the outskirts of town, don Juan stopped walking and moved to the side of the paved highway. He sat down by some huge boulders that had been dynamited from the face of the mountain when they cut the road and signaled me to join him. We usually stopped there to talk or rest on our way to the nearby mountains. Don Juan announced that this trip was going to be long and that we might be in the mountains for days.

"We are going to talk now about the third abstract core," don Juan said. "It is called the trickery of the spirit, or the trickery of the abstract, or *stalking* oneself, or dusting the link."

I was surprised at the variety of names, but said nothing. I waited for him to continue his explanation.

"And again, as with the first and second core," he

went on, "it could be a story in itself. The story says that after knocking on the door of that man we've been talking about, and having no success with him, the spirit used the only means available: trickery. After all, the spirit had resolved previous impasses with trickery. It was obvious that if it wanted to make an impact on this man it had to cajole him. So the spirit began to instruct the man on the mysteries of sorcery. And the sorcery apprenticeship became what it is: a route of artifice and subterfuge.

"The story says that the spirit cajoled the man by making him shift back and forth between levels of awareness to show him how to save energy needed to strengthen his connecting link."

Don Juan told me that if we apply his story to a modern setting we had the case of the nagual, the living conduit of the spirit, repeating the structure of this abstract core and resorting to artifice and subterfuge in order to teach.

Suddenly he stood and started to walk toward the mountain range. I followed him and we started our climb, side by side.

In the very late afternoon we reached the top of the high mountains. Even at that altitude it was still very warm. All day we had followed a nearly invisible trail. Finally we reached a small clearing, an ancient lookout post commanding the north and west.

We sat there and don Juan returned our conversation to the sorcery stories. He said that now I knew the story of *intent* manifesting itself to the nagual Elías and the story of the spirit knocking on the nagual Julian's door. And I knew how he had met the spirit, and I certainly could not forget how I had met it. All these stories, he declared, had the same structure; only the characters differed. Each story was an abstract tragicomedy with one abstract player, *intent*, and two human actors, the nagual and his apprentice. The script was the abstract core.

I thought I had finally understood what he meant, but I could not quite explain even to myself what it was I understood, nor could I explain it to don Juan. When I tried to put my thoughts into words I found myself babbling.

Don Juan seemed to recognize my state of mind. He suggested that I relax and listen. He told me his next story was about the process of bringing an apprentice into the realm of the spirit, a process sorcerers called the trickery of the spirit, or dusting the connecting link to *intent*.

"I've already told you the story of how the nagual Julian took me to his house after I was shot and tended my wound until I recovered," don Juan continued. "But I didn't tell you how he dusted my link, how he taught me to *stalk* myself.

"The first thing a nagual does with his prospective apprentice is to trick him. That is, he gives him a jolt on his connecting link to the spirit. There are two ways of doing this. One is through seminormal channels, which I used with you, and the other is by means of outright sorcery, which my benefactor used on me."

Don Juan again told me the story of how his benefactor had convinced the people who had gathered at the road that the wounded man was his son. Then he had paid some men to carry don Juan, unconscious from shock and loss of blood, to his own house. Don Juan woke there, days later, and found a kind old man and his fat wife tending his wound.

The old man said his name was Belisario and that his wife was a famous healer and that both of them were healing his wound. Don Juan told them he had no money, and Belisario suggested that when he recovered, payment of some sort could be arranged.

Don Juan said that he was thoroughly confused, which was nothing new to him. He was just a muscular, reckless twenty-year-old Indian, with no brains, no formal education, and a terrible temper. He had no conception of gratitude. He thought it was very kind of the old man and his wife to have helped him, but his intention was to wait for his wound to heal and then simply vanish in the middle of the night.

When he had recovered enough and was ready to flee, old Belisario took him into a room and in trembling whispers disclosed that the house where they were staying belonged to a monstrous man who was holding him and his wife prisoner. He asked don Juan to help them to regain their freedom, to escape from their captor and tormentor. Before don Juan could reply, a monstrous fish-faced man right out of a horror tale burst into the room, as if he had been listening behind the door. He was greenish-gray, had only one unblinking eye in the middle of his forehead, and was as big as a door. He lurched at don Juan, hissing like a serpent, ready to tear him apart, and frightened him so greatly that he fainted.

"His way of giving me a jolt on my connecting link with the spirit was masterful." Don Juan laughed. "My benefactor, of course, had shifted me into heightened awareness prior to the monster's entrance, so that what I actually *saw* as a monstrous man was what sorcerers call an inorganic being, a formless energy field."

Don Juan said that he knew countless cases in which his benefactor's devilishness created hilariously embarrassing situations for all his apprentices, especially for don Juan himself, whose seriousness and stiffness made him the perfect subject for his benefactor's didactic jokes. He added as an afterthought that it went without saying that these jokes entertained his benefactor immensely.

"If you think I laugh at you—which I do—it's nothing compared with how he laughed at me," don Juan continued. "My devilish benefactor had learned to weep to hide his laughter. You just can't imagine how he used to cry when I first began my apprenticeship."

Continuing with his story, don Juan stated that his life was never the same after the shock of *seeing* that monstrous man. His benefactor made sure of it. Don Juan explained that once a nagual has introduced his prospective disciple, especially his nagual disciple, to trickery he must struggle to assure his compliance. This compliance could be of two different kinds. Either the prospective disciple is so disciplined and tuned that only his decision to join the nagual is needed, as had been the case with young Talía. Or the prospective disciple is someone with little or no discipline, in which case a nagual has to expend time and a great deal of labor to convince his disciple.

In don Juan's case, because he was a wild young peasant without a thought in his head, the process of reeling him in took bizarre turns.

Soon after the first jolt, his benefactor gave him a second one by showing don Juan his ability to transform himself. One day his benefactor became a young man. Don Juan was incapable of conceiving of this transformation as anything but an example of a consummate actor's art.

"How did he accomplish those changes?" I asked.

"He was both a magician and an artist," don Juan replied. "His magic was that he transformed himself by moving his assemblage point into the position that would bring on whatever particular change he desired. And his art was the perfection of his transformations."

"I don't quite understand what you're telling me," I said.

Don Juan said that perception is the hinge for every-

For all the sorcerers of don Juan's party the death defier was a most vivid character. According to them, the death defier was a sorcerer of ancient times. He had succeeded in surviving to the present day by manipulating his assemblage point, making it move in specific ways to specific locations within his total energy field. Such maneuvers had permitted his awareness and life force to persist.

Don Juan had told me about the agreement that the seers of his lineage had entered into with the death defier centuries before. He made gifts to them in exchange for vital energy. Because of this agreement, they considered him their ward and called him "the tenant."

Don Juan had explained that sorcerers of ancient times were expert at making the assemblage point move. In doing so they had discovered extraordinary things about perception, but they had also discovered how easy it was to get lost in aberration. The death defier's situation was for don Juan a classic example of an aberration.

Don Juan used to repeat every chance he could that if the assemblage point was pushed by someone who not only *saw* it but also had enough energy to move it, it slid, within the luminous ball, to whatever location the pusher directed. Its brilliance was enough to light up the threadlike energy fields it touched. The resulting perception of the world was as complete as, but not the same as, our normal perception of everyday life, therefore, sobriety was crucial to dealing with the moving of the assemblage point.

Continuing his story, don Juan said that he quickly became accustomed to thinking of the old man who had saved his life as really a young man masquerading as old. But one day the young man was again the old Belisario don Juan had first met. He and the woman don Juan thought was his wife packed their bags, and two smiling men with a team of mules appeared out of nowhere.

Don Juan laughed, savoring his story. He said that while the muleteers packed the mules, Belisario pulled him aside and pointed out that he and his wife were again disguised. He was again an old man, and his beautiful wife was a fat irascible Indian.

"I was so young and stupid that only the obvious had value for me," don Juan continued. "Just a couple of days before, I had seen his incredible transformation from a feeble man in his seventies to a vigorous young man in his mid-twenties, and I took his word that old age was just a disguise. His wife had also changed from a sour, fat Indian to a beautiful slender young woman. The woman, of course, hadn't transformed herself the way my benefactor had. He had simply changed the woman. Of course, I could have seen everything at that time, but wisdom always comes to us painfully and in driblets."

Don Juan said that the old man assured him that his wound was healed although he did not feel quite well yet. He then embraced don Juan and in a truly sad voice whispered, "The monster has liked you so much that he has released me and my wife from bondage and taken you as his sole servant."

"I would have laughed at him," don Juan went on, "had it not been for a deep animal growling and a frightening rattle that came from the monster's rooms."

Don Juan's eyes were shining with inner delight. I wanted to remain serious, but could not help laughing.

Belisario, aware of don Juan's fright, apologized profusely for the twist of fate that had liberated him and imprisoned don Juan. He clicked his tongue in disgust and cursed the monster. He had tears in his eyes when he listed all the chores the monster wanted done daily. And when don Juan protested, he confided, in low tones, that there was no way to escape, because the monster's knowledge of witchcraft was unequaled.

Don Juan asked Belisario to recommend some line of action. And Belisario went into a long explanation about plans of action being appropriate only if one were dealing with average human beings. In the human context, we can plan and plot and, depending on luck, plus our cunning and dedication, can succeed. But in the face of the unknown, specifically don Juan's situation, the only hope of survival was to acquiesce and understand.

Belisario confessed to don Juan in a barely audible murmur that to make sure the monster never came after him, he was going to the state of Durango to learn sorcery. He asked don Juan if he, too, would consider learning sorcery. And don Juan, horrified at the thought, said that he would have nothing to do with witches.

Don Juan held his sides laughing and admitted that he enjoyed thinking about how his benefactor must have relished their interplay. Especially when he himself, in a frenzy of fear and passion, rejected the bona fide invitation to learn sorcery, saying, "I am an Indian. I was born to hate and fear witches."

Belisario exchanged looks with his wife and his body began to convulse. Don Juan realized he was weeping silently, obviously hurt by the rejection. His wife had to prop him up until he regained his composure.

As Belisario and his wife were walking away, he turned and gave don Juan one more piece of advice. He said that the monster abhorred women, and don Juan should be on the lookout for a male replacement on the off chance that the monster would like him enough to switch slaves. But he should not raise his hopes, because it was going to be years before he could even leave the house. The monster liked to make sure his slaves were loyal or at least obedient.

Don Juan could stand it no longer. He broke down, began to weep, and told Belisario that no one was going to enslave him. He could always kill himself. The old man was very moved by don Juan's outburst and confessed that he had had the same idea, but, alas, the monster was able to read his thoughts and had prevented him from taking his own life every time he had tried.

Belisario made another offer to take don Juan with him to Durango to learn sorcery. He said it was the only possible solution. And don Juan told him his solution was like jumping from the frying pan into the fire.

Belisario began to weep loudly and embraced don Juan. He cursed the moment he had saved the other man's life and swore that he had no idea they would trade places. He blew his nose, and looking at don Juan with burning eyes, said, "Disguise is the only way to survive. If you don't behave properly, the monster can steal your soul and turn you into an idiot who does his chores, and nothing more. Too bad I don't have time to teach you acting." Then he wept even more.

Don Juan, choking with tears, asked him to describe how he could disguise himself. Belisario confided that the monster had terrible eyesight, and recommended that don Juan experiment with various clothes that suited his fancy. He had, after all, years ahead of him to try different disguises. He embraced don Juan at the door, weeping openly. His wife touched don Juan's hand shyly. And then they were gone.

"Never in my life, before or after, have I felt such terror and despair," don Juan said. "The monster rattled things inside the house as if he were waiting impatiently for me. I sat down by the door and whined like a dog in pain. Then I vomited from sheer fear.''

Don Juan sat for hours incapable of moving. He dared not leave, nor did he dare go inside. It was no exaggeration to say that he was actually about to die when he saw Belisario waving his arms, frantically trying to catch his attention from the other side of the street. Just seeing him again gave don Juan instantaneous relief. Belisario was squatting by the sidewalk watching the house. He signaled don Juan to stay put.

After an excruciatingly long time, Belisario crawled a few feet on his hands and knees toward don Juan, then squatted again, totally immobile. Crawling in that fashion, he advanced until he was at don Juan's side. It took him hours. A lot of people had passed by, but no one seemed to have noticed don Juan's despair or the old man's actions. When the two of them were side by side, Belisario whispered that he had not felt right leaving don Juan like a dog tied to a post. His wife had objected, but he had returned to attempt to rescue him. After all, it was thanks to don Juan that he had gained his freedom.

He asked don Juan in a commanding whisper whether he was ready and willing to do anything to escape this. And don Juan assured him that he would do anything. In the most surreptitious manner, Belisario handed don Juan a bundle of clothes. Then he outlined his plan. Don Juan was to go to the area of the house farthest from the monster's rooms and slowly change his clothes, taking off one item of clothing at a time, starting with his hat, leaving the shoes for last. Then he was to put all his clothes on a wooden frame, a mannequin-like structure he was to build, efficiently and quickly, as soon as he was inside the house.

The next step of the plan was for don Juan to put on the only disguise that could fool the monster: the clothes in the bundle.

Don Juan ran into the house and got everything ready. He built a scarecrow-like frame with poles he found in the back of the house, took off his clothes and put them on it. But when he opened the bundle he got the surprise of his life. The bundle consisted of women's clothes!

"I felt stupid and lost," don Juan said, "and was just about to put my own clothes back on when I heard the inhuman growls of that monstrous man. I had been reared to despise women, to believe their only function was to take care of men. Putting on women's clothes to me was tantamount to becoming a woman. But my fear of the monster was so intense that I closed my eyes and put on the damned clothes."

I looked at don Juan, imagining him in women's clothes. It was an image so utterly ridiculous that against my will I broke into a belly laugh.

Don Juan said that when old Belisario, waiting for him across the street, saw don Juan in disguise, he began to weep uncontrollably. Weeping, he guided don Juan to the outskirts of town where his wife was waiting with the two muleteers. One of them very daringly asked Belisario if he was stealing the weird girl to sell her to a whorehouse. The old man wept so hard he seemed on the verge of fainting. The young muleteers did not know what to do, but Belisario's wife, instead of commiserating, began to scream with laughter. And don Juan could not understand why.

The party began to move in the dark. They took little-traveled trails and moved steadily north. Belisario did not speak much. He seemed to be frightened and expecting trouble. His wife fought with him all the time and complained that they had thrown away their chance for freedom by taking don Juan along. Belisario gave her strict orders not to mention it again for fear the muleteers would discover that don Juan was in disguise. He cautioned don Juan that because he did not know how to behave convincingly like a woman, he should act as if he were a girl who was a little touched in the head.

Within a few days don Juan's fear subsided a great deal. In fact, he became so confident that he could not even remember having been afraid. If it had not been for the clothes he was wearing, he could have imagined the whole experience had been a bad dream.

Wearing women's clothes under those conditions, entailed, of course, a series of drastic changes. Belisario's wife coached don Juan, with true seriousness, in every aspect of being a woman. Don Juan helped her cook, wash clothes, gather firewood. Belisario shaved don Juan's head and put a strong-smelling medicine on it, and told the muleteers that the girl had had an infestation of lice. Don Juan said that since he was still a beardless youth it was not really difficult to pass as a woman. But he felt disgusted with himself, and with all those people, and, above all, with his fate. To end up wearing women's clothes and doing women's chores was more than he could bear.

One day he had enough. The muleteers were the final straw. They expected and demanded that this strange girl wait on them hand and foot. Don Juan said that he also had to be on permanent guard, because they would make passes.

I felt compelled to ask a question.

"Were the muleteers in cahoots with your benefactor?" I asked.

"No," he replied and began to laugh uproariously. "They were just two nice people who had fallen temporarily under his spell. He had hired their mules to carry medicinal plants and told them that he would pay handsomely if they would help him kidnap a young woman.''

The scope of the nagual Julian's actions staggered my imagination. I pictured don Juan fending off sexual advances and hollered with laughter.

Don Juan continued his account. He said that he told the old man sternly that the masquerade had lasted long enough, the men were making sexual advances. Belisario nonchalantly advised him to be more understanding, because men will be men, and began to weep again, completely baffling don Juan, who found himself furiously defending women.

He was so passionate about the plight of women that he scared himself. He told Belisario that he was going to end up in worse shape than he would have, had he stayed as the monster's slave.

Don Juan's turmoil increased when the old man wept uncontrollably and mumbled inanities: life was sweet, the little price one had to pay for it was a joke, the monster would devour don Juan's soul and not even allow him to kill himself. "Flirt with the muleteers," he advised don Juan in a conciliatory tone and manner. "They are primitive peasants. All they want is to play, so push them back when they shove you. Let them touch your leg. What do you care?'' And again, he wept unrestrainedly. Don Juan asked him why he wept like that. "Because you are perfect for all this," he said and his body twisted with the force of his sobbing.

Don Juan thanked him for his good feelings and for all the trouble he was taking on his account. He told Belisario he now felt safe and wanted to leave.

"The art of *stalking* is learning all the quirks of your disguise," Belisario said, paying no attention to what don Juan was telling him. "And it is to learn them so well no one will know you are disguised. For that you need to be ruthless, cunning, patient, and sweet."

Don Juan had no idea what Belisario was talking about. Rather than finding out, he asked him for some men's clothes. Belisario was very understanding. He gave don Juan some old clothes and a few pesos. He promised don Juan that his disguise would always be there in case he needed it, and pressed him vehemently to come to Durango with him to learn sorcery and free himself from the monster for good. Don Juan said no and thanked him. So Belisario bid him good-bye and patted him on the back repeatedly and with considerable force.

Don Juan changed his clothes and asked Belisario for directions. He answered that if don Juan followed the trail north, sooner or later he would reach the next town. He said that the two of them might even cross paths again since they were all going in the same general direction—away from the monster.

Don Juan took off as fast as he could, free at last. He must have walked four or five miles before he found signs of people. He knew that a town was nearby and thought that perhaps he could get work there until he decided where he was going. He sat down to rest for a moment, anticipating the normal difficulties a stranger would find in a small out-of-the-way town, when from the corner of his eye he saw a movement in the bushes by the mule trail. He felt someone was watching him. He became so thoroughly terrified that he jumped up and started to run in the direction of the town; the monster jumped at him lurching out to grab his neck. He missed by an inch. Don Juan screamed as he had never screamed before, but still had enough self-control to turn and run back in the direction from which he had come.

While don Juan ran for his life, the monster pursued him, crashing through the bushes only a few feet away. Don Juan said that it was the most frightening sound he had ever heard. Finally he saw the mules moving slowly in the distance, and he yelled for help.

Belisario recognized don Juan and ran toward him displaying overt terror. He threw the bundle of women's clothes at don Juan shouting, "Run like a woman, you fool."

Don Juan admitted that he did not know how he had the presence of mind to run like a woman, but he did it. The monster stopped chasing him. And Belisario told him to change quickly while he held the monster at bay.

Don Juan joined Belisario's wife and the smiling muleteers without looking at anybody. They doubled back and took other trails. Nobody spoke for days; then Belisario gave him daily lessons. He told don Juan that Indian women were practical and went directly to the heart of things, but that they were also very shy, and that when challenged they showed the physical signs of fright in shifty eyes, tight mouths, and enlarged nostrils. All these signs were accompanied by a fearful stubbornness, followed by shy laughter.

He made don Juan practice his womanly behavior skills in every town they passed through. And don Juan honestly believed he was teaching him to be an actor. But Belisario insisted that he was teaching him the art of *stalking*. He told don Juan that *stalking* was an art applicable to everything, and that there were four steps to learning it: ruthlessness, cunning, patience, and sweetness.

I felt compelled to interrupt his account once more.

"But isn't *stalking* taught in deep, heightened awareness?" I asked.

"Of course," he replied with a grin. "But you have to understand that for some men wearing women's clothes is the door into heightened awareness. In fact, such means are more effective than pushing the assemblage point, but are very difficult to arrange."

Don Juan said that his benefactor drilled him daily in the four moods of *stalking* and insisted that don Juan understand that ruthlessness should not be harshness, cunning should not be cruelty, patience should not be negligence, and sweetness should not be foolishness.

He taught him that these four steps had to be practiced and perfected until they were so smooth they were unnoticeable. He believed women to be natural *stalkers*. And his conviction was so strong he maintained that only in a woman's disguise could any man really learn the art of *stalking*.

"I went with him to every market in every town we passed and haggled with everyone," don Juan went on. "My benefactor used to stay to one side watching me. 'Be ruthless but charming,' he used to say. 'Be cunning but nice. Be patient but active. Be sweet but lethal. Only women can do it. If a man acts this way he's being prissy.' "

And as if to make sure don Juan stayed in line, the monstrous man appeared from time to time. Don Juan caught sight of him, roaming the countryside. He would see him most often after Belisario gave him a vigorous back massage, supposedly to alleviate a sharp nervous pain in his neck. Don Juan laughed and said that he had no idea he was being manipulated into heightened awareness.

"It took us one month to reach the city of Durango," don Juan said. "In that month, I had a brief sample of the four moods of *stalking*. It really didn't change me much, but it gave me a chance to have an inkling of what being a woman was like."

THE FOUR MOODS OF *STALKING*

Don Juan said that I should sit there at that ancient lookout post and use the pull of the earth to move my assemblage point and recall other states of heightened awareness in which he had taught me *stalking*.

"In the past few days, I have mentioned many times the four moods of *stalking*," he went on. "I have mentioned ruthlessness, cunning, patience, and sweetness, with the hope that you might remember what I taught you about them. It would be wonderful if you could use these four moods as the ushers to bring you into a total recollection."

He kept quiet for what seemed an inordinately long moment. Then he made a statement which should not have surprised me, but did. He said he had taught me the four moods of *stalking* in northern Mexico with the help of Vicente Medrano and Silvio Manuel. He did not elaborate but let his statement sink in. I tried to remember but finally gave up and wanted to shout that I could not remember something that never happened.

As I was struggling to voice my protest, anxious thoughts began to cross my mind. I knew don Juan had not said what he had just to annoy me. As I always did when asked to remember heightened awareness, I became obsessively conscious that there was really no continuity to the events I had experienced under his guidance. Those events were not strung together as the events in my daily life were, in a linear sequence. It was perfectly possible he was right. In don Juan's world, I had no business being certain of anything.

I tried to voice my doubts but he refused to listen and urged me to recollect. By then it was quite dark.

It had gotten windy, but I did not feel the cold. Don Juan had given me a flat rock to place on my sternum. My awareness was keenly tuned to everything around. I felt an abrupt pull, which was neither external nor internal, but rather the sensation of a sustained tugging at an unidentifiable part of myself. Suddenly I began to remember with shattering clarity a meeting I had had years before. I remembered events and people so vividly that it frightened me. I felt a chill.

I told all this to don Juan, who did not seem impressed or concerned. He urged me not to give in to mental or physical fear.

My recollection was so phenomenal that it was as if I were reliving the experience. Don Juan kept quiet. He did not even look at me. I felt numbed. The sensation of numbness passed slowly.

I repeated the same things I always said to don Juan when I remembered an event with no linear existence.

"How can this be, don Juan? How could I have forgotten all this?"

And he reaffirmed the same things he always did.

"This type of remembering or forgetting has nothing to do with normal memory," he assured me. "It has to do with the movement of the assemblage point."

He affirmed that although I possessed total knowledge of what *intent* is, I did not command that knowledge yet. Knowing what *intent* is means that one can, at any time, explain that knowledge or use it. A nagual by the force of his position is obliged to command his knowledge in this manner.

"What did you recollect?" he asked me.

"The first time you told me about the four moods of *stalking*," I said.

Some process, inexplicable in terms of my usual awareness of the world, had released a memory which a minute before had not existed. And I recollected an entire sequence of events that had happened many years before.

Just as I was leaving don Juan's house in Sonora, he had asked me to meet him the following week around noon, across the U.S. border, in Nogales, Arizona, in the Greyhound bus depot.

I arrived about an hour early. He was standing by the door. I greeted him. He did not answer but hurriedly pulled me aside and whispered that I should take my hands out of my pockets. I was dumbfounded. He did not give me time to respond, but said that my fly was open, and it was shamefully evident that I was sexually aroused.

The speed with which I rushed to cover myself was phenomenal. By the time I realized it was a crude joke we were on the street. Don Juan was laughing, slapping me on the back repeatedly and forcefully, as if he were just celebrating the joke. Suddenly I found myself in a state of heightened awareness.

We walked into a coffee shop and sat down. My mind was so clear I wanted to look at everything, *see* the essence of things.

"Don't waste energy!" don Juan commanded in a stern voice. "I brought you here to discover if you can eat when your assemblage point has moved. Don't try to do more than that."

But then a man sat down at the table in front of me, and all my attention became trapped by him.

"Move your eyes in circles," don Juan commanded. "Don't look at that man."

I found it impossible to stop watching the man. I felt irritated by don Juan's demands.

"What do you *see*?" I heard don Juan ask.

I was *seeing* a luminous cocoon made of transparent wings which were folded over the cocoon itself. The wings unfolded, fluttered for an instant, peeled off,

71

fell, and were replaced by new wings, which repeated the same process.

Don Juan boldly turned my chair until I was facing the wall.

"What a waste," he said in a loud sigh, after I described what I had *seen*. "You have exhausted nearly all your energy. Restrain yourself. A warrior needs focus. Who gives a damn about wings on a luminous cocoon?"

He said that heightened awareness was like a springboard. From it one could jump into infinity. He stressed, over and over, that when the assemblage point was dislodged, it either became lodged again at a position very near its customary one or continued moving on into infinity.

"People have no idea of the strange power we carry within ourselves," he went on. "At this moment, for instance, you have the means to reach infinity. If you continue with your needless behavior, you may succeed in pushing your assemblage point beyond a certain threshold, from which there is no return."

I understood the peril he was talking about, or rather I had the bodily sensation that I was standing on the brink of an abyss, and that if I leaned forward I would fall into it.

"Your assemblage point moved to heightened awareness," he continued, "because I have lent you my energy."

We ate in silence, very simple food. Don Juan did not allow me to drink coffee or tea.

"While you are using my energy," he said, "you're not in your own time. You are in mine. I drink water."

As we were walking back to my car I felt a bit nauseous. I staggered and almost lost my balance. It was a sensation similar to that of walking while wearing glasses for the first time.

"Get hold of yourself," don Juan said, smiling.

"Where we're going, you'll need to be extremely precise."

He told me to drive across the international border into the twin city of Nogales, Mexico. While I was driving, he gave me directions: which street to take, when to make right or left hand turns, how fast to go.

"I know this area," I said quite peeved. "Tell me where you want to go and I'll take you there. Like a taxi driver."

"O.K.," he said. "Take me to 1573 Heavenward Avenue."

I did not know Heavenward Avenue, or if such a street really existed. In fact, I had the suspicion he had just concocted a name to embarrass me. I kept silent. There was a mocking glint in his shiny eyes.

"Egomania is a real tyrant," he said. "We must work ceaselessly to dethrone it."

He continued to tell me how to drive. Finally he asked me to stop in front of a one-story, light-beige house on a corner lot, in a well-to-do neighborhood.

There was something about the house that immediately caught my eye: a thick layer of ocher gravel all around it. The solid street door, the window sashes, and the house trim were all painted ocher, like the gravel. All the visible windows had closed venetian blinds. To all appearances it was a typical suburban middle-class dwelling.

We got out of the car. Don Juan led the way. He did not knock or open the door with a key, but when we got to it, the door opened silently on oiled hinges—all by itself, as far as I could detect.

Don Juan quickly entered. He did not invite me in. I just followed him. I was curious to see who had opened the door from the inside, but there was no one there.

The interior of the house was very soothing. There were no pictures on the smooth, scrupulously clean walls. There were no lamps or book shelves either. A golden yellow tile floor contrasted most pleasingly with the off-white color of the walls. We were in a small and narrow hall that opened into a spacious living room with a high ceiling and a brick fireplace. Half the room was completely empty, but next to the fireplace was a semicircle of expensive furniture: two large beige couches in the middle, flanked by two armchairs covered in fabric of the same color. There was a heavy, round, solid oak coffee table in the center. Judging from what I was seeing around the house, the people who lived there appeared to be well off, but frugal. And they obviously liked to sit around the fire.

Two men, perhaps in their mid-fifties, sat in the armchairs. They stood when we entered. One of them was Indian, the other Latin American. Don Juan introduced me first to the Indian, who was nearer to me.

"This is Silvio Manuel," don Juan said to me. "He's the most powerful and dangerous sorcerer of my party, and the most mysterious too."

Silvio Manuel's features were out of a Mayan fresco. His complexion was pale, almost yellow. I thought he looked Chinese. His eyes were slanted, but without the epicanthic fold. They were big, black, and brilliant. He was beardless. His hair was jet-black with specks of gray in it. He had high cheekbones and full lips. He was perhaps five feet seven, thin, wiry, and he wore a yellow sport shirt, brown slacks, and a thin beige jacket. Judging from his clothes and general mannerisms, he seemed to be Mexican-American.

I smiled and extended my hand to Silvio Manuel, but he did not take it. He nodded perfunctorily.

"And this is Vicente Medrano," don Juan said, turning to the other man. "He's the most knowledgeable and the oldest of my companions. He is oldest not in terms of age, but because he was my benefactor's first disciple."

Vicente nodded just as perfunctorily as Silvio Manuel had, and also did not say a word.

He was a bit taller than Silvio Manuel, but just as lean. He had a pinkish complexion and a neatly trimmed beard and mustache. His features were almost delicate: a thin, beautifully chiseled nose, a small mouth, thin lips. Bushy, dark eyebrows contrasted with his graying beard and hair. His eyes were brown and also brilliant and laughed in spite of his frowning expression.

He was conservatively dressed in a greenish seersucker suit and open-collared sport shirt. He too seemed to be Mexican-American. I guessed him to be the owner of the house.

In contrast, don Juan looked like an Indian peon. His straw hat, his worn-out shoes, his old khaki pants and plaid shirt were those of a gardener or a handyman.

The impression I had, upon seeing all three of them together, was that don Juan was in disguise. The military image came to me that don Juan was the commanding officer of a clandestine operation, an officer who, no matter how hard he tried, could not hide his years of command.

I also had the feeling that they must all have been around the same age, although don Juan looked much older than the other two, yet seemed infinitely stronger.

"I think you already know that Carlos is by far the biggest indulger I have ever met," don Juan told them with a most serious expression. "Bigger even than our benefactor. I assure you that if there is someone who takes indulging seriously, this is the man."

I laughed, but no one else did. The two men observed me with a strange glint in their eyes.

"For sure you'll make a memorable trio," don Juan continued. "The oldest and most knowledgeable, the most dangerous and powerful, and the most self-indulgent.''

They still did not laugh. They scrutinized me until I became self-conscious. Then Vicente broke the silence.

"I don't know why you brought him inside the house," he said in a dry, cutting tone. "He's of little use to us. Put him out in the backyard."

"And tie him," Silvio Manuel added.

Don Juan turned to me. "Come on," he said in a soft voice and pointed with a quick sideways movement of his head to the back of the house.

It was more than obvious that the two men did not like me. I did not know what to say. I was definitely angry and hurt, but those feelings were somehow deflected by my state of heightened awareness.

We walked into the backyard. Don Juan casually picked up a leather rope and twirled it around my neck with tremendous speed. His movements were so fast and so nimble that an instant later, before I could realize what was happening, I was tied at the neck, like a dog, to one of the two cinder-block columns supporting the heavy roof over the back porch.

Don Juan shook his head from side to side in a gesture of resignation or disbelief and went back into the house as I began to yell at him to untie me. The rope was so tight around my neck it prevented me from screaming as loud as I would have liked.

I could not believe what was taking place. Containing my anger, I tried to undo the knot at my neck. It was so compact that the leather strands seemed glued together. I hurt my nails trying to pull them apart.

I had an attack of uncontrollable wrath and growled like an impotent animal. Then I grabbed the rope, twisted it around my forearms, and bracing my feet against the cinder-block column, pulled. But the leather was too tough for the strength of my muscles.

I felt humiliated and scared. Fear brought me a moment of sobriety. I knew I had let don Juan's false aura of reasonableness deceive me.

I assessed my situation as objectively as I could and saw no way to escape except by cutting the leather rope. I frantically began to rub it against the sharp corner of the cinder-block column. I thought that if I could rip the rope before any of the men came to the back, I had a chance to run to my car and take off, never to return.

I puffed and sweated and rubbed the rope until I had nearly worn it through. Then I braced one foot against the column, wrapped the rope around my forearms again, and pulled it desperately until it snapped, throwing me back into the house.

As I crashed backward through the open door, don Juan, Vicente, and Silvio Manuel were standing in the middle of the room, applauding.

"What a dramatic reentry," Vicente said, helping me up. "You fooled me. I didn't think you were capable of such explosions."

Don Juan came to me and snapped the knot open, freeing my neck from the piece of rope around it.

I was shaking with fear, exertion, and anger. In a faltering voice, I asked don Juan why he was tormenting me like this. The three of them laughed and at that moment seemed the farthest thing from threatening.

"We wanted to test you and find out what sort of a man you really are," don Juan said.

He led me to one of the couches and politely offered me a seat. Vicente and Silvio Manuel sat in the armchairs, don Juan sat facing me on the other couch.

I laughed nervously but was no longer apprehensive about my situation, nor about don Juan and his friends. All three regarded me with frank curiosity. Vicente could not stop smiling, although he seemed to be trying desperately to appear serious. Silvio Manuel shook his head rhythmically as he stared at me. His eyes were unfocused but fixed on me.

"We tied you down," don Juan went on, "because we wanted to know whether you are sweet or patient or ruthless or cunning. We found out you are none of those things. Rather you're a king-sized indulger, just as I had said.

"If you hadn't indulged in being violent, you would certainly have noticed that the formidable knot in the rope around your neck was a fake. It snaps. Vicente designed that knot to fool his friends."

"You tore the rope violently. You're certainly not sweet," Silvio Manuel said.

They were all quiet for a moment, then began to laugh.

"You're neither ruthless nor cunning," don Juan went on. "If you were, you would easily have snapped open both knots and run away with a valuable leather rope. You're not patient either. If you were, you would have whined and cried until you realized that there was a pair of clippers by the wall with which you could have cut the rope in two seconds and saved yourself all the agony and exertion.

"You can't be taught, then, to be violent or obtuse. You already are that. But you can learn to be ruthless, cunning, patient, and sweet."

Don Juan explained to me that ruthlessness, cunning, patience, and sweetness were the essence of *stalking*. They were the basics that with all their ramifications had to be taught in careful, meticulous steps.

He was definitely addressing me, but he talked looking at Vicente and Silvio Manuel, who listened with utmost attention and shook their heads in agreement from time to time.

He stressed repeatedly that teaching *stalking* was one of the most difficult things sorcerers did. And he insisted that no matter what they themselves did to teach me *stalking,* and no matter what I believed to the contrary, it was impeccability which dictated their acts.

"Rest assured we know what we're doing. Our benefactor, the nagual Julian, saw to it," don Juan said, and all three of them broke into such uproarious laughter that I felt quite uncomfortable. I did not know what to think.

Don Juan reiterated that a very important point to consider was that, to an onlooker, the behavior of sorcerers might appear malicious, when in reality their behavior was always impeccable.

"How can you tell the difference, if you're at the receiving end?" I asked.

"Malicious acts are performed by people for personal gain," he said. "Sorcerers, though, have an ulterior purpose for their acts, which has nothing to do with personal gain. The fact that they enjoy their acts does not count as gain. Rather, it is a condition of their character. The average man acts only if there is the chance for profit. Warriors say they act not for profit but for the spirit."

I thought about it. Acting without considering gain was truly an alien concept. I had been reared to invest and to hope for some kind of reward for everything I did.

Don Juan must have taken my silence and thoughtfulness as skepticism. He laughed and looked at his two companions.

"Take the four of us, as an example," he went on. "You, yourself, believe that you're investing in this situation and eventually you are going to profit from it. If you get angry with us, or if we disappoint you, you may resort to malicious acts to get even with us. We, on the contrary, have no thought of personal gain. Our acts are dictated by impeccability—we can't be angry or disillusioned with you."

Don Juan smiled and told me that from the moment we had met at the bus depot that day, everything he had done to me, although it might not have seemed so, was dictated by impeccability. He explained that he needed to get me into an unguarded position to help me enter heightened awareness. It was to that end that he had told me my fly was open.

"It was a way of jolting you," he said with a grin. "We are crude Indians, so all our jolts are somehow primitive. The more sophisticated the warrior, the greater his finesse and elaboration of his jolts. But I have to admit we got a big kick out of our crudeness, especially when we tied you at the neck like a dog."

The three of them grinned and then laughed quietly as if there was someone else inside the house whom they did not want to disturb.

In a very low voice don Juan said that because I was in a state of heightened awareness, I could understand more readily what he was going to tell me about the two masteries: *stalking* and *intent*. He called them the crowning glory of sorcerers old and new, the very thing sorcerers were concerned with today, just as sorcerers had been thousands of years before. He asserted that *stalking* was the beginning, and that before anything could be attempted on the warrior's path, warriors must learn to *stalk;* next they must learn to *intend*, and only then could they move their assemblage point at will.

I knew exactly what he was talking about. I knew, without knowing how, what moving the assemblage point could accomplish. But I did not have the words to explain what I knew. I tried repeatedly to voice my knowledge to them. They laughed at my failures and coaxed me to try again.

"How would you like it if I articulate it for you?" don Juan asked. "I might be able to find the very words you want to use but can't."

From his look, I decided he was seriously asking my permission. I found the situation so incongruous that I began to laugh.

Don Juan, displaying great patience, asked me again, and I got another attack of laughter. Their look of surprise and concern told me my reaction was incomprehensible to them. Don Juan got up and announced that I was too tired and it was time for me to return to the world of ordinary affairs.

"Wait, wait," I pleaded. "I am all right. I just find it funny that you should be asking me to give you permission."

"I have to ask your permission," don Juan said, "because you're the only one who can allow the words pent up inside you to be tapped. I think I made the mistake of assuming you understand more than you do. Words are tremendously powerful and important and are the magical property of whoever has them.

"Sorcerers have a rule of thumb: they say that the deeper the assemblage point moves, the greater the feeling that one has knowledge and no words to explain it. Sometimes the assemblage point of average persons can move without a known cause and without their being aware of it, except that they become tongue-tied, confused, and evasive."

Vicente interrupted and suggested I stay with them a while longer. Don Juan agreed and turned to face me.

"The very first principle of *stalking* is that a warrior stalks himself," he said. "He *stalks* himself ruthlessly, cunningly, patiently, and sweetly."

I wanted to laugh, but he did not give me time. Very succinctly he defined *stalking* as the art of using behavior in novel ways for specific purposes. He said that normal human behavior in the world of everyday life was routine. Any behavior that broke from routine caused an unusual effect on our total being. That unusual effect was what sorcerers sought, because it was cumulative.

He explained that the sorcerer seers of ancient times, through their *seeing*, had first noticed that unusual behavior produced a tremor in the assemblage point. They soon discovered that if unusual behavior was practiced systematically and directed wisely, it eventually forced the assemblage point to move.

"The real challenge for those sorcerer seers," don Juan went on, "was finding a system of behavior that was neither petty nor capricious, but that combined the morality and the sense of beauty which differentiates sorcerer seers from plain witches."

He stopped talking, and they all looked at me as if searching for signs of fatigue in my eyes or face.

"Anyone who succeeds in moving his assemblage point to a new position is a sorcerer," don Juan continued. "And from that new position, he can do all kinds of good and bad things to his fellow men. Being a sorcerer, therefore, can be like being a cobbler or a baker. The quest of sorcerer seers is to go beyond that stand. And to do that, they need morality and beauty."

He said that for sorcerers *stalking* was the foundation on which everything else they did was built.

"Some sorcerers object to the term *stalking*," he went on, "but the name came about because it entails surreptitious behavior.

"It's also called the art of stealth, but that term is equally unfortunate. We ourselves, because of our nonmilitant temperament, call it the art of controlled folly. You can call it anything you wish. We, however, will continue with the term *stalking* since it's so easy to say *stalker* and, as my benefactor used to say, so awkward to say *controlled folly maker*."

At the mention of their benefactor, they laughed like children.

I understood him perfectly. I had no questions or doubts. If anything, I had the feeling that I needed to hold onto every word don Juan was saying to anchor myself. Otherwise my thoughts would have run ahead of him.

I noticed that my eyes were fixed on the movement of his lips as my ears were fixed on the sound of his words. But once I realized this, I could no longer follow him. My concentration was broken. Don Juan continued talking, but I was not listening. I was wondering about the inconceivable possibility of living permanently in heightened awareness. I asked myself what would the survival value be? Would one be able to assess situations better? Be quicker than the average man, or perhaps more intelligent?

Don Juan suddenly stopped talking and asked me what I was thinking about.

"Ah, you're so very practical," he commented after I had told him my reveries. "I thought that in heightened awareness your temperament was going to be more artistic, more mystical."

Don Juan turned to Vicente and asked him to answer my question. Vicente cleared his throat and dried his hands by rubbing them against his thighs. He gave the clear impression of suffering from stage fright. I felt sorry for him. My thoughts began to spin. And when I heard him stammering, an image burst into my mind—the image I had always had of my father's timidity, his fear of people. But before I had time to surrender myself to that image, Vicente's eyes flared with some strange inner luminosity. He made a comically serious face at me and then spoke with authority and a professorial manner.

"To answer your question," he said, "there is no survival value in heightened awareness; otherwise the thing man is or does, and that perception is ruled by the location of the assemblage point. Therefore, if that point changes positions, man's perception of the world changes accordingly. The sorcerer who knew exactly where to place his assemblage point could become anything he wanted.

"The nagual Julian's proficiency in moving his assemblage point was so magnificent that he could elicit the subtlest transformations," don Juan continued. "When a sorcerer becomes a crow, for instance, it is definitely a great accomplishment. But it entails a vast and therefore a gross shift of the assemblage point. However, moving it to the position of a fat man, or an old man, requires the minutest shift and the keenest knowledge of human nature."

"I'd rather avoid thinking or talking about those things as facts," I said.

Don Juan laughed as if I had said the funniest thing imaginable.

"Was there a reason for your benefactor's transformations?" I asked. "Or was he just amusing himself?"

"Don't be stupid. Warriors don't do anything just to amuse themselves," he replied. "His transformations were strategical. They were dictated by need, like his transformation from old to young. Now and then there were funny consequences, but that's another matter."

I reminded him that I had asked before how his benefactor learned those transformations. He had told me then that his benefactor had a teacher, but would not tell me who.

"That very mysterious sorcerer who is our ward taught him," don Juan replied curtly.

"What mysterious sorcerer is that?" I asked.

"The death defier," he said and looked at me questioningly.

whole human race would be there. They are safe from that, though, because it's so hard to get into it. There is always, however, the remote possibility that an average man might enter into such a state. If he does, he ordinarily succeeds in confusing himself, sometimes irreparably."

The three of them exploded with laughter.

"Sorcerers say that heightened awareness is the portal of *intent*," don Juan said. "And they use it as such. Think about it."

I was staring at each of them in turn. My mouth was open, and I felt that if I kept it open I would be able to understand the riddle eventually. I closed my eyes and the answer came to me. I felt it. I did not think it. But I could not put it into words, no matter how hard I tried.

"There, there," don Juan said, "you've gotten another sorcerer's answer all by yourself, but you still don't have enough energy to flatten it and turn it into words."

The sensation I was experiencing was more than just that of being unable to voice my thoughts; it was like reliving something I had forgotten ages ago: not to know what I felt because I had not yet learned to speak, and therefore lacked the resources to translate my feelings into thoughts.

"Thinking and saying exactly what you want to say requires untold amounts of energy," don Juan said and broke into my feelings.

The force of my reverie had been so intense it had made me forget what had started it. I stared dumbfounded at don Juan and confessed I had no idea what they or I had said or done just a moment before. I remembered the incident of the leather rope and what don Juan had told me immediately afterward, but I could not recall the feeling that had flooded me just moments ago.

"You're going the wrong way," don Juan said. "You're trying to remember thoughts the way you normally do, but this is a different situation. A second ago you had an overwhelming feeling that you knew something very specific. Such feelings cannot be recollected by using memory. You have to recall them by *intending* them back."

He turned to Silvio Manuel, who had stretched out in the armchair, his legs under the coffee table. Silvio Manuel looked fixedly at me. His eyes were black, like two pieces of shiny obsidian. Without moving a muscle, he let out a piercing birdlike scream.

"Intent!!" he yelled. *"Intent!! Intent!!!"*

With each scream his voice became more and more inhuman and piercing. The hair on the back of my neck stood on end. I felt goose bumps on my skin. My mind, however, instead of focusing on the fright I was experiencing, went directly to recollecting the feeling I had had. But before I could savor it completely, the feeling expanded and burst into something else. And then I understood not only why heightened awareness was the portal of *intent*, but I also understood what *intent* was. And, above all, I understood that that knowledge could not be turned into words. That knowledge was there for everyone. It was there to be felt, to be used, but not to be explained. One could come into it by changing levels of awareness, therefore, heightened awareness was an entrance. But even the entrance could not be explained. One could only make use of it.

There was still another piece of knowledge that came to me that day without any coaching: that the natural knowledge of *intent* was available to anyone, but the command of it belonged to those who probed it.

I was terribly tired by this time, and doubtlessly as a result of that, my Catholic upbringing came to bear heavily on my reactions. For a moment I believed that *intent* was God.

I said as much to don Juan, Vicente and Silvio Manuel. They laughed. Vicente, still in his professorial tone, said that it could not possibly be God, because *intent* was a force that could not be described, much less represented.

"Don't be presumptuous," don Juan said to me sternly. "Don't try to speculate on the basis of your first and only trial. Wait until you command your knowledge, then decide what is what."

Remembering the four moods of *stalking* exhausted me. The most dramatic result was a more than ordinary indifference. I would not have cared if I had dropped dead, nor if don Juan had. I did not care whether we stayed at that ancient lookout post overnight or started back in the pitch-dark.

Don Juan was very understanding. He guided me by the hand, as if I were blind, to a massive rock, and helped me sit with my back to it. He recommended that I let natural sleep return me to a normal state of awareness.

4

The Descent of the Spirit

SEEING THE SPIRIT

Right after a late lunch, while we were still at the table, don Juan announced that the two of us were going to spend the night in the sorcerers' cave and that we had to be on our way. He said that it was imperative that I sit there again, in total darkness, to allow the rock formation and the sorcerers' *intent* to move my assemblage point.

I started to get up from my chair, but he stopped me. He said that there was something he wanted to explain to me first. He stretched out, putting his feet on the seat of a chair, then leaned back into a relaxed, comfortable position.

"As I *see* you in greater detail," don Juan said, "I notice more and more how similar you and my benefactor are."

I felt so threatened that I did not let him continue. I told him that I could not imagine what those similarities were, but if there were any—a possibility I did not consider reassuring—I would appreciate it if he told me about them, to give me a chance to correct or avoid them.

Don Juan laughed until tears were rolling down his cheeks.

"One of the similarities is that when you act, you act very well," he said, "but when you think, you always trip yourself up. My benefactor was like that. He didn't think too well."

I was just about to defend myself, to say there was nothing wrong with my thinking, when I caught a glint of mischievousness in his eyes. I stopped cold. Don Juan noticed my shift and laughed with a note of surprise. He must have been anticipating the opposite.

"What I mean, for instance, is that you only have problems understanding the spirit when you think about it," he went on with a chiding smile. "But when you act, the spirit easily reveals itself to you. My benefactor was that way.

"Before we leave for the cave, I am going to tell you a story about my benefactor and the fourth abstract core.

"Sorcerers believe that until the very moment of the spirit's descent, any of us could walk away from the spirit; but not afterwards."

Don Juan deliberately stopped to urge me, with a movement of his eyebrows, to consider what he was telling me.

"The fourth abstract core is the full brunt of the spirit's descent," he went on. "The fourth abstract core is an act of revelation. The spirit reveals itself to us. Sorcerers describe it as the spirit lying in ambush and then descending on us, its prey. Sorcerers say that the spirit's descent is always shrouded. It happens and yet it seems not to have happened at all."

I became very nervous. Don Juan's tone of voice

was giving me the feeling that he was preparing to spring something on me at any moment.

He asked me if I remembered the moment the spirit descended on me, sealing my permanent allegiance to the abstract.

I had no idea what he was talking about.

"There is a threshold that once crossed permits no retreat," he said. "Ordinarily, from the moment the spirit knocks, it is years before an apprentice reaches that threshold. Sometimes, though, the threshold is reached almost immediately. My benefactor's case is an example."

Don Juan said every sorcerer should have a clear memory of crossing that threshold so he could remind himself of the new state of his perceptual potential. He explained that one did not have to be an apprentice of sorcery to reach this threshold, and that the only difference between an average man and a sorcerer, in such cases, is what each emphasizes. A sorcerer emphasizes crossing this threshold and uses the memory of it as a point of reference. An average man does not cross the threshold and does his best to forget all about it.

I told him that I did not agree with his point, because I could not accept that there was only one threshold to cross.

Don Juan looked heavenward in dismay and shook his head in a joking gesture of despair. I proceeded with my argument, not to disagree with him, but to clarify things in my mind. Yet I quickly lost my impetus. Suddenly I had the feeling I was sliding through a tunnel.

"Sorcerers say that the fourth abstract core happens when the spirit cuts our chains of self-reflection," he said. "Cutting our chains is marvelous, but also very undesirable, for nobody wants to be free."

The sensation of sliding through a tunnel persisted

for a moment longer, and then everything became clear to me. And I began to laugh. Strange insights pent up inside me were exploding into laughter.

Don Juan seemed to be reading my mind as if it were a book.

"What a strange feeling: to realize that everything we think, everything we say depends on the position of the assemblage point," he remarked.

And that was exactly what I had been thinking and laughing about.

"I know that at this moment your assemblage point has shifted," he went on, "and you have understood the secret of our chains. They imprison us, but by keeping us pinned down on our comfortable spot of self-reflection, they defend us from the onslaughts of the unknown."

I was having one of those extraordinary moments in which everything about the sorcerers' world was crystal clear. I understood everything.

"Once our chains are cut," don Juan continued, "we are no longer bound by the concerns of the daily world. We are still in the daily world, but we don't belong there anymore. In order to belong we must share the concerns of people, and without chains we can't."

Don Juan said that the nagual Elías had explained to him that what distinguishes normal people is that we share a metaphorical dagger: the concerns of our self-reflection. With this dagger, we cut ourselves and bleed; and the job of our chains of self-reflection is to give us the feeling that we are bleeding together, that we are sharing something wonderful: our humanity. But if we were to examine it, we would discover that we are bleeding alone; that we are not sharing anything; that all we are doing is toying with our manageable, unreal, man-made reflection.

"Sorcerers are no longer in the world of daily affairs,'' don Juan went on, ''because they are no longer prey to their self-reflection.''

Don Juan then began his story about his benefactor and the descent of the spirit. He said that the story started right after the spirit had knocked on the young actor's door.

I interrupted don Juan and asked him why he consistently used the terms ''young man'' or ''young actor'' to refer to the nagual Julian.

''At the time of this story, he wasn't the nagual,'' don Juan replied. ''He was a young actor. In my story, I can't just call him Julian, because to me he was always the nagual Julian. As a sign of deference for his lifetime of impeccability, we always prefix 'nagual' to a nagual's name.''

Don Juan proceeded with his story. He said that the nagual Elías had stopped the young actor's death by making him shift into heightened awareness, and following hours of struggle, the young actor regained consciousness. The nagual Elías did not mention his name, but he introduced himself as a professional healer who had stumbled onto the scene of a tragedy, where two persons had nearly died. He pointed to the young woman, Talía, stretched out on the ground. The young man was astonished to see her lying unconscious next to him. He remembered seeing her as she ran away. It startled him to hear the old healer explain that doubtlessly God had punished Talía for her sins by striking her with lightning and making her lose her mind.

''But how could there be lightning if it's not even raining?'' the young actor asked in a barely audible voice. He was visibly affected when the old Indian replied that God's ways couldn't be questioned.

Again I interrupted don Juan. I was curious to know if the young woman really had lost her mind. He reminded me that the nagual Elías delivered a shattering blow to her assemblage point. He said that she had not lost her mind, but that as a result of the blow she slipped in and out of heightened awareness, creating a serious threat to her health. After a gigantic struggle, however, the nagual Elías helped her to stabilize her assemblage point and she entered permanently into heightened awareness.

Don Juan commented that women are capable of such a master stroke: they can permanently maintain a new position of their assemblage point. And Talía was peerless. As soon as her chains were broken, she immediately understood everything and complied with the nagual's designs.

Don Juan, recounting his story, said that the nagual Elías—who was not only a superb *dreamer*, but also a superb *stalker*—had *seen* that the young actor was spoiled and conceited, but only seemed to be hard and calloused. The nagual knew that if he brought forth the idea of God, sin, and retribution, the actor's religious beliefs would make his cynical attitude collapse.

Upon hearing about God's punishment, the actor's facade began to crumble. He started to express remorse, but the nagual cut him short and forcefully stressed that when death was so near, feelings of guilt no longer mattered.

The young actor listened attentively, but, although he felt very ill, he did not believe that he was in danger of dying. He thought that his weakness and fainting had been brought on by his loss of blood.

As if he had read the young actor's mind, the nagual explained to him that those optimistic thoughts were out of place, that his hemorrhaging would have been fatal had it not been for the plug that he, as a healer, had created.

"When I struck your back, I put in a plug to stop the draining of your life force," the nagual said to the skeptical young actor. "Without that restraint, the unavoidable process of your death would continue. If you don't believe me, I'll prove it to you by removing the plug with another blow."

As he spoke, the nagual Elías tapped the young actor on his right side by his ribcage. In a moment the young man was retching and choking. Blood poured out of his mouth as he coughed uncontrollably. Another tap on his back stopped the agonizing pain and retching. But it did not stop his fear, and he passed out.

"I can control your death for the time being," the nagual said when the young actor regained consciousness. "How long I can control it depends on you, on how faithfully you acquiesce to everything I tell you to do."

The nagual said that the first requirements of the young man were total immobility and silence. If he did not want his plug to come out, the nagual added, he had to behave as if he had lost his powers of motion and speech. A single twitch or a single utterance would be enough to restart his dying.

The young actor was not accustomed to complying with suggestions or demands. He felt a surge of anger. As he started to voice his protest, the burning pain and convulsions started up again.

"Stay with it, and I will cure you," the nagual said. "Act like the weak, rotten imbecile you are, and you will die."

The actor, a proud young man, was numbed by the insult. Nobody had ever called him a weak, rotten imbecile. He wanted to express his fury, but his pain was so severe that he could not react to the indignity.

"If you want me to ease your pain, you must obey me blindly," the nagual said with frightening coldness. "Signal me with a nod. But know now that the moment you change your mind and act like the shameful moron you are, I'll immediately pull the plug and leave you to die."

With his last bit of strength the actor nodded his assent. The nagual tapped him on his back and his pain vanished. But along with the searing pain, something else vanished: the fog in his mind. And then the young actor knew everything without understanding anything. The nagual introduced himself again. He told him that his name was Elías, and that he was the nagual. And the actor knew what it all meant.

The nagual Elías then shifted his attention to the semi-conscious Talía. He put his mouth to her left ear and whispered commands to her in order to make her assemblage point stop its erratic shifting. He soothed her fear by telling her, in whispers, stories of sorcerers who had gone through the same thing she was experiencing. When she was fairly calm, he introduced himself as the nagual Elías, a sorcerer; and then he attempted with her the most difficult thing in sorcery: moving the assemblage point beyond the sphere of the world we know.

Don Juan remarked that seasoned sorcerers are capable of moving beyond the world we know, but that inexperienced persons are not. The nagual Elías always maintained that ordinarily he would not have dreamed of attempting such a feat, but on that day something other than his knowledge or his volition was making him act. Yet the maneuver worked. Talía moved beyond the world we know and came safely back.

Then the nagual Elías had another insight. He sat between the two people stretched out on the ground —the actor was naked, covered only by the nagual Elías's riding coat—and reviewed their situation. He told them they had both, by the force of circumstances, fallen into a trap set by the spirit itself. He, the nagual, was the active part of that trap, because by encountering them under the conditions he had, he had been forced to become their temporary protector and to engage his knowledge of sorcery in order to help them. As their temporary protector it was his duty to warn them that they were about to reach a unique threshold; and that it was up to them, both individually and together, to attain that threshold by entering a mood of abandon but not recklessness; a mood of caring but not indulgence. He did not want to say more for fear of confusing them or influencing their decision. He felt that if they were to cross that threshold, it had to be with minimal help from him.

The nagual then left them alone in that isolated spot and went to the city to arrange for medicinal herbs, mats, and blankets to be brought to them. His idea was that in solitude they would attain and cross that threshold.

For a long time the two young people lay next to each other, immersed in their own thoughts. The fact that their assemblage points had shifted meant that they could think in greater depth than ordinarily, but it also meant that they worried, pondered, and were afraid in equally greater depth.

Since Talía could talk and was a bit stronger, she broke their silence; she asked the young actor if he was afraid. He nodded affirmatively. She felt a great compassion for him and took off a shawl she was wearing to put over his shoulders, and she held his hand.

The young man did not dare voice what he felt. His fear that his pain would recur if he spoke was too great and too vivid. He wanted to apologize to her; to tell her that his only regret was having hurt her, and that it did not matter that he was going to die—for he knew with certainty that he was not going to survive the day.

Talía's thoughts were on the same subject. She said

that she too had only one regret: that she had fought him hard enough to bring on his death. She was very peaceful now, a feeling which, agitated as she always was and driven by her great strength, was unfamiliar to her. She told him that her death was very near, too, and that she was glad it all would end that day.

The young actor, hearing his own thoughts being spoken by Talía, felt a chill. A surge of energy came to him then and made him sit up. He was not in pain, nor was he coughing. He took in great gulps of air, something he had no memory of having done before. He took the girl's hand and they began to talk without vocalizing.

Don Juan said it was at that instant that the spirit came to them. And they *saw*. They were deeply Catholic, and what they saw was a vision of heaven, where everything was alive, bathed in light. They *saw* a world of miraculous sights.

When the nagual returned, they were exhausted, although not injured. Talía was unconscious, but the young man had managed to remain aware by a supreme effort of self-control. He insisted on whispering something in the nagual's ear.

"We saw heaven," he whispered, tears rolling down his cheeks.

"You saw more than that," the nagual Elías retorted. "You *saw* the spirit."

Don Juan said that since the spirit's descent is always shrouded, naturally, Talía and the young actor could not hold onto their vision. They soon forgot it, as anyone would. The uniqueness of their experience was that, without any training and without being aware of it, they had *dreamed together* and had *seen* the spirit. For them to have achieved this with such ease was quite out of the ordinary.

"Those two were really the most remarkable beings I have ever met," don Juan added.

I, naturally, wanted to know more about them. But don Juan would not indulge me. He said that this was all there was about his benefactor and the fourth abstract core.

He seemed to remember something he was not telling me and laughed uproariously. Then he patted me on the back and told me it was time to set out for the cave.

When we got to the rock ledge it was almost dark. Don Juan sat down hurriedly, in the same position as the first time. He was to my right, touching me with his shoulder. He immediately seemed to enter into a deep state of relaxation, which pulled me into total immobility and silence. I could not even hear his breathing. I closed my eyes, and he nudged me to warn me to keep them open.

By the time it became completely dark, an immense fatigue had begun to make my eyes sore and itchy. Finally I gave up my resistance and was pulled into the deepest, blackest sleep I have ever had. Yet I was not totally asleep. I could feel the thick blackness around me. I had an entirely physical sensation of wading through blackness. Then it suddenly became reddish, then orange, then glaring white, like a terribly strong neon light. Gradually I focused my vision until I saw I was still sitting in the same position with don Juan—but no longer in the cave. We were on a mountaintop looking down over exquisite flatlands with mountains in the distance. This beautiful prairie was bathed in a glow that, like rays of light, emanated from the land itself. Wherever I looked, I saw familiar features: rocks, hills, rivers, forests, canyons, enhanced and transformed by their inner vibration, their inner glow. This glow that was so pleasing to my eyes also tingled out of my very being.

"Your assemblage point has moved," don Juan seemed to say to me.

The words had no sound; nevertheless I knew what he had just said to me. My rational reaction was to try to explain to myself that I had no doubt heard him as I would have if he had been talking in a vacuum, probably because my ears had been temporarily affected by what was transpiring.

"Your ears are fine. We are in a different realm of awareness," don Juan again seemed to say to me.

I could not speak. I felt the lethargy of deep sleep preventing me from saying a word, yet I was as alert as I could be.

"What's happening?" I thought.

"The cave made your assemblage point move," don Juan thought, and I heard his thoughts as if they were my own words, voiced to myself.

I sensed a command that was not expressed in thoughts. Something ordered me to look again at the prairie.

As I stared at the wondrous sight, filaments of light began to radiate from everything on that prairie. At first it was like the explosion of an infinite number of short fibers, then the fibers became long threadlike strands of luminosity bundled together into beams of vibrating light that reached infinity. There was really no way for me to make sense of what I was seeing, or to describe it, except as filaments of vibrating light. The filaments were not intermingled or entwined. Although they sprang, and continued to spring, in every direction, each one was separate, and yet all of them were inextricably bundled together.

"You are *seeing* the Eagle's emanations and the force that keeps them apart and bundles them together," don Juan thought.

The instant I caught his thought the filaments of light seemed to consume all my energy. Fatigue overwhelmed me. It erased my vision and plunged me into darkness.

When I became aware of myself again, there was something so familiar around me, although I could not tell what it was, that I believed myself to be back in a normal state of awareness. Don Juan was asleep beside me, his shoulder against mine.

Then I realized that the darkness around us was so intense that I could not even see my hands. I speculated that fog must have covered the ledge and filled the cave. Or perhaps it was the wispy low clouds that descended every rainy night from the higher mountains like a silent avalanche. Yet in spite of the total blackness, somehow I saw that don Juan had opened his eyes immediately after I became aware, although he did not look at me. Instantly I realized that seeing him was not a consequence of light on my retina. It was, rather, a bodily sense.

I became so engrossed in observing don Juan without my eyes that I was not paying attention to what he was telling me. Finally he stopped talking and turned his face to me as if to look me in the eye.

He coughed a couple of times to clear his throat and started to talk in a very low voice. He said that his benefactor used to come to the cave quite often, both with him and with his other disciples, but more often by himself. In that cave his benefactor *saw* the same prairie we had just *seen,* a vision that gave him the idea of describing the spirit as the flow of things.

Don Juan repeated that his benefactor was not a good thinker. Had he been, he would have realized in an instant that what he had *seen* and described as the flow of things was *intent*, the force that permeates everything. Don Juan added that if his benefactor ever became aware of the nature of his *seeing* he didn't reveal it. And he, himself, had the idea that his benefactor never knew it. Instead, his benefactor believed that he had *seen* the flow of things, which was the absolute truth, but not the way he meant it.

Don Juan was so emphatic about this that I wanted to ask him what the difference was, but I could not speak. My throat seemed frozen. We sat there in complete silence and immobility for hours. Yet I did not experience any discomfort. My muscles did not get tired, my legs did not fall asleep, my back did not ache.

When he began to talk again, I did not even notice the transition, and I readily abandoned myself to listening to his voice. It was a melodic, rhythmical sound that emerged from the total blackness that surrounded me.

He said that at that very moment I was not in my normal state of awareness nor was I in heightened awareness. I was suspended in a lull, in the blackness of nonperception. My assemblage point had moved away from perceiving the daily world, but it had not moved enough to reach and light a totally new bundle of energy fields. Properly speaking, I was caught between two perceptual possibilities. This in-between state, this lull of perception had been reached through the influence of the cave, which was itself guided by the *intent* of the sorcerers who carved it.

Don Juan asked me to pay close attention to what he was going to say next. He said that thousands of years ago, by means of *seeing,* sorcerers became aware that the earth was sentient and that its awareness could affect the awareness of humans. They tried to find a way to use the earth's influence on human awareness and they discovered that certain caves were most effective. Don Juan said that the search for caves became nearly full-time work for those sorcerers, and that through their endeavors they were able to discover a variety of uses for a variety of cave configurations. He added that out of all that work the only result pertinent to us was this particular cave and its capacity to move the assemblage point until it reached a lull of perception.

As don Juan spoke, I had the unsettling sensation that something was clearing in my mind. Something was funnelling my awareness into a long narrow channel. All the superfluous half-thoughts and feelings of my normal awareness were being squeezed out.

Don Juan was thoroughly aware of what was happening to me. I heard his soft chuckle of satisfaction. He said that now we could talk more easily and our conversation would have more depth.

I remembered at that moment scores of things he had explained to me before. For instance, I knew that I was *dreaming*. I was actually sound asleep yet I was totally aware of myself through my second attention —the counterpart of my normal attentiveness. I was certain I was asleep because of a bodily sensation plus a rational deduction based on statements that don Juan had made in the past. I had just *seen* the Eagle's emanations, and don Juan had said that it was impossible for sorcerers to have a sustained view of the Eagle's emanations in any way except in *dreaming*, therefore I had to be *dreaming*.

Don Juan had explained that the universe is made up of energy fields which defy description or scrutiny. He had said that they resembled filaments of ordinary light, except that light is lifeless compared to the Eagle's emanations, which exude awareness. I had never, until this night, been able to *see* them in a sustained manner, and indeed they were made out of a light that was alive. Don Juan had maintained in the past that my knowledge and control of *intent* were not adequate to withstand the impact of that sight. He had explained that normal perception occurs when *intent*, which is pure energy, lights up a portion of the luminous filaments inside our cocoon, and at the same time brightens a long extension of the same luminous filaments extending into infinity outside our cocoon. Extraordinary perception, *seeing,* occurs when by the force of *intent,* a different cluster of energy fields energizes and lights up. He had said that when a crucial number of energy fields are lit up inside the luminous cocoon, a sorcerer is able to *see* the energy fields themselves.

On another occasion don Juan had recounted the rational thinking of the early sorcerers. He told me that, through their *seeing,* they realized that awareness took place when the energy fields inside our luminous cocoon were *aligned* with the same energy fields outside. And they believed they had discovered *alignment* as the source of awareness.

Upon close examination, however, it became evident that what they had called *alignment* of the Eagle's emanations did not entirely explain what they were *seeing.* They had noticed that only a very small portion of the total number of luminous filaments inside the cocoon was energized while the rest remained unaltered. *Seeing* these few filaments energized had created a false discovery. The filaments did not need to be *aligned* to be lit up, because the ones inside our cocoon were the same as those outside. Whatever energized them was definitely an independent force. They felt they could not continue to call it awareness, as they had, because awareness was the glow of the energy fields being lit up. So the force that lit up the fields was named *will.*

Don Juan had said that when their *seeing* became still more sophisticated and effective, they realized that *will* was the force that kept the Eagle's emanations separated and was not only responsible for our awareness, but also for everything in the universe. They *saw* that this force had total consciousness and that it sprang from the very fields of energy that made the universe. They decided then that *intent* was a more appropriate name for it than *will*. In the long run, however, the name proved disadvantageous, because it does not describe its overwhelming importance nor the living connection it has with everything in the universe.

Don Juan had asserted that our great collective flaw is that we live our lives completely disregarding that connection. The busyness of our lives, our relentless interests, concerns, hopes, frustrations, and fears take precedence, and on a day-to-day basis we are unaware of being linked to everything else.

Don Juan had stated his belief that the Christian idea of being cast out from the Garden of Eden sounded to him like an allegory for losing our silent knowledge, our knowledge of *intent*. Sorcery, then, was a going back to the beginning, a return to paradise.

We stayed seated in the cave in total silence, perhaps for hours, or perhaps it was only a few instants. Suddenly don Juan began to talk, and the unexpected sound of his voice jarred me. I did not catch what he said. I cleared my throat to ask him to repeat what he had said, and that act brought me completely out of my reflectiveness. I quickly realized that the darkness around me was no longer impenetrable. I could speak now. I felt I was back in my normal state of awareness.

In a calm voice don Juan told me that for the very first time in my life I had *seen* the spirit, the force that sustains the universe. He emphasized that *intent* is not something one might use or command or move in any way—nevertheless, one could use it, command it, or move it as one desires. This contradiction, he said, is the essence of sorcery. To fail to understand it had brought generations of sorcerers unimaginable pain and sorrow. Modern-day naguals, in an effort to avoid paying this exorbitant price in pain, had developed a code of behavior called the warrior's way, or the impeccable action, which prepared sorcerers by enhancing their sobriety and thoughtfulness.

Don Juan explained that at one time in the remote past, sorcerers were deeply interested in the general connecting link that *intent* has with everything. And by focusing their second attention on that link, they acquired not only direct knowledge but also the ability to manipulate that knowledge and perform astounding deeds. They did not acquire, however, the soundness of mind needed to manage all that power.

So in a judicious mood, sorcerers decided to focus their second attention solely on the connecting link of creatures who have awareness. This included the entire range of existing organic beings as well as the entire range of what sorcerers call inorganic beings, or allies, which they described as entities with awareness, but no life as we understand life. This solution was not successful either, because it, too, failed to bring them wisdom.

In their next reduction, sorcerers focused their attention exclusively on the link that connects human beings with *intent*. The end result was very much as before.

Then, sorcerers sought a final reduction. Each sorcerer would be concerned solely with his individual connection. But this proved to be equally ineffective.

Don Juan said that although there were remarkable differences among those four areas of interest, one was as corrupting as another. So in the end sorcerers concerned themselves exclusively with the capacity that their individual connecting link with *intent* had to set them free to light the fire from within.

He asserted that all modern-day sorcerers have to struggle fiercely to gain soundness of mind. A nagual has to struggle especially hard because he has more strength, a greater command over the energy fields that determine perception, and more training in and familiarity with the intricacies of silent knowledge, which is nothing but direct contact with *intent*.

Examined in this way, sorcery becomes an attempt to reestablish our knowledge of *intent* and regain use of it without succumbing to it. And the abstract cores of the sorcery stories are shades of realization, degrees of our being aware of *intent*.

I understood don Juan's explanation with perfect clarity. But the more I understood and the clearer his statements became, the greater my sense of loss and despondency. At one moment I sincerely considered ending my life right there. I felt I was damned. Nearly in tears, I told don Juan that there was no point in his continuing his explanation, for I knew that I was about to lose my clarity of mind, and that when I reverted to my normal state of awareness I would have no memory of having *seen* or heard anything. My mundane consciousness would impose its lifelong habit of repetition and the reasonable predictability of its logic. That was why I felt damned. I told him that I resented my fate.

Don Juan responded that even in heightened awareness I thrived on repetition, and that periodically I would insist on boring him by describing my attacks of feeling worthless. He said that if I had to go under it should be fighting, not apologizing or feeling sorry for myself, and that it did not matter what our specific fate was as long as we faced it with ultimate abandon.

His words made me feel blissfully happy. I repeated over and over, tears streaming down my cheeks, that I agreed with him. There was such profound happiness in me I suspected my nerves were getting out of hand. I called upon all my forces to stop this and I felt the sobering effect of my mental brakes. But as this happened, my clarity of mind began to diffuse. I silently fought—trying to be both less sober and less nervous. Don Juan did not make a sound and left me alone.

By the time I had reestablished my balance, it was almost dawn. Don Juan stood, stretched his arms above his head and tensed his muscles, making his joints crack. He helped me up and commented that I had spent a most enlightening night: I had experienced what the spirit was and had been able to summon hidden strength to accomplish something, which on the surface amounted to calming my nervousness, but at a deeper level it had actually been a very successful, volitional movement of my assemblage point.

He signaled then that it was time to start on our way back.

THE SOMERSAULT OF THOUGHT

We walked into his house around seven in the morning, in time for breakfast. I was famished but not tired. We had left the cave to climb down to the valley at dawn. Don Juan, instead of following the most direct route, made a long detour that took us along the river. He explained that we had to collect our wits before we got home.

I answered it was very kind of him to say "our wits" when I was the only one whose wits were disordered. But he replied that he was acting not out of kindness but out of warrior's training. A warrior, he said, was on permanent guard against the roughness of human behavior. A warrior was magical and ruthless, a maverick with the most refined taste and manners, whose wordly task was to sharpen, yet disguise, his cutting edges so that no one would be able to suspect his ruthlessness.

After breakfast I thought it would be wise to get some sleep, but don Juan contended I had no time to waste. He said that all too soon I would lose the little clarity I still had, and if I went to sleep I would lose it all.

"It doesn't take a genius to figure out that there is hardly any way to talk about *intent*," he said quickly as he scrutinized me from head to toe. "But making this statement doesn't mean anything. It is the reason why sorcerers rely instead on the sorcery stories. And their hope is that someday the abstract cores of the stories will make sense to the listener."

I understood what he was saying, but I still could not conceive what an abstract core was or what it was supposed to mean to me. I tried to think about it. Thoughts barraged me. Images passed rapidly through my mind giving me no time to think about them. I could not slow them down enough even to recognize them. Finally anger overpowered me and I slammed my fist on the table.

Don Juan shook from head to toe, choking with laughter.

"Do what you did last night," he urged me, winking. "Slow yourself down."

My frustration made me very aggressive. I immediately put forth some senseless arguments; then I became aware of my error and apologized for my lack of restraint.

"Don't apologize," he said. "I should tell you that the understanding you're after is impossible at this time. The abstract cores of the sorcery stories will say nothing to you now. Later—years later, I mean—they may make perfect sense to you."

I begged don Juan not to leave me in the dark, to

discuss the abstract cores. It was not at all clear to me what he wanted me to do with them. I assured him that my present state of heightened awareness could be very helpful to me in allowing me to understand his discussion. I urged him to hurry, for I could not guarantee how long this state would last. I told him that soon I would return to my normal state and would become a bigger idiot than I was at that moment. I said it half in jest. His laughter told me that he had taken it as such, but I was deeply affected by my own words. A tremendous sense of melancholy overtook me.

Don Juan gently took my arm, pulled me to a comfortable armchair, then sat down facing me. He gazed fixedly into my eyes, and for a moment I was incapable of breaking the force of his stare.

"Sorcerers constantly *stalk* themselves," he said in a reassuring voice, as if trying to calm me with the sound of his voice.

I wanted to say that my nervousness had passed and that it had probably been caused by my lack of sleep, but he did not allow me to say anything.

He assured me that he had already taught me everything there was to know about *stalking*, but I had not yet retrieved my knowledge from the depth of heightened awareness, where I had it stored. I told him I had the annoying sensation of being bottled up. I felt there was something locked inside me, something that made me slam doors and kick tables, something that frustrated me and made me irascible.

"That sensation of being bottled up is experienced by every human being," he said. "It is a reminder of our existing connection with *intent*. For sorcerers this sensation is even more acute, precisely because their goal is to sensitize their connecting link until they can make it function at will.

"When the pressure of their connecting link is too great, sorcerers relieve it by *stalking* themselves."

"I still don't think I understand what you mean by *stalking*," I said. "But at a certain level I think I know exactly what you mean."

"I'll try to help you clarify what you know, then," he said. "*Stalking* is a procedure, a very simple one. *Stalking* is special behavior that follows certain principles. It is secretive, furtive, deceptive behavior designed to deliver a jolt. And, when you *stalk* yourself you jolt yourself, using your own behavior in a ruthless, cunning way."

He explained that when a sorcerer's awareness became bogged down with the weight of his perceptual input, which was what was happening to me, the best, or even perhaps the only, remedy was to use the idea of death to deliver that *stalking* jolt.

"The idea of death therefore is of monumental importance in the life of a sorcerer," don Juan continued. "I have shown you innumerable things about death to convince you that the knowledge of our impending and unavoidable end is what gives us sobriety. Our most costly mistake as average men is indulging in a sense of immortality. It is as though we believe that if we don't think about death we can protect ourselves from it."

"You must agree, don Juan, not thinking about death certainly protects us from worrying about it."

"Yes, it serves that purpose," he conceded. "But that purpose is an unworthy one for average men and a travesty for sorcerers. Without a clear view of death, there is no order, no sobriety, no beauty. Sorcerers struggle to gain this crucial insight in order to help them realize at the deepest possible level that they have no assurance whatsoever their lives will continue beyond the moment. That realization gives sorcerers the courage to be patient and yet take action, courage to be acquiescent without being stupid.''

Don Juan fixed his gaze on me. He smiled and shook his head.

"Yes," he went on. "The idea of death is the only thing that can give sorcerers courage. Strange, isn't it? It gives sorcerers the courage to be cunning without being conceited, and above all it gives them courage to be ruthless without being self-important.''

He smiled again and nudged me. I told him I was absolutely terrified by the idea of my death, that I thought about it constantly, but it certainly didn't give me courage or spur me to take action. It only made me cynical or caused me to lapse into moods of profound melancholy.

"Your problem is very simple," he said. "You become easily obsessed. I have been telling you that sorcerers *stalk* themselves in order to break the power of their obsessions. There are many ways of *stalking* oneself. If you don't want to use the idea of your death, use the poems you read me to *stalk* yourself.''

"I beg your pardon?"

"I have told you that there are many reasons I like poems," he said. "What I do is *stalk* myself with them. I deliver a jolt to myself with them. I listen, and as you read, I shut off my internal dialogue and let my inner silence gain momentum. Then the combination of the poem and the silence delivers the jolt.''

He explained that poets unconsciously long for the sorcerers' world. Because they are not sorcerers on the path of knowledge, longing is all they have.

"Let us see if you can feel what I'm talking about," he said, handing me a book of poems by José Gorostiza.

I opened it at the bookmark and he pointed to the poem he liked.

. . . this incessant stubborn dying,
this living death,
that slays you, oh God,
in your rigorous handiwork,
in the roses, in the stones,
in the indomitable stars
and in the flesh that burns out,
like a bonfire lit by a song,
a dream,
a hue that hits the eye.

. . . and you, yourself,
perhaps have died eternities of ages out there,
without us knowing about it,
we dregs, crumbs, ashes of you;
you that still are present,
like a star faked by its very light,
an empty light without star
that reaches us,
hiding
its infinite catastrophe.

"As I hear the words," don Juan said when I had finished reading, "I feel that that man is *seeing* the essence of things and I can *see* with him. I don't care what the poem is about. I care only about the feeling the poet's longing brings me. I borrow his longing, and with it I borrow the beauty. And marvel at the fact that he, like a true warrior, lavishes it on the recipients, the beholders, retaining for himself only his longing. This jolt, this shock of beauty, is *stalking*."

I was very moved. Don Juan's explanation had touched a strange chord in me.

"Would you say, don Juan, that death is the only real enemy we have?" I asked him a moment later.

"No," he said with conviction. "Death is not an

enemy, although it appears to be. Death is not our destroyer, although we think it is."

"What is it, then, if not our destroyer?" I asked.

"Sorcerers say death is the only worthy opponent we have," he replied. "Death is our challenger. We are born to take that challenge, average men or sorcerers. Sorcerers know about it; average men do not."

"I personally would say, don Juan, life, not death, is the challenge."

"Life is the process by means of which death challenges us," he said. "Death is the active force. Life is the arena. And in that arena there are only two contenders at any time: oneself and death."

"I would think, don Juan, that we human beings are the challengers," I said.

"Not at all," he retorted. "We are passive. Think about it. If we move, it's only when we feel the pressure of death. Death sets the pace for our actions and feelings and pushes us relentlessly until it breaks us and wins the bout, or else we rise above all possibilities and defeat death.

"Sorcerers defeat death and death acknowledges the defeat by letting the sorcerers go free, never to be challenged again."

"Does that mean that sorcerers become immortal?"

"No. It doesn't mean that," he replied. "Death stops challenging them, that's all."

"But what does that mean, don Juan?" I asked.

"It means thought has taken a somersault into the inconceivable," he said.

"What is a somersault of thought into the inconceivable?" I asked, trying not to sound belligerent. "The problem you and I have is that we do not share the same meanings."

"You're not being truthful," don Juan interrupted. "You understand what I mean. For you to demand a rational explanation of 'a somersault of thought into the inconceivable' is a travesty. You know exactly what it is."

"No, I don't," I said.

And then I realized that I did, or rather, that I intuited what it meant. There was some part of me that could transcend my rationality and understand and explain, beyond the level of metaphor, a somersault of thought into the inconceivable. The trouble was that part of me was not strong enough to surface at will.

I said as much to don Juan, who laughed and commented that my awareness was like a yo-yo. Sometimes it rose to a high spot and my command was keen, while at others it descended and I became a rational moron. But most of the time it hovered at an unworthy median where I was neither fish nor fowl.

"A somersault of thought into the inconceivable," he explained with an air of resignation, "is the descent of the spirit; the act of breaking our perceptual barriers. It is the moment in which man's perception reaches its limits. Sorcerers practice the art of sending scouts, advance runners, to probe our perceptual limits. This is another reason I like poems. I take them as advance runners. But, as I've said to you before, poets don't know as exactly as sorcerers what those advance runners can accomplish."

In the early evening, don Juan said that we had many things to discuss and asked me if I wanted to go for a walk. I was in a peculiar state of mind. Earlier I had noticed a strange aloofness in myself that came and went. At first I thought it was physical fatigue clouding my thoughts. But my thoughts were crystal clear. So I became convinced that my strange detachment was a product of my shift to heightened awareness.

We left the house and strolled around the town's plaza. I quickly asked don Juan about my aloofness before he had a chance to begin on anything else. He explained it as a shift of energy. He said that as the energy that was ordinarily used to maintain the fixed position of the assemblage point became liberated, it focused automatically on that connecting link. He assured me that there were no techniques or maneuvers for a sorcerer to learn beforehand to move energy from one place to the other. Rather it was a matter of an instantaneous shift taking place once a certain level of proficiency had been attained.

I asked him what the level of proficiency was. Pure understanding, he replied. In order to attain that instantaneous shift of energy, one needed a clear connection with *intent,* and to get a clear connection one needed only to *intend* it through pure understanding.

Naturally I wanted him to explain pure understanding. He laughed and sat down on a bench.

"I'm going to tell you something fundamental about sorcerers and their acts of sorcery," he went on. "Something about the somersault of their thought into the inconceivable."

He said that some sorcerers were storytellers. Storytelling for them was not only the advance runner that probed their perceptual limits but their path to perfection, to power, to the spirit. He was quiet for a moment, obviously searching for an appropriate example. Then he reminded me that the Yaqui Indians had a collection of historical events they called "the memorable dates." I knew that the memorable dates were oral accounts of their history as a nation when they waged war against the invaders of their homeland: the Spaniards first, the Mexicans later. Don Juan, a Yaqui himself, stated emphatically that the memorable dates were accounts of their defeats and disintegration.

"So, what would you say," he asked me, "since you are a learned man, about a sorcerer storyteller's taking an account from the memorable dates—let's say, for example, the story of Calixto Muni—and changing the ending so that instead of describing how Calixto Muni was drawn and quartered by the Spanish executioners, which is what happened, he tells a story of Calixto Muni the victorious rebel who succeeded in liberating his people?"

I knew the story of Calixto Muni. He was a Yaqui Indian who, according to the memorable dates, served for many years on a buccaneer ship in the Caribbean in order to learn war strategy. Then he returned to his native Sonora, managed to start an uprising against the Spaniards and declared a war of independence, only to be betrayed, captured, and executed.

Don Juan coaxed me to comment. I told him I would have to assume that changing the factual account in the manner he was describing would be a psychological device, a sort of wishful thinking on the sorcerer storyteller's part. Or perhaps it would be a personal, idiosyncratic way of alleviating frustration. I added that I would even call such a sorcerer storyteller a patriot because he was unable to accept bitter defeat.

Don Juan laughed until he was choking.

"But it's not a matter of one sorcerer storyteller," he argued. "They all do that."

"Then it's a socially sanctioned device to express the wishful thinking of a whole society," I retorted. "A socially accepted way of releasing psychological stress collectively."

"Your argument is glib and convincing and reasonable," he commented. "But because your spirit is dead, you can't see the flaw in your argument."

He eyed me as if coaxing me to understand what he was saying. I had no comment, and anything I might have said would have made me sound peevish.

"The sorcerer storyteller who changes the ending of the 'factual' account," he said, "does it at the di-

115

rection and under the auspices of the spirit. Because he can manipulate his elusive connection with *intent*, he can actually change things. The sorcerer storyteller signals that he has *intended* it by taking off his hat, putting it on the ground, and turning it a full three hundred and sixty degrees counterclockwise. Under the auspices of the spirit, that simple act plunges him into the spirit itself. He has let his thought somersault into the inconceivable."

Don Juan lifted his arm above his head and pointed for an instant to the sky above the horizon.

"Because his pure understanding is an advance runner probing that immensity out there," don Juan went on, "the sorcerer storyteller knows without a shadow of doubt that somewhere, somehow, in that infinity, at this very moment the spirit has descended. Calixto Muni is victorious. He has delivered his people. His goal has transcended his person."

MOVING THE ASSEMBLAGE POINT

A couple of days later, don Juan and I made a trip to the mountains. Halfway up the foothills we sat down to rest. Earlier that day, don Juan had decided to find an appropriate setting in which to explain some intricate aspects of the mastery of awareness. Usually he preferred to go to the closer western range of mountains. This time, however, he chose the eastern peaks. They were much higher and farther away. To me they seemed more ominous, darker, and more massive. But I could not tell whether this impression was my own or if I had somehow absorbed don Juan's feelings about these mountains.

I opened my backpack. The women seers from don Juan's group had prepared it for me and I discovered that they had packed some cheese. I experienced a moment of annoyance, because while I liked cheese, it did not agree with me. Yet I was incapable of refusing it whenever it was made available.

Don Juan had pointed this out as a true weakness and had made fun of me. I was embarrassed at first but found that when I did not have cheese around I did not miss it. The problem was that the practical jokers in don Juan's group always packed a big chunk of cheese for me, which, of course, I always ended up eating.

"Finish it in one sitting," don Juan advised me with a mischievous glint in his eyes. "That way you won't have to worry about it anymore."

Perhaps influenced by his suggestion, I had the most intense desire to devour the whole chunk. Don Juan laughed so much I suspected that once again he had schemed with his group to set me up.

In a more serious mood, he suggested that we spend the night there in the foothills and take a day or two to reach the higher peaks. I agreed.

Don Juan casually asked me if I had recalled anything about the four moods of *stalking*. I admitted that I had tried, but that my memory had failed me.

"Don't you remember my teaching you the nature of ruthlessness?" he asked. "Ruthlessness, the opposite of self-pity?"

I could not remember. Don Juan appeared to be considering what to say next. Then he stopped. The corners of his mouth dropped in a gesture of sham impotence. He shrugged his shoulders, stood up and quickly walked a short distance to a small level spot on top of a hill.

"All sorcerers are ruthless," he said, as we sat down on the flat ground. "But you know this. We have discussed this concept at length."

After a long silence, he said that we were going to continue discussing the abstract cores of the sorcery stories, but that he intended to talk less and less about them because the time was approaching when it would be up to me to discover them and allow them to reveal their meaning.

"As I have already told you," he said, "the fourth abstract core of the sorcery stories is called the descent of the spirit, or being moved by *intent*. The story says that in order to let the mysteries of sorcery reveal themselves to the man we've been talking about, it was necessary for the spirit to descend on that man. The spirit chose a moment when the man was distracted, unguarded, and, showing no pity, the spirit let its presence by itself move the man's assemblage point to a specific position. This spot was known to sorcerers from then on as the place of no pity. Ruthlessness became, in this way, the first principle of sorcery.

"The first principle should not be confused with the first effect of sorcery apprenticeship, which is the shift between normal and heightened awareness."

"I don't understand what you are trying to tell me," I complained.

"What I want to say is that, to all appearances, having the assemblage point shift is the first thing that actually happens to a sorcery apprentice," he replied. "So, it is only natural for an apprentice to assume that this is the first principle of sorcery. But it is not. Ruthlessness is the first principle of sorcery. But we have discussed this before. Now I am only trying to help you remember."

I could honestly have said that I had no idea what he was talking about, but I also had the strange sensation that I did.

"Bring back the recollection of the first time I taught you ruthlessness," he urged. "Recollecting has to do with moving the assemblage point."

He waited a moment to see whether I was following his suggestion. Since it was obvious that I could not, he continued his explanation. He said that, mysterious as the shift into heightened awareness was, all that one needed to accomplish it was the presence of the spirit.

I remarked that his statements that day either were extremely obscure or I was terribly dense, because I could not follow his line of thought at all. He replied firmly that my confusion was unimportant and insisted that the only thing of real importance was that I understand that the mere contact with the spirit could bring about any movement of the assemblage point.

"I've told you the nagual is the conduit of the spirit," he went on. "Since he spends a lifetime impeccably redefining his connecting link with *intent,* and since he has more energy than the average man, he can let the spirit express itself through him. So, the first thing the sorcerer apprentice experiences is a shift in his level of awareness, a shift brought about simply by the presence of the nagual. And what I want you to know is that there really is no procedure involved in making the assemblage point move. The spirit touches the apprentice and his assemblage point moves. It is as simple as that."

I told him that his assertions were disturbing because they contradicted what I had painfully learned to accept through personal experience: that heightened awareness was feasible as a sophisticated, although inexplicable, maneuver performed by don Juan by means of which he manipulated my perception. Throughout the years of our association, he had time after time made me enter into heightened awareness by striking me on my back. I pointed out this contradiction.

He replied that striking my back was more a trick to trap my attention and remove doubts from my mind than a bona fide maneuver to manipulate my perception. He called it a simple trick, in keeping with his moderate personality. He commented, not quite as a joke, that I was lucky he was a plain man, not given to weird behavior. Otherwise, instead of simple tricks, I would have had to endure bizarre rituals before he could remove all doubts from my mind, to let the spirit move my assemblage point.

"What we need to do to allow magic to get hold of us is to banish doubt from our minds," he said. "Once doubts are banished, anything is possible."

He reminded me of an event I had witnessed some months before in Mexico City, which I had found to be incomprehensible until he had explained it, using the sorcerers' paradigm.

What I had witnessed was a surgical operation performed by a famous psychic healer. A friend of mine was the patient. The healer was a woman who entered a very dramatic trance to operate on him.

I was able to observe that, using a kitchen knife, she cut his abdominal cavity open in the umbilical region, detached his diseased liver, washed it in a bucket of alcohol, put it back in and closed the bloodless opening with just the pressure of her hands.

There had been a number of people in the semidark room, witnesses to the operation. Some of them seemed to be interested observers like myself. The others seemed to be the healer's helpers.

After the operation, I talked briefly to three of the observers. They all agreed that they had witnessed the same events I had. When I talked to my friend, the patient, he reported that he had felt the operation as a dull, constant pain in his stomach and a burning sensation on his right side.

I had narrated all of this to don Juan and I had even ventured a cynical explanation. I had told him that the semidarkness of the room, in my opinion, lent itself perfectly to all kinds of sleight of hand, which could have accounted for the sight of the internal organs being pulled out of the abdominal cavity and washed in alcohol. The emotional shock caused by the healer's dramatic trance—which I also considered trickery—helped to create an atmosphere of almost religious faith.

Don Juan immediately pointed out that this was a cynical opinion, not a cynical explanation, because it did not explain the fact that my friend had really gotten well. Don Juan had then proposed an alternative view based on sorcerers' knowledge. He had explained that the event hinged on the salient fact that the healer was capable of moving the assemblage point of the exact number of people in her audience. The only trickery involved—if one could call it trickery— was that the number of people present in the room could not exceed the number she could handle.

Her dramatic trance and the accompanying histrionics were, according to him, either well-thought-out devices the healer used to trap the attention of those present or unconscious maneuvers dictated by the spirit itself. Whichever, they were the most appropriate means whereby the healer could foster the unity of thought needed to remove doubt from the minds of those present and force them into heightened awareness.

When she cut the body open with a kitchen knife and removed the internal organs it was not, don Juan had stressed, sleight of hand. These were bona fide events, which, by virtue of taking place in heightened awareness, were outside the realm of everyday judgment.

I had asked don Juan how the healer could manage to move the assemblage points of those people without touching them. His reply had been that the healer's power, a gift or a stupendous accomplishment, was to serve as a conduit for the spirit. It was the spirit, he had said, and not the healer, which had moved those assemblage points.

"I explained to you then, although you didn't understand a word of it," don Juan went on, "that the healer's art and power was to remove doubts from the minds of those present. By doing this, she was able to allow the spirit to move their assemblage points. Once those points had moved, everything was possible. They had entered into the realm where miracles are commonplace."

He asserted emphatically that the healer must also have been a sorceress, and that if I made an effort to remember the operation, I would remember that she had been ruthless with the people around her, especially the patient.

I repeated to him what I could recall of the session. The pitch and tone of the healer's flat, feminine voice changed dramatically when she entered a trance into a raspy, deep, male voice. That voice announced that the spirit of a warrior of pre-Columbian antiquity had possessed the healer's body. Once the announcement was made, the healer's attitude changed dramatically. She was possessed. She was obviously absolutely sure of herself, and she proceeded to operate with total certainty and firmness.

"I prefer the word 'ruthlessness' to 'certainty' and 'firmness,'" don Juan commented, then continued. "That healer had to be ruthless to create the proper setting for the spirit's intervention."

He asserted that events difficult to explain, such as that operation, were really very simple. They were made difficult by our insistence upon thinking. If we did not think, everything fit into place.

"That is truly absurd, don Juan," I said and really meant it.

I reminded him that he demanded serious thinking of all his apprentices, and even criticized his own teacher for not being a good thinker.

"Of course I insist that everyone around me think clearly," he said. "And I explain, to anyone who wants to listen, that the only way to think clearly is to not think at all. I was convinced you understood this sorcerers' contradiction."

In a loud voice I protested the obscurity of his statements. He laughed and made fun of my compulsion to defend myself. Then he explained again that for a sorcerer there were two types of thinking. One was average day-to-day thinking, which was ruled by the normal position of his assemblage point. It was muddled thinking that did not really answer his needs and left great murkiness in his head. The other was precise thinking. It was functional, economical, and left very few things unexplained. Don Juan remarked that for this type of thinking to prevail the assemblage point had to move. Or at least the day-to-day type thinking had to stop to allow the assemblage point to shift. Thus the apparent contradiction, which was really no contradiction at all.

"I want you to recall something you have done in the past," he said. "I want you to recall a special movement of your assemblage point. And to do this, you have to stop thinking the way you normally think. Then the other, the type I call clear thinking, will take over and make you recollect."

"But how do I stop thinking?" I asked, although I knew what he was going to reply.

"By *intending* the movement of your assemblage point," he said. "*Intent* is beckoned with the eyes."

I told don Juan that my mind was shifting back and forth between moments of tremendous lucidity, when everything was crystal clear, and lapses into profound mental fatigue during which I could not understand what he was saying. He tried to put me at ease, explaining that my instability was caused by a slight fluctuation of my assemblage point, which had not stabilized in the new position it had reached some years earlier. The fluctuation was the result of left-over feelings of self-pity.

"What new position is that, don Juan?" I asked.

"Years ago—and this is what I want you to recollect—your assemblage point reached the place of no pity," he replied.

"I beg your pardon?" I said.

"The place of no pity is the site of ruthlessness," he said. "But you know all this. For the time being, though, until you recollect, let's say that ruthlessness, being a specific position of the assemblage point, is shown in the eyes of sorcerers. It's like a shimmering film over the eyes. The eyes of sorcerers are brilliant. The greater the shine, the more ruthless the sorcerer is. At this moment, your eyes are dull."

He explained that when the assemblage point moved to the place of no pity, the eyes began to shine. The firmer the grip of the assemblage point on its new position, the more the eyes shone.

"Try to recall what you already know about this," he urged me.

He kept quiet for a moment, then spoke without looking at me.

"Recollecting is not the same as remembering," he continued. "Remembering is dictated by the day-to-day type of thinking, while recollecting is dictated by the movement of the assemblage point. A recapitulation of their lives, which sorcerers do, is the key to moving their assemblage points. Sorcerers start their recapitulation by thinking, by remembering the most important acts of their lives. From merely thinking about them they then move on to actually being at the site of the event. When they can do that—be at the site of the event—they have successfully shifted their assemblage point to the precise spot it was when the event took place. Bringing back the total event by means of shifting the assemblage point is known as sorcerers' recollection.''

He stared at me for an instant as if trying to make sure I was listening.

''Our assemblage points are constantly shifting,'' he explained, ''imperceptible shifts. Sorcerers believe that in order to make their assemblage points shift to precise spots we must engage *intent*. Since there is no way of knowing what *intent* is, sorcerers let their eyes beckon it.''

''All this is truly incomprehensible to me,'' I said.

Don Juan put his hands behind his head and lay down on the ground. I did the same. We remained quiet for a long time. The wind scudded the clouds. Their movement almost made me feel dizzy. And the dizziness changed abruptly into a familiar sense of anguish.

Every time I was with don Juan, I felt, especially in moments of rest and quiet, an overwhelming sensation of despair—a longing for something I could not describe. When I was alone, or with other people, I was never a victim of this feeling. Don Juan had explained that what I felt and interpreted as longing was in fact the sudden movement of my assemblage point.

When don Juan started to speak, all of a sudden the sound of his voice jolted me and I sat up.

''You must recollect the first time your eyes

shone," he said, "because that was the first time your assemblage point reached the place of no pity. Ruthlessness possessed you then. Ruthlessness makes sorcerers' eyes shine, and that shine beckons *intent*. Each spot to which their assemblage points move is indicated by a specific shine of their eyes. Since their eyes have their own memory, they can call up the recollection of any spot by calling up the specific shine associated with that spot."

He explained that the reason sorcerers put so much emphasis on the shine of their eyes and on their gaze is because the eyes are directly connected to *intent*. Contradictory as it might sound, the truth is that the eyes are only superficially connected to the world of everyday life. Their deeper connection is to the abstract. I could not conceive how my eyes could store that sort of information, and I said as much. Don Juan's reply was that man's possibilities are so vast and mysterious that sorcerers, rather than thinking about them, had chosen to explore them, with no hope of ever understanding them.

I asked him if an average man's eyes were also affected by *intent*.

"Of course!" he exclaimed. "You know all this. But you know it at such a deep level that it is silent knowledge. You haven't sufficient energy to explain it, even to yourself.

"The average man knows the same thing about his eyes, but he has even less energy than you. The only advantages sorcerers may have over average men is that they have stored their energy, which means a more precise, clearer connecting link with *intent*. Naturally, it also means they can recollect at will, using the shine of their eyes to move their assemblage points."

Don Juan stopped talking and fixed me with his gaze. I clearly felt his eyes guiding, pushing and pulling something indefinite in me. I could not break away from his stare. His concentration was so intense it actually caused a physical sensation in me: I felt as if I were inside a furnace. And, quite abruptly, I was looking inward. It was a sensation very much like being in an absentminded reverie, but with the strange accompanying sensation of an intense awareness of myself and an absence of thoughts. Supremely aware, I was looking inward, into nothingness.

With a gigantic effort, I pulled myself out of it and stood up.

"What did you do to me, don Juan?"

"Sometimes you are absolutely unbearable," he said. "Your wastefulness is infuriating. Your assemblage point was just in the most advantageous spot to recollect anything you wanted, and what did you do? You let it all go, to ask me what I did to you."

He kept silent for a moment, and then smiled as I sat down again.

"But being annoying is really your greatest asset," he added. "So why should I complain?"

Both of us broke into a loud laugh. It was a private joke.

Years before, I had been both very moved and very confused by don Juan's tremendous dedication to helping me. I could not imagine why he should show me such kindness. It was evident that he did not need me in any way in his life. He was obviously not investing in me. But I had learned, through life's painful experiences, that nothing was free; and being unable to foresee what don Juan's reward would be made me tremendously uneasy.

One day I asked don Juan point-blank, in a very cynical tone, what he was getting out of our association. I said that I had not been able to guess.

"Nothing you would understand," he replied.

His answer annoyed me. Belligerently I told him I was not stupid, and he could at least try to explain it to me.

"Well, let me just say that, although you could understand it, you are certainly not going to like it," he said with the smile he always had when he was setting me up. "You see, I really want to spare you."

I was hooked, and I insisted that he tell me what he meant.

"Are you sure you want to hear the truth?" he asked, knowing I could never say no, even if my life depended on it.

"Of course I want to hear whatever it is you're dangling in front of me," I said cuttingly.

He started to laugh as if at a big joke; the more he laughed, the greater my annoyance.

"I don't see what's so funny," I said.

"Sometimes the underlying truth shouldn't be tampered with," he said. "The underlying truth here is like a block at the bottom of a big pile of things, a cornerstone. If we take a hard look at the bottom block, we might not like the results. I prefer to avoid that."

He laughed again. His eyes, shining with mischievousness, seemed to invite me to pursue the subject further. And I insisted again that I had to know what he was talking about. I tried to sound calm but persistent.

"Well, if that is what you want," he said with the air of one who had been overwhelmed by the request. "First of all, I'd like to say that everything I do for you is free. You don't have to pay for it. As you know, I've been impeccable with you. And as you also know, my impeccability with you is not an investment. I am not grooming you to take care of me when I am too feeble to look after myself. But I do get something of incalculable value out of our association, a sort of reward for dealing impeccably with that bottom block I've mentioned. And what I get is the very thing you are perhaps not going to understand or like."

He stopped and peered at me, with a devilish glint in his eyes.

"Tell me about it, don Juan!" I exclaimed, irritated with his delaying tactics.

"I want you to bear in mind that I am telling you at your insistence," he said, still smiling.

He paused again. By then I was fuming.

"If you judge me by my actions with you," he said, "you would have to admit that I have been a paragon of patience and consistency. But what you don't know is that to accomplish this I have had to fight for impeccability as I have never fought before. In order to spend time with you, I have had to transform myself daily, restraining myself with the most excruciating effort."

Don Juan had been right. I did not like what he said. I tried not to lose face and made a sarcastic comeback.

"I'm not that bad, don Juan," I said.

My voice sounded surprisingly unnatural to me.

"Oh, yes, you are that bad," he said with a serious expression. "You are petty, wasteful, opinionated, coercive, short-tempered, conceited. You are morose, ponderous, and ungrateful. You have an inexhaustible capacity for self-indulgence. And worst of all, you have an exalted idea of yourself, with nothing whatever to back it up.

"I could sincerely say that your mere presence makes me feel like vomiting."

I wanted to get angry. I wanted to protest, to complain that he had no right to talk to me that way, but I could not utter a single word. I was crushed. I felt numb.

My expression, upon hearing the bottom truth, must

have been something, for don Juan broke into such gales of laughter I thought he was going to choke.

"I told you you were not going to like it or understand it," he said. "Warriors' reasons are very simple, but their finesse is extreme. It is a rare opportunity for a warrior to be given a genuine chance to be impeccable in spite of his basic feelings. You gave me such a unique chance. The act of giving freely and impeccably rejuvenates me and renews my wonder. What I get from our association is indeed of incalculable value to me. I am in your debt."

His eyes were shining, but without mischievousness, as he peered at me.

Don Juan began to explain what he had done.

"I am the nagual, I moved your assemblage point with the shine of my eyes," he said matter-of-factly. "The nagual's eyes can do that. It's not difficult. After all, the eyes of all living beings can move someone else's assemblage point, especially if their eyes are focused on *intent*. Under normal conditions, however, people's eyes are focused on the world, looking for food . . . looking for shelter. . . ."

He nudged my shoulder.

"Looking for love," he added and broke into a loud laugh.

Don Juan constantly teased me about my "looking for love." He never forgot a naive answer I once gave him when he had asked me what I actively looked for in life. He had been steering me toward admitting that I did not have a clear goal, and he roared with laughter when I said that I was looking for love.

"A good hunter mesmerizes his prey with his eyes," he went on. "With his gaze he moves the assemblage point of his prey, and yet his eyes are on the world, looking for food."

I asked him if sorcerers could mesmerize people

with their gaze. He chuckled and said that what I really wanted to know was if I could mesmerize women with my gaze, in spite of the fact that my eyes were focused on the world, looking for love. He added, seriously, that the sorcerers' safety valve was that by the time their eyes were really focused on *intent*, they were no longer interested in mesmerizing anyone.

"But, for sorcerers to use the shine of their eyes to move their own or anyone else's assemblage point," he continued, "they have to be ruthless. That is, they have to be familiar with that specific position of the assemblage point called the place of no pity. This is especially true for the naguals."

He said that each nagual developed a brand of ruthlessness specific to him alone. He took my case as an example and said that, because of my unstable natural configuration, I appeared to seers as a sphere of luminosity not composed of four balls compressed into one —the usual structure of a nagual—but as a sphere composed of only three compressed balls. This configuration made me automatically hide my ruthlessness behind a mask of indulgence and laxness.

"Naguals are very misleading," don Juan went on. "They always give the impression of something they are not, and they do it so completely that everybody, including those who know them best, believe their masquerade."

"I really don't understand how you can say that I am masquerading, don Juan," I protested.

"You pass yourself off as an indulgent, relaxed man," he said. "You give the impression of being generous, of having great compassion. And everybody is convinced of your genuineness. They can even swear that that is the way you are."

"But that *is* the way I am!"

Don Juan doubled up with laughter.

The direction the conversation had taken was not to my liking. I wanted to set the record straight. I argued vehemently that I was truthful in everything I did, and challenged him to give me an example of my being otherwise. He said I compulsively treated people with unwarranted generosity, giving them a false sense of my ease and openness. And I argued that being open was my nature. He laughed and retorted that if this were the case, why should it be that I always demanded, without voicing it, that the people I dealt with be aware I was deceiving them? The proof was that when they failed to be aware of my ploy and took my pseudo-laxness at face value, I turned on them with exactly the cold ruthlessness I was trying to mask.

His comments made me feel desperate, because I couldn't argue with them. I remained quiet. I did not want to show that I was hurt. I was wondering what to do when he stood and started to walk away. I stopped him by holding his sleeve. It was an unplanned move on my part which startled me and made him laugh. He sat down again with a look of surprise on his face.

"I didn't mean to be rude," I said, "but I've got to know more about this. It upsets me."

"Make your assemblage point move," he urged. "We've discussed ruthlessness before. Recollect it!"

He eyed me with genuine expectation although he must have seen that I could not recollect anything, for he continued to talk about the naguals' patterns of ruthlessness. He said that his own method consisted of subjecting people to a flurry of coercion and denial, hidden behind sham understanding and reasonableness.

"What about all the explanations you give me?" I asked. "Aren't they the result of genuine reasonableness and desire to help me understand?"

"No," he replied. "They are the result of my ruthlessness."

I argued passionately that my own desire to understand was genuine. He patted me on the shoulder and explained that my desire to understand was genuine, but my generosity was not. He said that naguals masked their ruthlessness automatically, even against their will.

As I listened to his explanation, I had the peculiar sensation in the back of my mind that at some point we had covered the concept of ruthlessness extensively.

"I'm not a rational man," he continued, looking into my eyes. "I only appear to be because my mask is so effective. What you perceive as reasonableness is my lack of pity, because that's what ruthlessness is: a total lack of pity.

"In your case, since you mask your lack of pity with generosity, you appear at ease, open. But actually you are as generous as I am reasonable. We are both fakes. We have perfected the art of disguising the fact that we feel no pity."

He said his benefactor's total lack of pity was masked behind the facade of an easygoing, practical joker with an irresistible need to poke fun at anyone with whom he came into contact.

"My benefactor's mask was that of a happy, unruffled man without a care in the world," don Juan continued. "But underneath all that he was, like all the naguals, as cold as the arctic wind."

"But you are not cold, don Juan," I said sincerely.

"Of course I am," he insisted. "The effectiveness of my mask is what gives you the impression of warmth."

He went on to explain that the nagual Elías's mask consisted of a maddening meticulousness about all details and accuracy, which created the false impression of attention and thoroughness.

He started to describe the nagual Elías's behavior. As he talked, he kept watching me. And perhaps because he was observing me so intently, I was unable to concentrate at all on what he was saying. I made a supreme effort to gather my thoughts.

He watched me for an instant, then went back to explaining ruthlessness, but I no longer needed his explanation. I told him that I had recollected what he wanted me to recollect: the first time my eyes had shone. Very early in my apprenticeship I had achieved —by myself—a shift in my level of awareness. My assemblage point reached the position called the place of no pity.

THE PLACE OF NO PITY

Don Juan told me that there was no need to talk about the details of my recollection, at least not at that moment, because talk was used only to lead one to recollecting. Once the assemblage point moved, the total experience was relived. He also told me the best way to assure a complete recollection was to walk around.

And so both of us stood up; walked very slowly and in silence, following a trail in those mountains, until I had recollected everything.

We were in the outskirts of Guaymas, in northern Mexico, on a drive from Nogales, Arizona, when it became evident to me that something was wrong with don Juan. For the last hour or so he had been unusually quiet and somber. I did not think anything of it, but then, abruptly, his body twitched out of control. His chin hit his chest as if his neck muscles could no longer support the weight of his head.

"Are you getting carsick, don Juan?" I asked, suddenly alarmed.

He did not answer. He was breathing through his mouth.

During the first part of our drive, which had taken several hours, he had been fine. We had talked a great deal about everything. When we had stopped in the city of Santa Ana to get gas, he was even doing pushouts against the roof of the car to loosen up the muscles of his shoulders.

"What's wrong with you, don Juan?" I asked.

I felt pangs of anxiety in my stomach. With his head down, he mumbled that he wanted to go to a particular restaurant and in a slow, faltering voice gave me precise directions on how to get there.

I parked my car on a side street, a block from the restaurant. As I opened the car door on my side, he held onto my arm with an iron grip. Painfully, and with my help, he dragged himself out of the car, over the driver's seat. Once he was on the sidewalk, he held onto my shoulders with both hands to straighten his back. In ominous silence, we shuffled down the street toward the dilapidated building where the restaurant was.

Don Juan was hanging onto my arm with all his weight. His breathing was so accelerated and the tremor in his body so alarming that I panicked. I stumbled and had to brace myself against the wall to keep us both from falling to the sidewalk. My anxiety was so intense I could not think. I looked into his eyes. They were dull. They did not have their usual shine.

We clumsily entered the restaurant and a solicitous waiter rushed over, as if on cue, to help don Juan.

"How are you feeling today?" he yelled into don Juan's ear.

He practically carried don Juan from the door to a table, seated him, and then disappeared.

"Does he know you, don Juan?" I asked when we were seated.

Without looking at me, he mumbled something unintelligible. I stood up and went to the kitchen to look for the busy waiter.

"Do you know the old man I am with?" I asked when I was able to corner him.

"Of course I know him," he said with the attitude of someone who has just enough patience to answer one question. "He's the old man who suffers from strokes."

That statement settled things for me. I knew then that don Juan had suffered a mild stroke while we were driving. There was nothing I could have done to avoid it but I felt helpless and apprehensive. The feeling that the worst had not yet happened made me feel sick to my stomach.

I went back to the table and sat down in silence. Suddenly the same waiter arrived with two plates of fresh shrimp and two large bowls of sea-turtle soup. The thought occurred to me that either the restaurant served only shrimp and sea-turtle soup or don Juan ate the same thing every time he was here.

The waiter talked so loudly to don Juan he could be heard above the clatter of customers.

"Hope you like your food!" he yelled. "If you need me, just lift your arm. I'll come right away."

Don Juan nodded his head affirmatively and the waiter left, after patting don Juan affectionately on the back.

Don Juan ate voraciously, smiling to himself from

time to time. I was so apprehensive that just the thought of food made me feel nauseous. But then I reached a familiar threshold of anxiety, and the more I worried the hungrier I became. I tried the food and found it incredibly good.

I felt somewhat better after having eaten, but the situation had not changed, nor had my anxiety diminished.

When don Juan was through eating, he shot his arm straight above his head. In a moment, the waiter came over and handed me the bill.

I paid him and he helped don Juan stand up. He guided him by the arm out of the restaurant. The waiter even helped him out to the street and said good-bye to him effusively.

We walked back to the car in the same laborious way, don Juan leaning heavily on my arm, panting and stopping to catch his breath every few steps. The waiter stood in the doorway, as if to make sure I was not going to let don Juan fall.

Don Juan took two or three full minutes to climb into the car.

"Tell me, what can I do for you, don Juan?" I pleaded.

"Turn the car around," he ordered in a faltering, barely audible voice. "I want to go to the other side of town, to the store. They know me there, too. They are my friends."

I told him I had no idea what store he was talking about. He mumbled incoherently and had a tantrum. He stamped on the floor of the car with both feet. He pouted and actually drooled on his shirt. Then he seemed to have an instant of lucidity. I got extremely nervous, watching him struggle to arrange his thoughts. He finally succeeded in telling me how to get to the store.

My discomfort was at its peak. I was afraid that the

stroke don Juan had suffered was more serious than I thought. I wanted to be rid of him, to take him to his family or his friends, but I did not know who they were. I did not know what else to do. I made a U-turn and drove to the store which he said was on the other side of town.

I wondered about going back to the restaurant to ask the waiter if he knew don Juan's family. I hoped someone in the store might know him. The more I thought about my predicament, the sorrier I felt for myself. Don Juan was finished. I had a terrible sense of loss, of doom. I was going to miss him, but my sense of loss was offset by my feeling of annoyance at being saddled with him at his worst.

I drove around for almost an hour looking for the store. I could not find it. Don Juan admitted that he might have made a mistake, that the store might be in a different town. By then I was completely exhausted and had no idea what to do next.

In my normal state of awareness I always had the strange feeling that I knew more about him than my reason told me. Now, under the pressure of his mental deterioration, I was certain, without knowing why, that his friends were waiting for him somewhere in Mexico, although I did not know where.

My exhaustion was more than physical. It was a combination of worry and guilt. It worried me that I was stuck with a feeble old man who might, for all I knew, be mortally ill. And I felt guilty for being so disloyal to him.

I parked my car near the waterfront. It took nearly ten minutes for don Juan to get out of the car. We walked toward the ocean, but as we got closer, don Juan shied like a mule and refused to go on. He mumbled that the water of Guaymas Bay scared him.

He turned around and led me to the main square: a dusty plaza without even benches. Don Juan sat down on the curb. A street-cleaning truck went by, rotating its steel brushes, but no water was squirting into them. The cloud of dust made me cough.

I was so disturbed by my situation that the thought of leaving him sitting there crossed my mind. I felt embarrassed at having had such a thought and patted don Juan's back.

"You must make an effort and tell me where I can take you," I said softly. "Where do you want me to go."

"I want you to go to hell!" he replied in a cracked, raspy voice.

Hearing him speak to me like this, I had the suspicion that don Juan might not have suffered from a stroke, but some other crippling brain condition that had made him lose his mind and become violent.

Suddenly he stood up and walked away from me. I noticed how frail he looked. He had aged in a matter of hours. His natural vigor was gone, and what I saw before me was a terribly old, weak man.

I rushed to lend him a hand. A wave of immense pity enveloped me. I saw myself old and weak, barely able to walk. It was intolerable. I was close to weeping, not for don Juan but for myself. I held his arm and made him a silent promise that I would look after him, no matter what.

I was lost in a reverie of self-pity when I felt the numbing force of a slap across my face. Before I recovered from the surprise, don Juan slapped me again across the back of my neck. He was standing facing me, shivering with rage. His mouth was half open and shook uncontrollably.

"Who are you?" he yelled in a strained voice.

He turned to a group of onlookers who had immediately gathered.

"I don't know who this man is," he said to them. "Help me. I'm a lonely old Indian. He's a foreigner and he wants to kill me. They do that to helpless old people, kill them for pleasure.''

There was a murmur of disapproval. Various young, husky men looked at me menacingly.

"What are you doing, don Juan?" I asked him in a loud voice. I wanted to reassure the crowd that I was with him.

"I don't know you," don Juan shouted. "Leave me alone."

He turned to the crowd and asked them to help him. He wanted them to restrain me until the police came.

"Hold him," he insisted. "And someone, please call the police. They'll know what to do with this man."

I had the image of a Mexican jail. No one would know where I was. The idea that months would go by before someone noticed my disappearance made me react with vicious speed. I kicked the first young man who came close to me, then took off at a panicked run. I knew I was running for my life. Several young men ran after me.

As I raced toward the main street, I realized that in a small city like Guaymas there were policemen all over the place patrolling on foot. There were none in sight, and before I ran into one, I entered the first store in my path. I pretended to be looking for curios.

The young men running after me went by noisily. I conceived a quick plan: to buy as many things as I could. I was counting on being taken for a tourist by the people in the store. Then I was going to ask someone to help me carry the packages to my car.

It took me quite a while to select what I wanted. I paid a young man in the store to help me carry my packages, but as I got closer to my car, I saw don Juan standing by it, still surrounded by people. He was talking to a policeman, who was taking notes.

It was useless. My plan had failed. There was no

way to get to my car. I instructed the young man to leave my packages on the sidewalk. I told him a friend of mine was going to drive by presently to take me to my hotel. He left and I remained hidden behind the packages I was holding in front of my face, out of sight of don Juan and the people around him.

I saw the policeman examining my California license plates. And that completely convinced me I was done for. The accusation of the crazy old man was too grave. And the fact that I had run away would have only reinforced my guilt in the eyes of any policeman. Besides, I would not have put it past the policeman to ignore the truth, just to arrest a foreigner.

I stood in a doorway for perhaps an hour. The policeman left, but the crowd remained around don Juan, who was shouting and agitatedly moving his arms. I was too far away to hear what he was saying but I could imagine the gist of his fast, nervous shouting.

I was in desperate need of another plan. I considered checking into a hotel and waiting there for a couple of days before venturing out to get my car. I thought of going back to the store and having them call a taxi. I had never had to hire a cab in Guaymas and I had no idea if there were any. But my plan died instantly with the realization that if the police were fairly competent, and had taken don Juan seriously, they would check the hotels. Perhaps the policeman had left don Juan in order to do just that.

Another alternative that crossed my mind was to get to the bus station and catch a bus to any town along the international border. Or to take any bus leaving Guaymas in any direction. I abandoned the idea immediately. I was sure don Juan had given my name to the policeman and the police had probably already alerted the bus companies.

My mind plunged into blind panic. I took short breaths to calm my nerves.

I noticed then that the crowd around don Juan was beginning to disperse. The policeman returned with a colleague, and the two of them moved away, walking slowly toward the end of the street. It was at that point that I felt a sudden uncontrollable urge. It was as if my body were disconnected from my brain. I walked to my car, carrying all the packages. Without even the slightest trace of fear or concern, I opened the trunk, put the packages inside, then opened the driver's door.

Don Juan was on the sidewalk, by my car, looking at me absentmindedly. I stared at him with a thoroughly uncharacteristic coldness. Never in my life had I had such a feeling. It was not hatred I felt, or even anger. I was not even annoyed with him. What I felt was not resignation or patience, either. And it was certainly not kindness. Rather it was a cold indifference, a frightening lack of pity. At that instant, I could not have cared less about what happened to don Juan or myself.

Don Juan shook his upper body the way a dog shakes itself dry after a swim. And then, as if all of it had only been a bad dream, he was again the man I knew. He quickly turned his jacket inside out. It was a reversible jacket, beige on one side and black on the other. Now he was wearing a black jacket. He threw his straw hat inside the car and carefully combed his hair. He pulled his shirt collar over the jacket collar, instantly making himself look younger. Without saying a word, he helped me put the rest of the packages in the car.

When the two policemen ran back to us, blowing their whistles, drawn by the noise of the car doors being opened and closed, don Juan very nimbly rushed to meet them. He listened to them attentively and assured them they had nothing to worry about. He explained that they must have encountered his father,

a feeble old Indian who suffered from brain damage.
As he talked to them, he opened and closed the car
doors, as if checking the locks. He moved the packages from the trunk to the back seat. His agility and
youthful strength were the opposite of the old man's
movements of a few minutes ago. I knew that he was
acting for the benefit of the policeman who had seen
him before. If I had been that man, there would have
been no doubt in my mind that I was now seeing the
son of the old brain-damaged Indian.

Don Juan gave them the name of the restaurant
where they knew his father and then bribed them
shamelessly.

I did not bother to say anything to the policemen.
There was something that made me feel hard, cold,
efficient, silent.

We got in the car without a word. The policemen
did not attempt to ask me anything. They seemed too
tired even to try. We drove away.

"What kind of act did you pull out there, don
Juan?" I asked, and the coldness in my tone surprised
me.

"It was the first lesson in ruthlessness," he said.

He remarked that on our way to Guaymas he had
warned me about the impending lesson on ruthlessness.

I confessed that I had not paid attention because I
had thought that we were just making conversation to
break the monotony of driving.

"I never just make conversation," he said sternly.
"You should know that by now. What I did this afternoon was to create the proper situation for you to
move your assemblage point to the precise spot where
pity disappears. That spot is known as the place of no
pity.

"The problem that sorcerers have to solve," he
went on, "is that the place of no pity has to be reached

143

with only minimal help. The nagual sets the scene, but it is the apprentice who makes his assemblage point move.

"Today you just did that. I helped you, perhaps a bit overdramatically, by moving my own assemblage point to a specific position that made me into a feeble and unpredictable old man. I was not just acting old and feeble. I *was* old."

The mischievous glint in his eyes told me that he was enjoying the moment.

"It was not absolutely necessary that I do that," he went on. "I could have directed you to move your assemblage point without the hard tactics, but I couldn't help myself. Since this event will never be repeated, I wanted to know whether or not I could act, in some measure, like my own benefactor. Believe me, I surprised myself as much as I must have surprised you."

I felt incredibly at ease. I had no problems in accepting what he was saying to me, and no questions, because I understood everything without needing him to explain.

He then said something which I already knew, but could not verbalize, because I would not have been able to find the appropriate words to describe it. He said that everything sorcerers did was done as a consequence of a movement of their assemblage points, and that such movements were ruled by the amount of energy sorcerers had at their command.

I mentioned to don Juan that I knew all that and much more. And he commented that inside every human being was a gigantic, dark lake of silent knowledge which each of us could intuit. He told me I could intuit it perhaps with a bit more clarity than the average man because of my involvement in the warrior's path. He then said that sorcerers were the only beings on earth who deliberately went beyond the intuitive level by training themselves to do two transcendental things: first, to conceive the existence of the assemblage point, and second, to make that assemblage point move.

He emphasized over and over that the most sophisticated knowledge sorcerers possessed was of our potential as perceiving beings, and the knowledge that the content of perception depended on the position of the assemblage point.

At that point I began to experience a unique difficulty in concentrating on what he was saying, not because I was distracted or fatigued, but because my mind, on its own, had started to play the game of anticipating his words. It was as if an unknown part of myself were inside me, trying unsuccessfully to find adequate words to voice a thought. As don Juan spoke, I felt I could anticipate how he was going to express my own silent thoughts. I was thrilled to realize his choice of words was always better than mine could have been. But anticipating his words also diminished my concentration.

I abruptly pulled over to the side of the road. And right there I had, for the first time in my life, a clear knowledge of a dualism in me. Two obviously separate parts were within my being. One was extremely old, at ease, indifferent. It was heavy, dark, and connected to everything else. It was the part of me that did not care, because it was equal to anything. It enjoyed things with no expectation. The other part was light, new, fluffy, agitated. It was nervous, fast. It cared about itself because it was insecure and did not enjoy anything, simply because it lacked the capacity to connect itself to anything. It was alone, on the surface, vulnerable. That was the part with which I looked at the world.

I deliberately looked around with that part. Everywhere I looked I saw extensive farmlands. And that

145

insecure, fluffy, and caring part of me got caught between being proud of the industriousness of man and being sad at the sight of the magnificent old Sonoran desert turned into an orderly scene of furrows and domesticated plants.

The old, dark, heavy part of me did not care. And the two parts entered into a debate. The fluffy part wanted the heavy part to care, and the heavy part wanted the other one to stop fretting, and to enjoy.

"Why did you stop?" don Juan asked.

His voice produced a reaction, but it would be inaccurate to say that it was I who reacted. The sound of his voice seemed to solidify the fluffy part, and suddenly I was recognizably myself.

I described to don Juan the realization I had just had about my dualism. As he began to explain it in terms of the position of the assemblage point I lost my solidity. The fluffy part became as fluffy as it had been when I first noticed my dualism, and once again I knew what don Juan was explaining.

He said that when the assemblage point moves and reaches the place of no pity, the position of rationality and common sense becomes weak. The sensation I was having of an older, dark, silent side was a view of the antecedents of reason.

"I know exactly what you are saying," I told him. "I know a great number of things, but I can't speak of what I know. I don't know how to begin."

"I have mentioned this to you already," he said. "What you are experiencing and call dualism is a view from another position of your assemblage point. From that position, you can feel the older side of man. And what the older side of man knows is called silent knowledge. It's a knowledge that you cannot yet voice."

"Why not?" I asked.

"Because in order to voice it, it is necessary for you

to have and use an inordinate amount of energy," he replied. "You don't at this time have that kind of energy to spare.

"Silent knowledge is something that all of us have," he went on. "Something that has complete mastery, complete knowledge of everything. But it cannot think, therefore, it cannot speak of what it knows.

"Sorcerers believe that when man became aware that he knew, and wanted to be conscious of what he knew, he lost sight of what he knew. This silent knowledge, which you cannot describe, is, of course, *intent* —the spirit, the abstract. Man's error was to want to know it directly, the way he knew everyday life. The more he wanted, the more ephemeral it became."

"But what does that mean in plain words, don Juan?" I asked.

"It means that man gave up silent knowledge for the world of reason," he replied. "The more he clings to the world of reason, the more ephemeral *intent* becomes."

I started the car and we drove in silence. Don Juan did not attempt to give me directions or tell me how to drive—a thing he often did in order to exacerbate my self-importance. I had no clear idea where I was going, yet something in me knew. I let that part take over.

Very late in the evening we arrived at the big house don Juan's group of sorcerers had in a rural area of the state of Sinaloa in northwestern Mexico. The journey seemed to have taken no time at all. I could not remember the particulars of our drive. All I knew about it was that we had not talked.

The house seemed to be empty. There were no signs of people living there. I knew, however, that don Juan's friends were in the house. I could feel their presence without actually having to see them.

Don Juan lit some kerosene lanterns and we sat

down at a sturdy table. It seemed that don Juan was getting ready to eat. I was wondering what to say or do when a woman entered noiselessly and put a large plate of food on the table. I was not prepared for her entrance, and when she stepped out of the darkness into the light, as if she had materialized out of nowhere, I gasped involuntarily.

"Don't be scared, it's me, Carmela," she said and disappeared, swallowed again by the darkness.

I was left with my mouth open in mid-scream. Don Juan laughed so hard that I knew everybody in the house must have heard him. I half expected them to come, but no one appeared.

I tried to eat, but I was not hungry. I began to think about the woman. I did not know her. That is, I could almost identify her, but I could not quite work my memory of her out of the fog that obscured my thoughts. I struggled to clear my mind. I felt that it required too much energy and I gave up.

Almost as soon as I had stopped thinking about her, I began to experience a strange, numbing anxiety. At first I believed that the dark, massive house, and the silence in and around it, were depressing. But then my anguish rose to incredible proportions, right after I heard the faint barking of dogs in the distance. For a moment I thought that my body was going to explode. Don Juan intervened quickly. He jumped to where I was sitting and pushed my back until it cracked. The pressure on my back brought me immediate relief.

When I had calmed down, I realized I had lost, together with the anxiety that had nearly consumed me, the clear sense of knowing everything. I could no longer anticipate how don Juan was going to articulate what I myself knew.

Don Juan then started a most peculiar explanation. First he said that the origin of the anxiety that had overtaken me with the speed of wildfire was the sudden movement of my assemblage point, caused by Carmela's sudden appearance, and by my unavoidable effort to move my assemblage point to the place where I would be able to identify her completely.

He advised me to get used to the idea of recurrent attacks of the same type of anxiety, because my assemblage point was going to keep moving.

"Any movement of the assemblage point is like dying," he said. "Everything in us gets disconnected, then reconnected again to a source of much greater power. That amplification of energy is felt as a killing anxiety."

"What am I to do when this happens?" I asked.

"Nothing," he said. "Just wait. The outburst of energy will pass. What's dangerous is not knowing what is happening to you. Once you know, there is no real danger."

Then he talked about ancient man. He said that ancient man knew, in the most direct fashion, what to do and how best to do it. But, because he performed so well, he started to develop a sense of selfness, which gave him the feeling that he could predict and plan the actions he was used to performing. And thus the idea of an individual "self" appeared; an individual self which began to dictate the nature and scope of man's actions.

As the feeling of the individual self became stronger, man lost his natural connection to silent knowledge. Modern man, being heir to that development, therefore finds himself so hopelessly removed from the source of everything that all he can do is express his despair in violent and cynical acts of self-destruction. Don Juan asserted that the reason for man's cynicism and despair is the bit of silent knowledge left in him, which does two things: one, it gives man an inkling of his ancient connection to the source of everything; and two, it makes man feel that without

149

this connection, he has no hope of peace, of satisfaction, of attainment.

I thought I had caught don Juan in a contradiction. I pointed out to him that he had once told me that war was the natural state for a warrior, that peace was an anomaly.

"That's right," he admitted. "But war, for a warrior, doesn't mean acts of individual or collective stupidity or wanton violence. War, for a warrior, is the total struggle against that individual self that has deprived man of his power."

Don Juan said then that it was time for us to talk further about ruthlessness—the most basic premise of sorcery. He explained that sorcerers had discovered that any movement of the assemblage point meant a movement away from the excessive concern with that individual self which was the mark of modern man. He went on to say that sorcerers believed it was the position of the assemblage point which made modern man a homicidal egotist, a being totally involved with his self-image. Having lost hope of ever returning to the source of everything, man sought solace in his selfness. And, in doing so, he succeeded in fixing his assemblage point in the exact position to perpetuate his self-image. It was therefore safe to say that any movement of the assemblage point away from its customary position resulted in a movement away from man's self-reflection and its concomitant: self-importance.

Don Juan described self-importance as the force generated by man's self-image. He reiterated that it is that force which keeps the assemblage point fixed where it is at present. For this reason, the thrust of the warriors' way is to dethrone self-importance. And everything sorcerers do is toward accomplishing this goal.

He explained that sorcerers had unmasked self-importance and found that it is self-pity masquerading as something else.

"It doesn't sound possible, but that is what it is," he said. "Self-pity is the real enemy and the source of man's misery. Without a degree of pity for himself, man could not afford to be as self-important as he is. However, once the force of self-importance is engaged, it develops its own momentum. And it is this seemingly independent nature of self-importance which gives it its fake sense of worth."

His explanation, which I would have found incomprehensible under normal conditions, seemed thoroughly cogent to me. But because of the duality in me, which still pertained, it appeared a bit simplistic. Don Juan seemed to have aimed his thoughts and words at a specific target. And I, in my normal state of awareness, was that target.

He continued his explanation, saying that sorcerers are absolutely convinced that by moving our assemblage points away from their customary position we achieve a state of being which could only be called ruthlessness. Sorcerers knew, by means of their practical actions, that as soon as their assemblage points move, their self-importance crumbles. Without the customary position of their assemblage points, their self-image can no longer be sustained. And without the heavy focus on that self-image, they lose their self-compassion, and with it their self-importance. Sorcerers are right, therefore, in saying that self-importance is merely self-pity in disguise.

He then took my experience of the afternoon and went through it step by step. He stated that a nagual in his role as leader or teacher has to behave in the most efficient, but at the same time most impeccable, way. Since it is not possible for him to plan the course of his actions rationally, the nagual always lets the spirit decide his course. For example, he said he had

had no plans to do what he did until the spirit gave him an indication, very early that morning while we were having breakfast in Nogales. He urged me to recall the event and tell him what I could remember.

I recalled that during breakfast I got very embarrassed because don Juan made fun of me.

"Think about the waitress," don Juan urged me.

"All I can remember about her is that she was rude."

"But what did she do?" he insisted. "What did she do while she waited to take our order?"

After a moment's pause, I remembered that she was a hard-looking young woman who threw the menu at me and stood there, almost touching me, silently demanding that I hurry up and order.

While she waited, impatiently tapping her big foot on the floor, she pinned her long black hair up on her head. The change was remarkable. She looked more appealing, more mature. I was frankly taken by the change in her. In fact, I overlooked her bad manners because of it.

"That was the omen," don Juan said. "Hardness and transformation were the indication of the spirit."

He said that his first act of the day, as a nagual, was to let me know his intentions. To that end, he told me in very plain language, but in a surreptitious manner, that he was going to give me a lesson in ruthlessness.

"Do you remember now?" he asked. "I talked to the waitress and to an old lady at the next table."

Guided by him in this fashion, I did remember don Juan practically flirting with an old lady and the ill-mannered waitress. He talked to them for a long time while I ate. He told them idiotically funny stories about graft and corruption in government, and jokes about farmers in the city. Then he asked the waitress if she was an American. She said no and laughed at the question. Don Juan said that that was good, because I was a Mexican-American in search of love. And I might as well start here, after eating such a good breakfast.

The women laughed. I thought they laughed at my being embarrassed. Don Juan said to them that, seriously speaking, I had come to Mexico to find a wife. He asked if they knew of any honest, modest, chaste woman who wanted to get married and was not too demanding in matters of male beauty. He referred to himself as my spokesman.

The women were laughing very hard. I was truly chagrined. Don Juan turned to the waitress and asked her if she would marry me. She said that she was engaged. It looked to me as though she was taking don Juan seriously.

"Why don't you let him speak for himself?" the old lady asked don Juan.

"Because he has a speech impediment," he said. "He stutters horribly."

The waitress said that I had been perfectly normal when I ordered my food.

"Oh! You're so observant," don Juan said. "Only when he orders food can he speak like anyone else. I've told him time and time again that if he wants to learn to speak normally, he has to be ruthless. I brought him here to give him some lessons in ruthlessness."

"Poor man," the old woman said.

"Well, we'd better get going if we are going to find love for him today," don Juan said as he stood to leave.

"You're serious about this marriage business," the young waitress said to don Juan.

"You bet," he replied. "I'm going to help him get what he needs so he can cross the border and go to the place of no pity."

I thought don Juan was calling either marriage or

the U.S.A. the place of no pity. I laughed at the metaphor and stuttered horribly for a moment, which scared the women half to death and made don Juan laugh hysterically.

"It was imperative that I state my purpose to you then," don Juan said, continuing his explanation. "I did, but it bypassed you completely, as it should have."

He said that from the moment the spirit manifested itself, every step was carried to its satisfactory completion with absolute ease. And my assemblage point reached the place of no pity, when, under the stress of his transformation, it was forced to abandon its customary place of self-reflection.

"The position of self-reflection," don Juan went on, "forces the assemblage point to assemble a world of sham compassion, but of very real cruelty and self-centeredness. In that world the only real feelings are those convenient for the one who feels them.

"For a sorcerer, ruthlessness is not cruelty. Ruthlessness is the opposite of self-pity or self-importance. Ruthlessness is sobriety."

5

The Requirements of Intent

BREAKING THE MIRROR OF
SELF-REFLECTION

We spent a night at the spot where I had recollected my experience in Guaymas. During that night, because my assemblage point was pliable, don Juan helped me to reach new positions, which immediately became blurry non-memories.

The next day I was incapable of remembering what had happened or what I had perceived; I had, nonetheless, the acute sensation of having had bizarre experiences. Don Juan agreed that my assemblage point had moved beyond his expectations, yet he refused to give me even a hint of what I had done. His only comment had been that some day I would recollect everything.

Around noon, we continued on up the mountains. We walked in silence and without stopping until late in the afternoon. As we slowly climbed a mildly steep mountain ridge, don Juan suddenly spoke. I did not understand any of what he was saying. He repeated it until I realized he wanted to stop on a wide ledge, visible from where we were. He was telling me that we would be protected there from the wind by the boulders and large, bushy shrubs.

"Tell me, which spot on the ledge would be the best for us to sit out all night?" he asked.

Earlier, as we were climbing, I had spotted the almost unnoticeable ledge. It appeared as a patch of darkness on the face of the mountain. I had identified it with a very quick glance. Now that don Juan was asking my opinion, I detected a spot of even greater darkness, one almost black, on the south side of the ledge. The dark ledge and the almost black spot in it did not generate any feeling of fear or anxiety. I felt that I liked that ledge. And I liked its dark spot even more.

"That spot there is very dark, but I like it," I said, when we reached the ledge.

He agreed that that was the best place to sit all night. He said it was a place with a special level of energy, and that he, too, liked its pleasing darkness.

We headed toward some protruding rocks. Don Juan cleared an area by the boulders and we sat with our backs against them.

I told him that on the one hand I thought it had been a lucky guess on my part to choose that very spot, but on the other I could not overlook the fact that I had perceived it with my eyes.

"I wouldn't say that you perceived it exclusively with your eyes," he said. "It was a bit more complex than that."

"What do you mean by that, don Juan?" I asked.

"I mean that you have possibilities you are not yet aware of," he replied. "Since you're quite careless, you may think that all of what you perceive is simply average sensory perception."

He said that if I doubted him, he dared me to go down to the base of the mountain again and corroborate what he was saying. He predicted that it would be impossible for me to see the dark ledge merely by looking at it.

I stated vehemently that I had no reason to doubt him. I was not going to climb down that mountain.

He insisted that we climb down. I thought he was doing it just to tease me. I got nervous, though, when it occurred to me that he might be serious. He laughed so hard he choked.

He commented on the fact that all animals could detect, in their surroundings, areas with special levels of energy. Most animals were frightened of these spots and avoided them. The exceptions were mountain lions and coyotes, which lay and even slept on such spots whenever they happened upon them. But, only sorcerers deliberately sought such spots for their effects.

I asked him what the effects were. He said that they gave out imperceptible jolts of invigorating energy, and he remarked that average men living in natural settings could find such spots, even though they were not conscious about having found them nor aware of their effects.

"How do they know they have found them?" I asked.

"They never do," he replied. "Sorcerers watching men travel on foot trails notice right away that men always become tired and rest right on the spot with a positive level of energy. If, on the other hand, they are going through an area with an injurious flow of energy, they become nervous and rush. If you ask them about it they will tell you they rushed through that area because they felt energized. But it is the opposite—the only place that energizes them is the place where they feel tired."

He said that sorcerers are capable of finding such spots by perceiving with their entire bodies minute surges of energy in their surroundings. The sorcerers' increased energy, derived from the curtailment of their self-reflection, allows their senses a greater range of perception.

"I've been trying to make clear to you that the only worthwhile course of action, whether for sorcerers or average men, is to restrict our involvement with our self-image," he continued. "What a nagual aims at with his apprentices is the shattering of their mirror of self-reflection."

He added that each apprentice was an individual case, and that the nagual had to let the spirit decide about the particulars.

"Each of us has a different degree of attachment to his self-reflection," he went on. "And that attachment is felt as need. For example, before I started on the path of knowledge, my life was endless need. And years after the nagual Julian had taken me under his wing, I was still just as needy, if not more so.

"But there are examples of people, sorcerers or average men, who need no one. They get peace, harmony, laughter, knowledge, directly from the spirit. They need no intermediaries. For you and for me, it's different. I'm your intermediary and the nagual Julian was mine. Intermediaries, besides providing a minimal chance—the awareness of *intent*—help shatter people's mirrors of self-reflection.

"The only concrete help you ever get from me is that I attack your self-reflection. If it weren't for that, you would be wasting your time. This is the only real help you've gotten from me."

"You've taught me, don Juan, more than anyone in my entire life," I protested.

"I've taught you all kinds of things in order to trap your attention," he said. "You'll swear, though, that that teaching has been the important part. It hasn't. There is very little value in instruction. Sorcerers maintain that moving the assemblage point is all that matters. And that movement, as you well know, depends on increased energy and not on instruction."

He then made an incongruous statement. He said that any human being who would follow a specific and simple sequence of actions can learn to move his assemblage point.

I pointed out that he was contradicting himself. To me, a sequence of actions meant instructions; it meant procedures.

"In the sorcerers' world there are only contradictions of terms," he replied. "In practice there are no contradictions. The sequence of actions I am talking about is one that stems from being aware. To become aware of this sequence you need a nagual. This is why I've said that the nagual provides a minimal chance, but that minimal chance is not instruction, like the instruction you need to learn to operate a machine. The minimal chance consists of being made aware of the spirit."

He explained that the specific sequence he had in mind called for being aware that self-importance is the force which keeps the assemblage point fixed. When self-importance is curtailed, the energy it requires is no longer expended. That increased energy then serves as the springboard that launches the assemblage point, automatically and without premeditation, into an inconceivable journey.

Once the assemblage point has moved, the movement itself entails moving from self-reflection, and this, in turn, assures a clear connecting link with the spirit. He commented that, after all, it was self-reflection that had disconnected man from the spirit in the first place.

"As I have already said to you," don Juan went on, "sorcery is a journey of return. We return victorious to the spirit, having descended into hell. And from hell we bring trophies. Understanding is one of our trophies.''

I told him that his sequence seemed very easy and very simple when he talked about it, but that when I had tried to put it into practice I had found it the total antithesis of ease and simplicity.

"Our difficulty with this simple progression," he said, "is that most of us are unwilling to accept that we need so little to get on with. We are geared to expect instruction, teaching, guides, masters. And when we are told that we need no one, we don't believe it. We become nervous, then distrustful, and finally angry and disappointed. If we need help, it is not in methods, but in emphasis. If someone makes us aware that we need to curtail our self-importance, that help is real.

"Sorcerers say we should need no one to convince us that the world is infinitely more complex than our wildest fantasies. So, why are we dependent? Why do we crave someone to guide us when we can do it ourselves? Big question, eh?"

Don Juan did not say anything else. Obviously, he wanted me to ponder the question. But I had other worries in my mind. My recollection had undermined certain foundations that I had believed unshakable, and I desperately needed him to redefine them. I broke the long silence and voiced my concern. I told him that I had come to accept that it was possible for me to forget whole incidents, from beginning to end, if they had taken place in heightened awareness. Up to that day I had had total recall of anything I had done under his guidance in my state of normal awareness. Yet, having had breakfast with him in Nogales had not existed in my mind prior to my recollecting it. And that event simply must have taken place in the world of everyday affairs.

"You are forgetting something essential," he said.

"The nagual's presence is enough to move the assemblage point. I have humored you all along with the nagual's blow. The blow between the shoulder blades that I have delivered is only a pacifier. It serves the purpose of removing your doubts. Sorcerers use physical contact as a jolt to the body. It doesn't do anything but give confidence to the apprentice who is being manipulated."

"Then who moves the assemblage point, don Juan?" I asked.

"The spirit does it," he replied in the tone of someone about to lose his patience.

He seemed to check himself and smiled and shook his head from side to side in a gesture of resignation.

"It's hard for me to accept," I said. "My mind is ruled by the principle of cause and effect."

He had one of his usual attacks of inexplicable laughter—inexplicable from my point of view, of course. I must have looked annoyed. He put his hand on my shoulder.

"I laugh like this periodically because you are demented," he said. "The answer to everything you ask me is staring you right in the eyes and you don't see it. I think dementia is your curse."

His eyes were so shiny, so utterly crazy and mischievous, that I ended up laughing myself.

"I have insisted to the point of exhaustion that there are no procedures in sorcery," he went on. "There are no methods, no steps. The only thing that matters is the movement of the assemblage point. And no procedure can cause that. It's an effect that happens all by itself."

He pushed me as if to straighten my shoulders, and then he peered at me, looking right into my eyes. My attention became riveted to his words.

"Let us see how you figure this out," he said. "I have just said that the movement of the assemblage

161

point happens by itself. But I have also said that the nagual's presence moves his apprentice's assemblage point and that the way the nagual masks his ruthlessness either helps or hinders that movement. How would you resolve this contradiction?"

I confessed that I had been just about to ask him about the contradiction, for I had been aware of it, but that I could not even begin to think of resolving it. I was not a sorcery practitioner.

"What are you, then?" he asked.

"I am a student of anthropology, trying to figure out what sorcerers do," I said.

My statement was not altogether true, but it was not a lie.

Don Juan laughed uncontrollably

"It's too late for that," he said. "Your assemblage point has moved already. And it is precisely that movement that makes one a sorcerer."

He stated that what seemed a contradiction was really the two sides of the same coin. The nagual entices the assemblage point into moving by helping to destroy the mirror of self-reflection. But that is all the nagual can do. The actual mover is the spirit, the abstract; something that cannot be seen or felt; something that does not seem to exist, and yet does. For this reason, sorcerers report that the assemblage point moves all by itself. Or they say that the nagual moves it. The nagual, being the conduit of the abstract, is allowed to express it through his actions.

I looked at don Juan questioningly.

"The nagual moves the assemblage point, and yet it is not he himself who does the actual moving," don Juan said. "Or perhaps it would be more appropriate to say that the spirit expresses itself in accordance with the nagual's impeccability. The spirit can move the assemblage point with the mere presence of an impeccable nagual."

He said that he had wanted to clarify this point, because, if it was misunderstood, it led a nagual back to self-importance and thus to his destruction.

He changed the subject and said that, because the spirit had no perceivable essence, sorcerers deal rather with the specific instances and ways in which they are able to shatter the mirror of self-reflection.

Don Juan noted that in this area it was important to realize the practical value of the different ways in which the naguals masked their ruthlessness. He said my mask of generosity, for example, was adequate for dealing with people on a shallow level, but useless for shattering their self-reflection because it forced me to demand an almost impossible decision on their part. I expected them to jump into the sorcerers' world without any preparation.

"A decision such as that jump must be prepared for," he went on. "And in order to prepare for it, any kind of mask for a nagual's ruthlessness will do, except the mask of generosity."

Perhaps because I desperately wanted to believe that I was truly generous, his comments on my behavior renewed my terrible sense of guilt. He assured me that I had nothing to be ashamed of, and that the only undesirable effect was that my pseudo-generosity did not result in positive trickery.

In this regard, he said, although I resembled his benefactor in many ways, my mask of generosity was too crude, too obvious to be of value to me as a teacher. A mask of reasonableness, such as his own, however, was very effective in creating an atmosphere propitious to moving the assemblage point. His disciples totally believed his pseudo-reasonableness. In fact, they were so inspired by it that he could easily trick them into exerting themselves to any degree.

"What happened to you that day in Guaymas was an example of how the nagual's masked ruthlessness shatters self-reflection,'' he continued. ''My mask was your downfall. You, like everyone around me, believed my reasonableness. And, of course, you expected, above all, the continuity of that reasonableness.

''When I faced you with not only the senile behavior of a feeble old man, but with the old man himself, your mind went to extremes in its efforts to repair my continuity and your self-reflection. And so you told yourself that I must have suffered a stroke.

''Finally, when it became impossible to believe in the continuity of my reasonableness, your mirror began to break down. From that point on, the shift of your assemblage point was just a matter of time. The only thing in question was whether it was going to reach the place of no pity.''

I must have appeared skeptical to don Juan, for he explained that the world of our self-reflection or of our mind was very flimsy and was held together by a few key ideas that served as its underlying order. When those ideas failed, the underlying order ceased to function.

''What are those key ideas, don Juan?'' I asked.

''In your case, in that particular instance, as in the case of the audience of that healer we talked about, continuity was the key idea,'' he replied.

''What is continuity?'' I asked.

''The idea that we are a solid block,'' he said. ''In our minds, what sustains our world is the certainty that we are unchangeable. We may accept that our behavior can be modified, that our reactions and opinions can be modified, but the idea that we are malleable to the point of changing appearances, to the point of being someone else, is not part of the underlying order of our self-reflection. Whenever a sorcerer interrupts that order, the world of reason stops.''

I wanted to ask him if breaking an individual's continuity was enough to cause the assemblage point to move. He seemed to anticipate my question. He said that that breakage was merely a softener. What helped the assemblage point move was the nagual's ruthlessness.

He then compared the acts he performed that afternoon in Guaymas with the actions of the healer we had previously discussed. He said that the healer had shattered the self-reflection of the people in her audience with a series of acts for which they had no equivalents in their daily lives—the dramatic spirit possession, changing voices, cutting the patient's body open. As soon as the continuity of the idea of themselves was broken, their assemblage points were ready to be moved.

He reminded me that he had described to me in the past the concept of stopping the world. He had said that stopping the world was as necessary for sorcerers as reading and writing was for me. It consisted of introducing a dissonant element into the fabric of everyday behavior for purposes of halting the otherwise smooth flow of ordinary events—events which were catalogued in our minds by our reason.

The dissonant element was called "not-doing," or the opposite of doing. "Doing" was anything that was part of a whole for which we had a cognitive account. Not-doing was an element that did not belong in that charted whole.

"Sorcerers, because they are *stalkers,* understand human behavior to perfection," he said. "They understand, for instance, that human beings are creatures of inventory. Knowing the ins and outs of a particular inventory is what makes a man a scholar or an expert in his field.

"Sorcerers know that when an average person's inventory fails, the person either enlarges his inventory or his world of self-reflection collapses. The average person is willing to incorporate new items into his inventory if they don't contradict the inventory's underlying order. But if the items contradict that order, the person's mind collapses. The inventory is the mind. Sorcerers count on this when they attempt to break the mirror of self-reflection."

He explained that that day he had carefully chosen the props for his act to break my continuity. He slowly transformed himself until he was indeed a feeble old man, and then, in order to reinforce the breaking of my continuity, he took me to a restaurant where they knew him as an old man.

I interrupted him. I had become aware of a contradiction I had not noticed before. He had said, at the time, that the reason he transformed himself was that he wanted to know what it was like to be old. The occasion was propitious and unrepeatable. I had understood that statement as meaning that he had not been an old man before. Yet at the restaurant they knew him as the feeble old man who suffered from strokes.

"The nagual's ruthlessness has many aspects," he said. "It's like a tool that adapts itself to many uses. Ruthlessness is a state of being. It is a level of *intent* that the nagual attains.

"The nagual uses it to entice the movement of his own assemblage point or those of his apprentices. Or he uses it to *stalk*. I began that day as a *stalker*, pretending to be old, and ended up as a genuinely old, feeble man. My ruthlessness, controlled by my eyes, made my own assemblage point move.

"Although I had been at the restaurant many times before as an old, sick man, I had only been *stalking*, merely playing at being old. Never before that day had my assemblage point moved to the precise spot of age and senility."

He said that as soon as he had *intended* to be old,

166

his eyes lost their shine, and I immediately noticed it. Alarm was written all over my face. The loss of the shine in his eyes was a consequence of using his eyes to *intend* the position of an old man. As his assemblage point reached that position, he was able to age in appearance, behavior, and feeling.

I asked him to clarify the idea of *intending* with the eyes. I had the faint notion I understood it, yet I could not formulate even to myself what I knew.

"The only way of talking about it is to say that *intent* is *intended* with the eyes," he said. "I know that it is so. Yet, just like you, I can't pinpoint what it is I know. Sorcerers resolve this particular difficulty by accepting something extremely obvious: human beings are infinitely more complex and mysterious than our wildest fantasies."

I insisted that he had not shed any light on the matter.

"All I can say is that the eyes do it," he said cuttingly. "I don't know how, but they do it. They summon *intent* with something indefinable that they have, something in their shine. Sorcerers say that *intent* is experienced with the eyes, not with the reason."

He refused to add anything and went back to explaining my recollection. He said that once his assemblage point had reached the specific position that made him genuinely old, doubts should have been completely removed from my mind. But due to the fact that I took pride in being super-rational, I immediately did my best to explain away his transformation.

"I've told you over and over that being too rational is a handicap," he said. "Human beings have a very deep sense of magic. We are part of the mysterious. Rationality is only a veneer with us. If we scratch that surface, we find a sorcerer underneath. Some of us, however, have great difficulty getting underneath the surface level; others do it with total ease. You and I are very alike in this respect—we both have to sweat blood before we let go of our self-reflection."

I explained to him that, for me, holding onto my rationality had always been a matter of life or death. Even more so when it came to my experiences in his world.

He remarked that that day in Guaymas my rationality had been exceptionally trying for him. From the start he had had to make use of every device he knew to undermine it. To that end, he began by forcibly putting his hands on my shoulders and nearly dragging me down with his weight. That blunt physical maneuver was the first jolt to my body. And this, together with my fear caused by his lack of continuity, punctured my rationality.

"But puncturing your rationality was not enough," don Juan went on. "I knew that if your assemblage point was going to reach the place of no pity, I had to break every vestige of my continuity. That was when I became really senile and made you run around town, and finally got angry at you and slapped you.

"You were shocked, but you were on the road to instant recovery when I gave your mirror of self-image what should have been its final blow. I yelled bloody murder. I didn't expect you to run away. I had forgotten about your violent outbursts."

He said that in spite of my on-the-spot recovery tactics, my assemblage point reached the place of no pity when I became enraged at his senile behavior. Or perhaps it had been the opposite: I became enraged because my assemblage point had reached the place of no pity. It did not really matter. What counted was that my assemblage point did arrive there.

Once it was there, my own behavior changed markedly. I became cold and calculating and indifferent to my personal safety.

I asked don Juan whether he had *seen* all this. I did

not remember telling him about it. He replied that to know what I was feeling all he had to do was introspect and remember his own experience.

He pointed out that my assemblage point became fixed in its new position when he reverted to his natural self. By then, my conviction about his normal continuity had suffered such a profound upheaval that continuity no longer functioned as a cohesive force. And it was at that moment, from its new position, that my assemblage point allowed me to build another type of continuity, one which I expressed in terms of a strange, detached hardness—a hardness that became my normal mode of behavior from then on.

"Continuity is so important in our lives that if it breaks it's always instantly repaired," he went on. "In the case of sorcerers, however, once their assemblage points reach the place of no pity, continuity is never the same.

"Since you are naturally slow, you haven't noticed yet that since that day in Guaymas you have become, among other things, capable of accepting any kind of discontinuity at its face value—after a token struggle of your reason, of course."

His eyes were shining with laughter.

"It was also that day that you acquired your masked ruthlessness," he went on. "Your mask wasn't as well developed as it is now, of course, but what you got then was the rudiments of what was to become your mask of generosity."

I tried to protest. I did not like the idea of masked ruthlessness, no matter how he put it.

"Don't use your mask on me," he said, laughing. "Save it for a better subject: someone who doesn't know you."

He urged me to recollect accurately the moment the mask came to me.

"As soon as you felt that cold fury coming over

you," he went on, "you had to mask it. You didn't joke about it, as my benefactor would have done. You didn't try to sound reasonable about it, like I would. You didn't pretend to be intrigued by it, like the nagual Elías would have. Those are the three nagual's masks I know. What did you do then? You calmly walked to your car and gave half of your packages away to the guy who was helping you carry them."

Until that moment I had not remembered that indeed someone helped me carry the packages. I told don Juan that I had seen lights dancing before my face, and I had thought I was seeing them because, driven by my cold fury, I was on the verge of fainting.

"You were not on the verge of fainting," don Juan answered. "You were on the verge of entering a *dreaming* state and *seeing* the spirit all by yourself, like Talía and my benefactor."

I said to don Juan that it was not generosity that made me give away the packages but cold fury. I had to do something to calm myself, and that was the first thing that occurred to me.

"But that's exactly what I've been telling you. Your generosity is not genuine," he retorted and began to laugh at my dismay.

THE TICKET TO IMPECCABILITY

It had gotten dark while don Juan was talking about breaking the mirror of self-reflection. I told him I was thoroughly exhausted, and we should cancel the rest of the trip and return home, but he maintained that we

had to use every minute of our available time to re-
view the sorcery stories or recollect by making my
assemblage point move as many times as possible.

I was in a complaining mood. I said that a state of
deep fatigue such as mine could only breed uncertainty and lack of conviction.

"Your uncertainty is to be expected," don Juan said
matter-of-factly. "After all, you are dealing with a
new type of continuity. It takes time to get used to it.
Warriors spend years in limbo where they are neither
average men nor sorcerers."

"What happens to them in the end?" I asked. "Do
they choose sides?"

"No. They have no choice," he replied. "All of
them become aware of what they already are: sorcerers. The difficulty is that the mirror of self-reflection
is extremely powerful and only lets its victims go after
a ferocious struggle."

He stopped talking and seemed lost in thought. His
body entered into the state of rigidity I had seen before
whenever he was engaged in what I characterized as
reveries, but which he described as instances in which
his assemblage point had moved and he was able to
recollect.

"I'm going to tell you the story of a sorcerer's ticket
to impeccability," he suddenly said after some thirty
minutes of total silence. "I'm going to tell you the
story of my death."

He began to recount what had happened to him after
his arrival in Durango still disguised in women's
clothes, following his month-long journey through
central Mexico. He said that old Belisario took him
directly to a hacienda to hide from the monstrous man
who was chasing him.

As soon as he arrived, don Juan—very daringly in
view of his taciturn nature—introduced himself to
everyone in the house. There were seven beautiful

women and a strange unsociable man who did not utter a single word. Don Juan delighted the lovely women with his rendition of the monstrous man's efforts to capture him. Above all, they were enchanted with the disguise which he still wore, and the story that went with it. They never tired of hearing the details of his trip, and all of them advised him on how to perfect the knowledge he had acquired during his journey. What surprised don Juan was their poise and assuredness, which were unbelievable to him.

The seven women were exquisite and they made him feel happy. He liked them and trusted them. They treated him with respect and consideration. But something in their eyes told him that under their facades of charm there existed a terrifying coldness, an aloofness he could never penetrate.

The thought occurred to him that in order for these strong and beautiful women to be so at ease and to have no regard for formalities, they had to be loose women. Yet it was obvious to him that they were not.

Don Juan was left alone to roam the property. He was dazzled by the huge mansion and its grounds. He had never seen anything like it. It was an old colonial house with a high surrounding wall. Inside were balconies with flowerpots and patios with enormous fruit trees that provided shade, privacy, and quiet.

There were large rooms, and on the ground floor airy corridors around the patios. On the upper floor there were mysterious bedrooms, where don Juan was not permitted to set foot.

During the following days don Juan was amazed by the profound interest the women took in his well-being. They did everything for him. They seemed to hang on his every word. Never before had people been so kind to him. But also, never before had he felt so solitary. He was always in the company of the beautiful, strange women, and yet he had never been so alone.

Don Juan believed that his feeling of aloneness came from being unable to predict the behavior of the women or to know their real feelings. He knew only what they told him about themselves.

A few days after his arrival, the woman who seemed to be their leader gave him some brand-new men's clothes and told him that his woman's disguise was no longer necessary, because whoever the monstrous man might have been, he was now nowhere in sight. She told him he was free to go whenever he pleased.

Don Juan begged to see Belisario, whom he had not seen since the day they arrived. The woman said that Belisario was gone. He had left word, however, that don Juan could stay in the house as long as he wanted —but only if he was in danger.

Don Juan declared he was in mortal danger. During his few days in the house, he had seen the monster constantly, always sneaking about the cultivated fields surrounding the house. The woman did not believe him and told him bluntly that he was a con artist, pretending to see the monster so they would take him in. She told him their house was not a place to loaf. She stated they were serious people who worked very hard and could not afford to keep a freeloader.

Don Juan was insulted. He stomped out of the house, but when he caught sight of the monster hiding behind the ornamental shrubbery bordering the walk, his fright immediately replaced his anger.

He rushed back into the house and begged the woman to let him stay. He promised to do peon labor for no wages if he could only remain at the hacienda.

She agreed, with the understanding that don Juan would accept two conditions: that he not ask any questions, and that he do exactly as he was told without requiring any explanations. She warned him that if he broke these rules his stay at the house would be in jeopardy.

"I stayed in the house really under protest," don Juan continued. "I did not like to accept her conditions, but I knew that the monster was outside. In the house I was safe. I knew that the monstrous man was always stopped at an invisible boundary that encircled the house, at a distance of perhaps a hundred yards. Within that circle I was safe. As far as I could discern, there must have been something about that house that kept the monstrous man away, and that was all I cared about.

"I also realized that when the people of the house were around me the monster never appeared."

After a few weeks with no change in his situation, the young man who don Juan believed had been living in the monster's house disguised as old Belisario reappeared. He told don Juan that he had just arrived, that his name was Julian, and that he owned the hacienda.

Don Juan naturally asked him about his disguise. But the young man, looking him in the eye and without the slightest hesitation, denied knowledge of any disguise.

"How can you stand here in my own house and talk such rubbish?" he shouted at don Juan. "What do you take me for?"

"But—you are Belisario, aren't you?" don Juan insisted.

"No," the young man said. "Belisario is an old man. I am Julian and I'm young. Don't you see?"

Don Juan meekly admitted that he had not been quite convinced that it was a disguise and immediately realized the absurdity of his statement. If being old was not a disguise, then it was a transformation, and that was even more absurd.

Don Juan's confusion increased by the moment. He asked about the monster and the young man replied that he had no idea what monster he was talking about. He conceded that don Juan must have been scared by something, otherwise old Belisario would not have given him sanctuary. But whatever reason don Juan had for hiding, it was his personal business.

Don Juan was mortified by the coldness of his host's tone and manner. Risking his anger, don Juan reminded him that they had met. His host replied that he had never seen him before that day, but that he was honoring Belisario's wishes as he felt obliged to do.

The young man added that not only was he the owner of the house but that he was also in charge of every person in that household, including don Juan, who, by the act of hiding among them, had become a ward of the house. If don Juan did not like the arrangement, he was free to go and take his chances with the monster no one else was able to see.

Before he made up his mind one way or another, don Juan judiciously decided to ask what being a ward of the house involved.

The young man took don Juan to a section of the mansion that was under construction and said that that part of the house was symbolic of his own life and actions. It was unfinished. Construction was indeed underway, but chances were it might never be completed.

"You are one of the elements of that incomplete construction," he said to don Juan. "Let's say that you are the beam that will support the roof. Until we put it in place and put the roof on top of it, we won't know whether it will support the weight. The master carpenter says it will. I am the master carpenter."

This metaphorical explanation meant nothing to don Juan, who wanted to know what was expected of him in matters of manual labor.

The young man tried another approach. "I'm a nagual," he explained. "I bring freedom. I'm the leader of the people in this house. You are in this house, and because of that you are part of it whether you like or not."

Don Juan looked at him dumbfounded, unable to say anything.

"I am the nagual Julian," his host said, smiling. "Without my intervention, there is no way to freedom."

Don Juan still did not understand. But he began to wonder about his safety in light of the man's obviously erratic mind. He was so concerned with this unexpected development that he was not even curious about the use of the word nagual. He knew that nagual meant sorcerer, yet he was unable to take in the total implication of the nagual Julian's words. Or perhaps, somehow, he understood it perfectly, although his conscious mind did not.

The young man stared at him for a moment and then said that don Juan's actual job would involve being his personal valet and assistant. There would be no pay for this, but excellent room and board. From time to time there would be other small jobs for don Juan, jobs requiring special attention. He was to be in charge of either doing the jobs himself or seeing that they got done. For these special services he would be paid small amounts of money which would be put into an account kept for him by the other members of the household. Thus, should he ever want to leave, there would be a small amount of cash to tide him over.

The young man stressed that don Juan should not consider himself a prisoner, but that if he stayed he would have to work. And still more important than the work were the three requirements he had to fulfill. He had to make a serious effort to learn everything the women taught him. His conduct with all the members of the household must be exemplary, which meant that he would have to examine his behavior and attitude toward them every minute of the day. And he was to address the young man, in direct conversation, as nagual, and when talking of him, to refer to him as the nagual Julian.

Don Juan accepted the terms grudgingly. But although he instantly plunged into his habitual sulkiness and moroseness, he learned his work quickly. What he did not understand was what was expected of him in matters of attitude and behavior. And even though he could not have put his finger on a concrete instance, he honestly believed that he was being lied to and exploited.

As his moroseness got the upper hand, he entered into a permanent sulk and hardly said a word to anyone.

It was then that the nagual Julian assembled all the members of his household and explained to them that even though he badly needed an assistant, he would abide by their decision. If they did not like the morose and unappealing attitude of his new orderly, they had the right to say so. If the majority disapproved of don Juan's behavior, the young man would have to leave and take his chances with whatever was waiting for him outside, be it a monster or his own fabrication.

The nagual Julian then led them to the front of the house and challenged don Juan to show them the monstrous man. Don Juan pointed him out, but no one else saw him. Don Juan ran frantically from one person to another, insisting that the monster was there, imploring them to help him. They ignored his pleas and called him crazy.

It was then that the nagual Julian put don Juan's fate to a vote. The unsociable man did not choose to vote. He shrugged his shoulders and walked away. All the women spoke out against don Juan's staying. They argued that he was simply too morose and bad-tempered. During the heat of the argument, however, the nagual Julian completely changed his attitude and became don Juan's defender. He suggested that the women might be misjudging the poor young man, that he was perhaps not crazy at all and maybe actually did see a monster. He said that perhaps his moroseness was the result of his worries. And a great fight ensued. Tempers flared, and in no time the women were yelling at the nagual.

Don Juan heard the argument but was past caring. He knew they were going to throw him out and that the monstrous man would certainly capture him and take him into slavery. In his utter helplessness he began to weep.

His despair and his tears swayed some of the enraged women. The leader of the women proposed another choice: a three-week trial period during which don Juan's actions and attitude would be evaluated daily by all the women. She warned don Juan that if there was one single complaint about his attitude during that time, he would be kicked out for good.

Don Juan recounted how the nagual Julian in a fatherly manner took him aside and proceeded to drive a wedge of fear into him. He whispered to don Juan that he knew for a fact that the monster not only existed but was roaming the property. Nevertheless, because of certain previous agreements with the women, agreements he could not divulge, he was not permitted to tell the women what he knew. He urged don Juan to stop demonstrating his stubborn, morose personality and pretend to be the opposite.

"Pretend to be happy and satisfied," he said to don Juan. "If you don't, the women will kick you out. That prospect alone should be enough to scare you. Use that fear as a real driving force. It's the only thing you have."

Any hesitation or second thoughts that don Juan might have had were instantly dispelled at the sight of the monstrous man. As the monster waited impatiently at the invisible line, he seemed aware of how precarious don Juan's position was. It was as if the monster were ravenously hungry, anxiously anticipating a feast.

The nagual Julian drove his wedge of fear a bit deeper.

"If I were you," he told don Juan, "I would behave like an angel. I'd act any way these women want me to, as long as it kept me from that hellish beast."

"Then you do see the monster?" don Juan asked.

"Of course I do," he replied. "And I also see that if you leave, or if the women kick you out, the monster will capture you and put you in chains. That will change your attitude for sure. Slaves don't have any choice but to behave well with their masters. They say that the pain inflicted by a monster like that is beyond anything."

Don Juan knew that his only hope was to make himself as congenial as he possibly could. The fear of falling prey to that monstrous man was indeed a powerful psychological force.

Don Juan told me that by some quirk in his own nature he was boorish only with the women; he never behaved badly in the presence of the nagual Julian. For some reason that don Juan could not determine, in his mind the nagual was not someone he could attempt to affect either consciously or subconsciously.

The other member of the household, the unsociable man, was of no consequence to don Juan. Don Juan had formed an opinion the moment he met him, and had discounted him. He thought that the man was weak, indolent, and overpowered by those beautiful women. Later on, when he was more aware of the nagual's personality, he knew that the man was definitely overshadowed by the glitter of the others.

As time passed, the nature of leadership and authority among them became evident to don Juan. He was surprised and somehow delighted to realize that no one was better or higher than another. Some of them performed functions of which the others were incapable, but that did not make them superior. It simply made them different. However, the ultimate decision in everything was automatically the nagual Julian's, and he apparently took great pleasure in expressing his decisions in the form of bestial jokes he played on everyone.

There was also a mystery woman among them. They referred to her as Talía, the nagual woman. Nobody told don Juan who she was, or what being the nagual woman meant. It was made clear to him, however, that one of the seven women was Talía. They all talked so much about her that don Juan's curiosity was aroused to tremendous heights. He asked so many questions that the woman who was the leader of the other women told him that she would teach him to read and write so that he might make better use of his deductive abilities. She said that he must learn to write things down rather than committing them to memory. In this fashion he would accumulate a huge collection of facts about Talía, facts that he ought to read and study until the truth became evident.

Perhaps anticipating the cynical retort he had in mind, she argued that, although it might seem an absurd endeavor, finding out who Talía was was one of the most difficult and rewarding tasks anyone could undertake.

That, she said, was the fun part. She added more seriously that it was imperative for don Juan to learn basic bookkeeping in order to help the nagual manage the property.

Immediately she started daily lessons and in one year don Juan had progressed so rapidly and extensively that he was able to read, write, and keep account books.

Everything had occurred so smoothly that he did not notice the changes in himself, the most remarkable of which was a sense of detachment. As far as he was concerned, he retained his impression that nothing was happening in the house, simply because he still was unable to identify with the members of the household. Those people were mirrors that did not yield reflection.

"I took refuge in that house for nearly three years," don Juan went on. "Countless things happened to me during that time, but I didn't think they were really important. Or at least I had chosen to consider them unimportant. I was convinced that for three years all I had done was hide, shake with fear, and work like a mule."

Don Juan laughed and told me that at one point, at the urging of the nagual Julian, he agreed to learn sorcery so that he might rid himself of the fear that consumed him each time he saw the monster keeping vigil. But although the nagual Julian talked to him a great deal, he seemed more interested in playing jokes on him. So he believed it was fair and accurate to say that he did not learn anything even loosely related to sorcery, simply because it was apparent that nobody in that house knew or practiced sorcery.

One day, however, he found himself walking purposefully, but without any volition on his part, toward the invisible line that held the monster at bay. The monstrous man was, of course, watching the house as usual. But that day, instead of turning back and running to seek shelter inside the house, don Juan kept walking. An incredible surge of energy made him advance with no concern for his safety.

A feeling of total detachment allowed him to face the monster that had terrorized him for so many years.

Don Juan expected the monster to lurch out and grab him by the throat, but that thought no longer created any terror in him. From a distance of a few inches he stared at the monstrous man for an instant and then stepped over the line. And the monster did not attack him, as don Juan had always feared he would, but became blurry. He lost his definition and turned into a misty whiteness, a barely perceptible patch of fog.

Don Juan advanced toward the fog and it receded as if in fear. He chased the patch of fog over the fields until he knew there was nothing left of the monster. He knew then that there had never been one. He could not, however, explain what he had feared. He had the vague sensation that although he knew exactly what the monster was, something was preventing him from thinking about it. He immediately thought that that rascal, the nagual Julian, knew the truth about what was happening. Don Juan would not have put it past the nagual Julian to play that kind of trick.

Before confronting him, don Juan gave himself the pleasure of walking unescorted all over the property. Never before had he been able to do that. Whenever he had needed to venture beyond that invisible line, he had been escorted by a member of the household. That had put a serious constraint on his mobility. The two or three times he had attempted to walk unescorted, he had found that he risked annihilation at the hands of the monstrous being.

Filled with a strange vigor, don Juan went into the house, but instead of celebrating his new freedom and power, he assembled the entire household and angrily demanded that they explain their lies. He accused them of making him work as their slave by playing on his fear of a nonexistent monster.

The women laughed as if he were telling the funniest joke. Only the nagual Julian seemed contrite, especially when don Juan, his voice cracking with resentment, described his three years of constant fear. The nagual Julian broke down and wept openly as don Juan demanded an apology for the shameful way he had been exploited.

"But we told you the monster didn't exist," one of the women said.

Don Juan glared at the nagual Julian, who cowered meekly.

"He knew the monster existed," don Juan yelled, pointing an accusing finger at the nagual.

But at the same time he was aware he was talking nonsense, because the nagual Julian had originally told him that the monster did not exist.

"The monster didn't exist," don Juan corrected himself, shaking with rage. "It was one of his tricks."

The nagual Julian, weeping uncontrollably, apologized to don Juan, while the women howled with laughter. Don Juan had never seen them laughing so hard.

"You knew all along that there was never any monster. You lied to me," he accused the nagual Julian, who, with his head down and his eyes filled with tears, admitted his guilt.

"I have certainly lied to you," he mumbled. "There was never any monster. What you saw as a monster was simply a surge of energy. Your fear made it into a monstrosity."

"You told me that that monster was going to devour me. How could you have lied to me like that?" don Juan shouted at him.

"Being devoured by that monster was symbolic," the nagual Julian replied softly. "Your real enemy is your stupidity. You are in mortal danger of being devoured by that monster now."

Don Juan yelled that he did not have to put up with silly statements. And he insisted they reassure him there were no longer any restrictions on his freedom to leave.

"You can go any time you want," the nagual Julian said curtly.

"You mean I can go right now?" don Juan asked.

"Do you want to?" the nagual asked.

"Of course, I want to leave this miserable place and the miserable bunch of liars who live here," don Juan shouted.

The nagual Julian ordered that don Juan's savings be paid him in full, and with shining eyes wished him happiness, prosperity, and wisdom.

The women did not want to say goodbye to him. They stared at him until he lowered his head to avoid their burning eyes.

Don Juan put his money in his pocket and without a backward glance walked out, glad his ordeal was over. The outside world was a question mark to him. He yearned for it. Inside that house he had been removed from it. He was young, strong. He had money in his pocket and a thirst for living.

He left them without saying thank you. His anger, bottled up by his fear for so long, was finally able to surface. He had even learned to like them—and now he felt betrayed. He wanted to run as far away from that place as he could.

In the city, he had his first unpleasant encounter. Traveling was very difficult and very expensive. He learned that if he wanted to leave the city at once he would not be able to choose his destination, but would have to wait for whatever muleteers were willing to take him. A few days later he left with a reputable muleteer for the port of Mazatlán.

"Although I was only twenty-three years old at the time," don Juan said, "I felt I had lived a full life. The only thing I had not experienced was sex. The nagual Julian had told me that it was the fact I had not been with a woman that gave me my strength and endurance, and that he had little time left to set things up before the world would catch up with me."

"What did he mean, don Juan?" I asked.

"He meant that I had no idea about the kind of hell I was heading for," don Juan replied, "and that he had very little time to set up my barricades, my silent protectors."

"What's a silent protector, don Juan?" I asked.

"It's a lifesaver," he said. "A silent protector is a surge of inexplicable energy that comes to a warrior when nothing else works.

"My benefactor knew what direction my life would take once I was no longer under his influence. So he struggled to give me as many sorcerers' options as possible. Those sorcerers' options were to be my silent protectors."

"What are sorcerers' options?" I asked.

"Positions of the assemblage point," he replied, "the infinite number of positions which the assemblage point can reach. In each and every one of those shallow or deep shifts, a sorcerer can strengthen his new continuity."

He reiterated that everything he had experienced either with his benefactor or while under his guidance had been the result of either a minute or a considerable shift of his assemblage point. His benefactor had made him experience countless sorcerers' options, more than the number that would normally be necessary, because he knew that don Juan's destiny would be to be called upon to explain what sorcerers were and what they did.

"The effect of those shifts of the assemblage point is cumulative," he continued. "It weighs on you whether you understand it or not. That accumulation worked for me, at the end.

"Very soon after I came into contact with the nagual, my point of assemblage moved so profoundly that I was capable of *seeing*. I *saw* an energy field as a monster. And the point kept on moving until I *saw* the monster as what it really was: an energy field. I had succeeded in *seeing*, and I didn't know it. I thought I had done nothing, had learned nothing. I was stupid beyond belief.''

''You were too young, don Juan,'' I said. ''You couldn't have done otherwise.''

He laughed. He was on the verge of replying, when he seemed to change his mind. He shrugged his shoulders and went on with his account.

Don Juan said that when he arrived in Mazatlán he was practically a seasoned muleteer, and was offered a permanent job running a mule train. He was very satisfied with the arrangements. The idea that he would be making the trip between Durango and Mazatlán pleased him no end. There were two things, however, that bothered him: first, that he had not yet been with a woman, and second, a strong but unexplainable urge to go north. He did not know why. He knew only that somewhere to the north something was waiting for him. The feeling persisted so strongly that in the end he was forced to refuse the security of a permanent job so he could travel north.

His superior strength and a new and unaccountable cunning enabled him to find jobs even where there were none to be had, as he steadily worked his way north to the state of Sinaloa. And there his journey ended. He met a young widow, like himself a Yaqui Indian, who had been the wife of a man to whom don Juan was indebted.

He attempted to repay his indebtedness by helping the widow and her children, and without being aware of it, he fell into the role of husband and father.

His new responsibilities put a great burden on him. He lost his freedom of movement and even his urge to

186

journey farther north. He felt compensated for that loss, however, by the profound affection he felt for the woman and her children.

"I experienced moments of sublime happiness as a husband and father," don Juan said. "But it was at those moments when I first noticed that something was terribly wrong. I realized that I was losing the feeling of detachment, the aloofness I had acquired during my time in the nagual Julian's house. Now I found myself identifying with the people who surrounded me."

Don Juan said that it took about a year of unrelenting abrasion to make him lose every vestige of the new personality he had acquired at the nagual's house. He had begun with a profound yet aloof affection for the woman and her children. This detached affection allowed him to play the role of husband and father with abandon and gusto. As time went by, his detached affection turned into a desperate passion that made him lose his effectiveness.

Gone was his feeling of detachment, which was what had given him the power to love. Without that detachment, he had only mundane needs, desperation, and hopelessness: the distinctive features of the world of everyday life. Gone as well was his enterprise. During his years at the nagual's house, he had acquired a dynamism that had served him well when he set out on his own.

But the most draining pain was knowing that his physical energy had waned. Without actually being in ill health, one day he became totally paralyzed. He did not feel pain. He did not panic. It was as if his body had understood that he would get the peace and quiet he so desperately needed only if it ceased to move.

As he lay helpless in bed, he did nothing but think. And he came to realize that he had failed because he did not have an abstract purpose. He knew that the people in the nagual's house were extraordinary because they pursued freedom as their abstract purpose. He did not understand what freedom was, but he knew that it was the opposite of his own concrete needs.

His lack of an abstract purpose had made him so weak and ineffective that he was incapable of rescuing his adopted family from their abysmal poverty. Instead, they had pulled him back to the very misery, sadness, and despair which he himself had known prior to encountering the nagual.

As he reviewed his life, he became aware that the only time he had not been poor and had not had concrete needs was during his years with the nagual. Poverty was the state of being that had reclaimed him when his concrete needs overpowered him.

For the first time since he had been shot and wounded so many years before, don Juan fully understood that the nagual Julian was indeed the nagual, the leader, and his benefactor. He understood what it was his benefactor had meant when he said to him that there was no freedom without the nagual's intervention. There was now no doubt in don Juan's mind that his benefactor and all the members of his benefactor's household were sorcerers. But what don Juan understood with the most painful clarity was that he had thrown away his chance to be with them.

When the pressure of his physical helplessness seemed unendurable, his paralysis ended as mysteriously as it had begun. One day he simply got out of bed and went to work. But his luck did not get any better. He could hardly make ends meet.

Another year passed. He did not prosper, but there was one thing in which he succeeded beyond his expectations: he made a total recapitulation of his life. He understood then why he loved and could not leave those children, and why he could not stay with them, and he also understood why he could neither act one way nor the other.

Don Juan knew that he had reached a complete impasse, and that to die like a warrior was the only action congruous with what he had learned at his benefactor's house. So every night, after a frustrating day of hardship and meaningless toil, he patiently waited for his death to come.

He was so utterly convinced of his end that his wife and her children waited with him—in a gesture of solidarity, they too wanted to die. All four sat in perfect immobility, night after night, without fail, and recapitulated their lives while they waited for death.

Don Juan had admonished them with the same words his benefactor had used to admonish him.

"Don't wish for it," his benefactor had said. "Just wait until it comes. Don't try to imagine what death is like. Just be there to be caught in its flow."

The time spent quietly strengthened them mentally, but physically their emaciated bodies told of their losing battle.

One day, however, don Juan thought his luck was beginning to change. He found temporary work with a team of farm laborers during the harvest season. But the spirit had other designs for him. A couple of days after he started work, someone stole his hat. It was impossible for him to buy a new one, but he had to have one to work under the scorching sun.

He fashioned a protection of sorts by covering his head with rags and handfuls of straw. His coworkers began to laugh and taunt him. He ignored them. Compared to the lives of the three people who depended on his labor, how he looked had little meaning for him. But the men did not stop. They yelled and laughed until the foreman, fearing that they would riot, fired don Juan.

A wild rage overwhelmed don Juan's sense of sobriety and caution. He knew he had been wronged. The moral right was with him. He let out a chilling, piercing scream, and grabbed one of the men, and lifted him over his shoulders, meaning to crack his back. But he thought of those hungry children. He thought of their disciplined little bodies as they sat with him night after night awaiting death. He put the man down and walked away.

Don Juan said that he sat down at the edge of the field where the men were working, and all the despair that had accumulated in him finally exploded. It was a silent rage, but not against the people around him. He raged against himself. He raged until all his anger was spent.

"I sat there in view of all those people and began to weep," don Juan continued. "They looked at me as if I were crazy, which I really was, but I didn't care. I was beyond caring.

"The foreman felt sorry for me and came over to give a word of advice. He thought I was weeping for myself. He couldn't have possibly known that I was weeping for the spirit."

Don Juan said that a silent protector came to him after his rage was spent. It was in the form of an unaccountable surge of energy that left him with the clear feeling that his death was imminent. He knew that he was not going to have time to see his adopted family again. He apologized to them in a loud voice for not having had the fortitude and wisdom necessary to deliver them from their hell on earth.

The farm workers continued to laugh and mock him. He vaguely heard them. Tears swelled in his chest as he addressed and thanked the spirit for having placed him in the nagual's path, giving him an undeserved chance to be free. He heard the howls of the uncomprehending men. He heard their insults and yells as if from within himself. They had the right to ridicule him. He had been at the portals of eternity and had been unaware of it.

"I understood how right my benefactor had been," don Juan said. "My stupidity was a monster and it had already devoured me. The instant I had that thought, I knew that anything I could say or do was useless. I had lost my chance. Now, I was only clowning for those men. The spirit could not possibly have cared about my despair. There were too many of us—men with our own petty private hells, born of our stupidity —for the spirit to pay attention.

"I knelt and faced the southeast. I thanked my benefactor again and told the spirit I was ashamed. So ashamed. And with my last breath I said goodbye to a world which could have been wonderful if I had had wisdom. An immense wave came for me then. I felt it, first. Then I heard it, and finally I saw it coming for me from the southeast, over the fields. It overtook me and its blackness covered me. And the light of my life was gone. My hell had ended. I was finally dead! I was finally free!"

Don Juan's story devastated me. He ignored all my efforts to talk about it. He said that at another time and in another setting we were going to discuss it. He demanded instead that we get on with what he had come to do: elucidate the mastery of awareness.

A couple of days later, as we were coming down from the mountains, he suddenly began to talk about his story. We had sat down to rest. Actually, I was the one who had stopped to catch my breath. Don Juan was not even breathing hard.

"The sorcerers' struggle for assuredness is the most dramatic struggle there is," don Juan said. "It's painful and costly. Many, many times it has actually cost sorcerers their lives."

He explained that in order for any sorcerer to have

complete certainty about his actions, or about his position in the sorcerers' world, or to be capable of utilizing intelligently his new continuity, he must invalidate the continuity of his old life. Only then can his actions have the necessary assuredness to fortify and balance the tenuousness and instability of his new continuity.

"The sorcerer seers of modern times call this process of invalidation the ticket to impeccability, or the sorcerers' symbolic but final death," don Juan said. "And in that field in Sinaloa, I got my ticket to impeccability. I died there. The tenuousness of my new continuity cost me my life."

"But did you die, don Juan, or did you just faint?" I asked, trying not to sound cynical.

"I died in that field," he said. "I felt my awareness flowing out of me and heading toward the Eagle. But as I had impeccably recapitulated my life, the Eagle did not swallow my awareness. The Eagle spat me out. Because my body was dead in the field, the Eagle did not let me go through to freedom. It was as if it told me to go back and try again.

"I ascended the heights of blackness and descended again to the light of the earth. And then I found myself in a shallow grave at the edge of the field, covered with rocks and dirt."

Don Juan said that he knew instantly what to do. After digging himself out he rearranged the grave to look as if a body were still there, and slipped away. He felt strong and determined. He knew that he had to return to his benefactor's house. But, before he started on his return journey, he wanted to see his family and explain to them that he was a sorcerer and for that reason he could not stay with them. He wanted to explain that his downfall had been not knowing that sorcerers can never make a bridge to join the people of the world. But, if people desire to do so, they have to make a bridge to join sorcerers.

"I went home," don Juan continued, "but the house was empty. The shocked neighbors told me that farm workers had come earlier with the news that I had dropped dead at work, and my wife and her children had left."

"How long were you dead, don Juan?" I asked.

"A whole day, apparently," he said.

Don Juan's smile played on his lips. His eyes seemed to be made of shiny obsidian. He was watching my reaction, waiting for my comments.

"What became of your family, don Juan?" I asked.

"Ah, the question of a sensible man," he remarked. "For a moment I thought you were going to ask me about my death!"

I confessed that I had been about to, but that I knew he was *seeing* my question as I formulated it in my mind, and just to be contrary I asked something else. I did not mean it as a joke, but it made him laugh.

"My family disappeared that day," he said. "My wife was a survivor. She had to be, with the conditions we lived under. Since I had been waiting for my death, she believed I had gotten what I wanted. There was nothing for her to do there, so she left.

"I missed the children and I consoled myself with the thought that it wasn't my fate to be with them. However, sorcerers have a peculiar bent. They live exclusively in the twilight of a feeling best described by the words 'and yet . . .' When everything is crumbling down around them, sorcerers accept that the situation is terrible, and then immediately escape to the twilight of 'and yet . . .'

"I did that with my feelings for those children and the woman. With great discipline—especially on the part of the oldest boy—they had recapitulated their lives with me. Only the spirit could decide the outcome of that affection.''

He reminded me that he had taught me how warriors acted in such situations. They did their utmost, and then, without any remorse or regrets, they relaxed and let the spirit decide the outcome.

"What was the decision of the spirit, don Juan?" I asked.

He scrutinized me without answering. I knew he was completely aware of my motive for asking. I had experienced a similar affection and a similar loss.

"The decision of the spirit is another basic core," he said. "Sorcery stories are built around it. We'll talk about that specific decision when we get to discussing that basic core.

"Now, wasn't there a question about my death you wanted to ask?"

"If they thought you were dead, why the shallow grave?" I asked. "Why didn't they dig a real grave and bury you?"

"That's more like you," he said laughing. "I asked the same question myself and I realized that all those farm workers were pious people. I was a Christian. Christians are not buried just like that, nor are they left to rot like dogs. I think they were waiting for my family to come and claim the body and give it a proper burial. But my family never came."

"Did you go and look for them, don Juan?" I asked.

"No. Sorcerers never look for anyone," he replied. "And I was a sorcerer. I had paid with my life for the mistake of not knowing I was a sorcerer, and that sorcerers never approach anyone.

"From that day on, I have only accepted the company or the care of people or warriors who are dead, as I am."

Don Juan said that he went back to his benefactor's house, where all of them knew instantly what he had discovered. And they treated him as if he had not left at all.

The nagual Julian commented that because of his peculiar nature don Juan had taken a long time to die.

"My benefactor told me then that a sorcerer's ticket to freedom was his death," don Juan went on. "He said that he himself had paid with his life for that ticket to freedom, as had everyone else in his household. And that now we were equals in our condition of being dead."

"Am I dead too, don Juan?" I asked.

"You are dead," he said. "The sorcerers' grand trick, however, is to be aware that they are dead. Their ticket to impeccability must be wrapped in awareness. In that wrapping, sorcerers say, their ticket is kept in mint condition.

"For sixty years, I've kept mine in mint condition."

6

Handling Intent

THE THIRD POINT

Don Juan often took me and the rest of his apprentices
on short trips to the western range nearby. On this
occasion we left at dawn, and late in the afternoon,
started back. I chose to walk with don Juan. To be
close to him always soothed and relaxed me; but being
with his volatile apprentices always produced in me
the opposite effect: they made me feel very tired.

As we all came down from the mountains, don Juan
and I made one stop before we reached the flatlands.
An attack of profound melancholy came upon me with
such speed and strength that all I could do was to sit
down. Then, following don Juan's suggestion, I lay on
my stomach, on top of a large round boulder.

The rest of the apprentices taunted me and continued walking. I heard their laughter and yelling become
faint in the distance. Don Juan urged me to relax and
let my assemblage point, which he said had moved
with sudden speed, settle into its new position.

"Don't fret," he advised me. "In a short while, you'll feel a sort of tug, or a pat on your back, as if someone has touched you. Then you'll be fine."

The act of lying motionless on the boulder, waiting to feel the pat on my back, triggered a spontaneous recollection so intense and clear that I never noticed the pat I was expecting. I was sure, however, that I got it, because my melancholy indeed vanished instantly.

I quickly described what I was recollecting to don Juan. He suggested I stay on the boulder and move my assemblage point back to the exact place it was when I experienced the event that I was recalling.

"Get every detail of it," he warned.

It had happened many years before. Don Juan and I had been at that time in the state of Chihuahua in northern Mexico, in the high desert. I used to go there with him because it was an area rich in the medicinal herbs he collected. From an anthropological point of view that area also held a tremendous interest for me. Archaeologists had found, not too long before, the remains of what they concluded was a large, prehistoric trading post. They surmised that the trading post, strategically situated in a natural passway, had been the epicenter of commerce along a trade route which joined the American Southwest to southern Mexico and Central America.

The few times I had been in that flat, high desert had reinforced my conviction that archaeologists were right in their conclusions that it was a natural passway. I, of course, had lectured don Juan on the influence of that passway in the prehistoric distribution of cultural traits on the North American continent. I was deeply interested at that time in explaining sorcery among the Indians of the American Southwest, Mexico, and Central America as a system of beliefs which had been transmitted along trade routes and which had served to create, at a certain abstract level, a sort of pre-Columbian pan-Indianism.

Don Juan, naturally, laughed uproariously every time I expounded my theories.

The event that I recollected had begun in the mid-afternoon. After don Juan and I had gathered two small sacks of some extremely rare medicinal herbs, we took a break and sat down on top of some huge boulders. But before we headed back to where I had left my car, don Juan insisted on talking about the art of *stalking*. He said that the setting was the most adequate one for explaining its intricacies, but that in order to understand them I first had to enter into heightened awareness.

I demanded that before he do anything he explain to me again what heightened awareness really was.

Don Juan, displaying great patience, discussed heightened awareness in terms of the movement of the assemblage point. As he kept talking, I realized the facetiousness of my request. I knew everything he was telling me. I remarked that I did not really need anything explained, and he said that explanations were never wasted, because they were imprinted in us for immediate or later use or to help prepare our way to reaching silent knowledge.

When I asked him to talk about silent knowledge in more detail, he quickly responded that silent knowledge was a general position of the assemblage point, that ages ago it had been man's normal position, but that, for reasons which would be impossible to determine, man's assemblage point had moved away from that specific location and adopted a new one called "reason."

Don Juan remarked that not every human being was a representative of this new position. The assemblage points of the majority of us were not placed squarely on the location of reason itself, but in its immediate vicinity. The same thing had been the case with silent knowledge: not every human being's assemblage point had been squarely on that location either.

He also said that "the place of no pity," being another position of the assemblage point, was the forerunner of silent knowledge, and that yet another position of the assemblage point called "the place of concern," was the forerunner of reason.

I found nothing obscure about those cryptic remarks. To me they were self-explanatory. I understood everything he said while I waited for his usual blow to my shoulder blades to make me enter into heightened awareness. But the blow never came, and I kept on understanding what he was saying without really being aware that I understood anything. The feeling of ease, of taking things for granted, proper to my normal consciousness, remained with me, and I did not question my capacity to understand.

Don Juan looked at me fixedly and recommended that I lie face down on top of a round boulder with my arms and legs spread like a frog.

I lay there for about ten minutes, thoroughly relaxed, almost asleep, until I was jolted out of my slumber by a soft, sustained hissing growl. I raised my head, looked up, and my hair stood on end. A gigantic, dark jaguar was squatting on a boulder, scarcely ten feet from me, right above where don Juan was sitting. The jaguar, its fangs showing, was glaring straight at me. He seemed ready to jump on me.

"Don't move!" don Juan ordered me softly. "And don't look at his eyes. Stare at his nose and don't blink. Your life depends on your stare."

I did what he told me. The jaguar and I stared at each other for a moment until don Juan broke the standoff by hurling his hat, like a Frisbee, at the jaguar's head. The jaguar jumped back to avoid being hit, and don Juan let out a loud, prolonged, and piercing whistle. He then yelled at the top of his voice and clapped his hands two or three times. It sounded like muffled gunshots.

Don Juan signaled me to come down from the boulder and join him. The two of us yelled and clapped our hands until he decided we had scared the jaguar away.

My body was shaking, yet I was not frightened. I told don Juan that what had caused me the greatest fear had not been the cat's sudden growl or his stare, but the certainty that the jaguar had been staring at me long before I had heard him and lifted my head.

Don Juan did not say a word about the experience. He was deep in thought. When I began to ask him if he had seen the jaguar before I had, he made an imperious gesture to quiet me. He gave me the impression he was ill at ease or even confused.

After a moment's silence, don Juan signaled me to start walking. He took the lead. We walked away from the rocks, zigzagging at a fast pace through the bush.

After about half an hour we reached a clearing in the chaparral where we stopped to rest for a moment. We had not said a single word and I was eager to know what don Juan was thinking.

"Why are we walking in this pattern?" I asked. "Wouldn't it be better to make a beeline out of here, and fast?"

"No!" he said emphatically. "It wouldn't be any good. That one is a male jaguar. He's hungry and he's going to come after us."

"All the more reason to get out of here fast," I insisted.

"It's not so easy," he said. "That jaguar is not encumbered by reason. He'll know exactly what to do to get us. And, as sure as I am talking to you, he'll read our thoughts."

"What do you mean, the jaguar reading our thoughts?" I asked.

"That is no metaphorical statement," he said. "I mean what I say. Big animals like that have the capacity to read thoughts. And I don't mean guess. I mean that they know everything directly."

"What can we do then?" I asked, truly alarmed.

"We ought to become less rational and try to win the battle by making it impossible for the jaguar to read us," he replied.

"How would being less rational help us?" I asked.

"Reason makes us choose what seems sound to the mind," he said. "For instance, your reason already told you to run as fast as you can in a straight line. What your reason failed to consider is that we would have had to run about six miles before reaching the safety of your car. And the jaguar will outrun us. He'll cut in front of us and be waiting in the most appropriate place to jump us.

"A better but less rational choice is to zigzag."

"How do you know that it's better, don Juan?" I asked.

"I know it because my connection to the spirit is very clear," he replied. "That is to say, my assemblage point is at the place of silent knowledge. From there I can discern that this is a hungry jaguar, but not one that has already eaten humans. And he's baffled by our actions. If we zigzag now, the jaguar will have to make an effort to anticipate us."

"Are there any other choices beside zigzagging?" I asked.

"There are only rational choices," he said. "And we don't have all the equipment we need to back up rational choices. For example, we can head for the high ground, but we would need a gun to hold it.

"We must match the jaguar's choices. Those choices are dictated by silent knowledge. We must do what silent knowledge tells us, regardless of how unreasonable it may seem."

He began his zigzagging trot. I followed him very closely, but I had no confidence that running like that would save us. I was having a delayed panic reaction. The thought of the dark, looming shape of the enormous cat obsessed me.

The desert chaparral consisted of tall, ragged bushes spaced four or five feet apart. The limited rainfall in the high desert did not allow the growth of plants with thick foliage or of dense underbrush. Yet the visual effect of the chaparral was of thickness and impenetrable growth.

Don Juan moved with extraordinary nimbleness and I followed as best as I could. He suggested that I watch where I stepped and make less noise. He said that the sound of branches cracking under my weight was a dead giveaway.

I deliberately tried to step in don Juan's tracks to avoid breaking dry branches. We zigzagged about a hundred yards in this manner before I caught sight of the jaguar's enormous dark mass no more than thirty feet behind me.

I yelled at the top of my voice. Without stopping, don Juan turned around quickly enough to see the big cat move out of sight. Don Juan let out another piercing whistle and kept clapping his hands, imitating the sound of muffled gunshots.

In a very low voice he said that cats did not like to go uphill and so we were going to cross, at top speed, the wide and deep ravine a few yards to my right.

He gave a signal to go and we thrashed through the bushes as fast as we could. We slid down one side of the ravine, reached the bottom, and rushed up the other side. From there we had a clear view of the slope, the bottom of the ravine, and the level ground where we had been. Don Juan whispered that the jaguar was following our scent, and that if we were lucky we would see him running to the bottom of the ravine, close to our tracks.

Gazing fixedly at the ravine below us, I waited anxiously to catch a glimpse of the animal. But I did not see him. I was beginning to think the jaguar might have run away when I heard the frightening growling of the big cat in the chaparral just behind us. I had the chilling realization that don Juan had been right. To get to where he was, the jaguar must have read our thoughts and crossed the ravine before we had.

Without uttering a single word, don Juan began running at a formidable speed. I followed and we zigzagged for quite a while. I was totally out of breath when we stopped to rest.

The fear of being chased by the jaguar had not, however, prevented me from admiring don Juan's superb physical prowess. He had run as if he were a young man. I began to tell him that he had reminded me of someone in my childhood who had impressed me deeply with his running ability, but he signaled me to stop talking. He listened attentively and so did I.

I heard a soft rustling in the underbrush, right ahead of us. And then the black silhouette of the jaguar was visible for an instant at a spot in the chaparral perhaps fifty yards from us.

Don Juan shrugged his shoulders and pointed in the direction of the animal.

"It looks like we're not going to shake him off," he said with a tone of resignation. "Let's walk calmly, as if we were taking a nice stroll in the park, and you tell me the story of your childhood. This is the right time and the right setting for it. A jaguar is after us with a ravenous appetite, and you are reminiscing about your past: the perfect not-doing for being chased by a jaguar."

He laughed loudly. But when I told him I had completely lost interest in telling the story, he doubled up with laughter.

"You are punishing me now for not wanting to listen to you, aren't you?" he asked.

And I, of course, began to defend myself. I told him his accusation was definitely absurd. I really had lost the thread of the story.

"If a sorcerer doesn't have self-importance, he doesn't give a rat's ass about having lost the thread of a story," he said with a malicious shine in his eyes. "Since you don't have any self-importance left, you should tell your story now. Tell it to the spirit, to the jaguar, and to me, as if you hadn't lost the thread at all."

I wanted to tell him that I did not feel like complying with his wishes, because the story was too stupid and the setting was overwhelming. I wanted to pick the appropriate setting for it, some other time, as he himself did with his stories.

Before I voiced my opinions, he answered me.

"Both the jaguar and I can read thoughts," he said, smiling. "If I choose the proper setting and time for my sorcery stories, it's because they are for teaching and I want to get the maximum effect from them."

He signaled me to start walking. We walked calmly, side by side. I said I had admired his running and his stamina, and that a bit of self-importance was at the core of my admiration, because I considered myself a good runner. Then I told him the story from my childhood I had remembered when I saw him running so well.

I told him I had played soccer as a boy and had run extremely well. In fact, I was so agile and fast that I felt I could commit any prank with impunity because I would be able to outrun anyone chasing me, especially the old policemen who patrolled the streets of my hometown on foot. If I broke a street light or something of the sort, all I had to do was to take off running and I was safe.

But one day, unbeknownst to me, the old policemen were replaced by a new police corps with military training. The disastrous moment came when I broke a window in a store and ran, confident that my speed was my safeguard. A young policeman took off after me. I ran as I had never run before, but it was to no avail. The officer, who was a crack center forward on the police soccer team, had more speed and stamina than my ten-year-old body could manage. He caught me and kicked me all the way back to the store with the broken window. Very artfully he named off all his kicks, as if he were training on a soccer field. He did not hurt me, he only scared me spitless, yet my intense humiliation was tempered by a ten-year-old's admiration for his prowess and his talent as a soccer player.

I told don Juan that I had felt the same with him that day. He was able to outrun me in spite of our age difference and my old proclivity for speedy getaways.

I also told him that for years I had been having a recurrent dream in which I ran so well that the young policeman was no longer able to overtake me.

"Your story is more important than I thought," don Juan commented. "I thought it was going to be a story about your mama spanking you."

The way he emphasized his words made his statement very funny and very mocking. He added that at certain times it was the spirit, and not our reason, which decided on our stories. This was one of those times. The spirit had triggered this particular story in my mind, doubtlessly because the story was concerned with my indestructible self-importance. He said that the torch of anger and humiliation had burned in me for years, and my feelings of failure and dejection were still intact.

"A psychologist would have a field day with your story and its present context," he went on. "In your mind, I must be identified with the young policeman who shattered your notion of invincibility."

Now that he mentioned it, I had to admit that that had been my feeling, although I would not consciously have thought of it, much less voiced it.

We walked in silence. I was so touched by his analogy that I completely forgot the jaguar stalking us, until a wild growl reminded me of our situation.

Don Juan directed me to jump up and down on the long, low branches of the shrubs and break off a couple of them to make a sort of long broom. He did the same. As we ran, we used them to raise a cloud of dust, stirring and kicking the dry, sandy dirt.

"That ought to worry the jaguar," he said when we stopped again to catch our breath. "We have only a few hours of daylight left. At night the jaguar is unbeatable, so we had better start running straight toward those rocky hills."

He pointed to some hills in the distance, perhaps half a mile south.

"We've got to go east," I said. "Those hills are too far south. If we go that way, we'll never get to my car."

"We won't get to your car today, anyway," he said calmly. "And perhaps not tomorrow either. Who is to say we'll ever get back to it?"

I felt a pang of fear, and then a strange peace took possession of me. I told don Juan that if death was going to take me in that desert chaparral I hoped it would be painless.

"Don't worry," he said. "Death is painful only when it happens in one's bed, in sickness. In a fight for your life, you feel no pain. If you feel anything, it's exultation."

He said that one of the most dramatic differences

between civilized men and sorcerers was the way in which death came to them. Only with sorcerer-warriors was death kind and sweet. They could be mortally wounded and yet would feel no pain. And what was even more extraordinary was that death held itself in abeyance for as long as the sorcerers needed it to do so.

"The greatest difference between an average man and a sorcerer is that a sorcerer commands his death with his speed," don Juan went on. "If it comes to that, the jaguar will not eat me. He'll eat you, because you don't have the speed to hold back your death."

He then elaborated on the intricacies of the sorcerers' idea of speed and death. He said that in the world of everyday life our word or our decisions could be reversed very easily. The only irrevocable thing in our world was death. In the sorcerers' world, on the other hand, normal death could be countermanded, but not the sorcerers' word. In the sorcerers' world decisions could not be changed or revised. Once they had been made, they stood forever.

I told him his statements, impressive as they were, could not convince me that death could be revoked. And he explained once more what he had explained before. He said that for a seer human beings were either oblong or spherical luminous masses of countless, static, yet vibrant fields of energy, and that only sorcerers were capable of injecting movement into those spheres of static luminosity. In a millisecond they could move their assemblage points to any place in their luminous mass. That movement and the speed with which it was performed entailed an instantaneous shift into the perception of another totally different universe. Or they could move their assemblage points, without stopping, across their entire fields of luminous energy. The force created by such movement was so intense that it instantly consumed their whole luminous mass.

He said that if a rockslide were to come crashing down on us at that precise moment, he would be able to cancel the normal effect of an accidental death. By using the speed with which his assemblage point would move, he could make himself change universes or make himself burn from within in a fraction of a second. I, on the other hand, would die a normal death, crushed by the rocks, because my assemblage point lacked the speed to pull me out.

I said it seemed to me that the sorcerers had just found an alternative way of dying, which was not the same as a cancellation of death. And he replied that all he had said was that sorcerers commanded their deaths. They died only when they had to.

Although I did not doubt what he was saying, I kept asking questions, almost as a game. But while he was talking, thoughts and unanchored memories about other perceivable universes were forming in my mind, as if on a screen.

I told don Juan I was thinking strange thoughts. He laughed and recommended I stick to the jaguar, because he was so real that he could only be a true manifestation of the spirit.

The idea of how real the animal was made me shudder. "Wouldn't it be better if we changed direction instead of heading straight for the hills?" I asked.

I thought that we could create a certain confusion in the jaguar with an unexpected change.

"It's too late to change direction," don Juan said. "The jaguar already knows that there is no place for us to go but the hills."

"That can't be true, don Juan!" I exclaimed.

"Why not?" he asked.

I told him that although I could attest to the animal's ability to be one jump ahead of us, I could not quite accept that the jaguar had the foresight to figure out where we wanted to go.

"Your error is to think of the jaguar's power in terms of his capacity to figure things out," he said. "He can't think. He only knows."

Don Juan said that our dust-raising maneuver was to confuse the jaguar by giving him sensory input on something for which we had no use. We could not develop a real feeling for raising dust though our lives depended on it.

"I truly don't understand what you are saying," I whined.

Tension was taking its toll on me. I was having a hard time concentrating.

Don Juan explained that human feelings were like hot or cold currents of air and could easily be detected by a beast. We were the senders, the jaguar was the receiver. Whatever feelings we had would find their way to the jaguar. Or rather, the jaguar could read any feelings that had a history of use for us. In the case of the dust-raising maneuver, the feeling we had about it was so out of the ordinary that it could only create a vacuum in the receiver.

"Another maneuver silent knowledge might dictate would be to kick up dirt," don Juan said.

He looked at me for an instant as if he were waiting for my reactions.

"We are going to walk very calmly now," he said. "And you are going to kick up dirt as if you were a ten-foot giant."

I must have had a stupid expression on my face. Don Juan's body shook with laughter.

"Raise a cloud of dust with your feet," he ordered me. "Feel huge and heavy."

I tried it and immediately had a sense of massiveness. In a joking tone, I commented that his power of suggestion was incredible. I actually felt gigantic and ferocious. He assured me that my feeling of size was not in any way the product of his suggestion, but the product of a shift of my assemblage point.

He said that men of antiquity became legendary because they knew by silent knowledge about the power to be obtained by moving the assemblage point. On a reduced scale sorcerers had recaptured that old power. With a movement of their assemblage points they could manipulate their feelings and change things. I was changing things by feeling big and ferocious. Feelings processed in that fashion were called *intent*.

"Your assemblage point has already moved quite a bit," he went on. "Now you are in the position of either losing your gain or making your assemblage point move beyond the place where it is now."

He said that possibly every human being under normal living conditions had had at one time or another the opportunity to break away from the bindings of convention. He stressed that he did not mean social convention, but the conventions binding our perception. A moment of elation would suffice to move our assemblage points and break our conventions. So, too, a moment of fright, ill health, anger, or grief. But ordinarily, whenever we had the chance to move our assemblage points we became frightened. Our religious, academic, social backgrounds would come into play. They would assure our safe return to the flock; the return of our assemblage points to the prescribed position of normal living.

He told me that all the mystics and spiritual teachers I knew of had done just that: their assemblage points moved, either through discipline or accident, to a certain point; and then they returned to normalcy carrying a memory that lasted them a lifetime.

"You can be a very pious, good boy," he went on, "and forget about the initial movement of your assemblage point. Or you can push beyond your reasonable limits. You are still within those limits.''

I knew what he was talking about, yet there was a strange hesitation in me making me vacillate.

Don Juan pushed his argument further. He said that the average man, incapable of finding the energy to perceive beyond his daily limits, called the realm of extraordinary perception sorcery, witchcraft, or the work of the devil, and shied away from it without examining it further.

''But you can't do that anymore,'' don Juan went on. ''You are not religious and you are much too curious to discard anything so easily. The only thing that could stop you now is cowardice.

''Turn everything into what it really is: the abstract, the spirit, the nagual. There is no witchcraft, no evil, no devil. There is only perception.''

I understood him. But I could not tell exactly what he wanted me to do.

I looked at don Juan, trying to find the most appropriate words. I seemed to have entered into an extremely functional frame of mind and did not want to waste a single word.

''Be gigantic!'' he ordered me, smiling. ''Do away with reason.''

Then I knew exactly what he meant. In fact, I knew that I could increase the intensity of my feelings of size and ferociousness until I actually could be a giant, hovering over the shrubs, seeing all around us.

I tried to voice my thoughts but quickly gave up. I became aware that don Juan knew all I was thinking, and obviously much, much more.

And then something extraordinary happened to me. My reasoning faculties ceased to function. Literally, I felt as though a dark blanket had covered me and obscured my thoughts. And I let go of my reason with the abandon of one who doesn't have a worry in the world. I was convinced that if I wanted to dispel the obscuring blanket, all I had to do was feel myself breaking through it.

In that state, I felt I was being propelled, set in motion. Something was making me move physically from one place to another. I did not experience any fatigue. The speed and ease with which I could move elated me.

I did not feel I was walking; I was not flying either. Rather I was being transported with extreme facility. My movements became jerky and ungraceful only when I tried to think about them. When I enjoyed them without thought, I entered into a unique state of physical elation for which I had no precedent. If I had had instances of that kind of physical happiness in my life, they must have been so short-lived that they had left no memory. Yet when I experienced that ecstasy I felt a vague recognition, as if I had once known it but had forgotten.

The exhilaration of moving through the chaparral was so intense that everything else ceased. The only things that existed for me were those periods of exhilaration and then the moments when I would stop moving and find myself facing the chaparral.

But even more inexplicable was the total bodily sensation of looming over the bushes which I had had since the instant I started to be moved.

At one moment, I clearly saw the figure of the jaguar up ahead of me. He was running away as fast as he could. I felt that he was trying to avoid the spines of the cactuses. He was being extremely careful about where he stepped.

I had the overwhelming urge to run after the jaguar and scare him into losing his caution. I knew that he would get pricked by the spines. A thought then erupted in my silent mind—I thought that the jaguar would be a more dangerous animal if he was hurt by the spines. That thought produced the same effect as someone waking me from a dream.

When I became aware that my thinking processes were functioning again, I found that I was at the base of a low range of rocky hills. I looked around. Don Juan was a few feet away. He seemed exhausted. He was pale and breathing very hard.

"What happened, don Juan?" I asked, after clearing my raspy throat.

"You tell me what happened," he gasped between breaths.

I told him what I had felt. Then I realized that I could barely see the top of the mountain directly in my line of vision. There was very little daylight left, which meant I had been running, or walking, for more than two hours.

I asked don Juan to explain the time discrepancy. He said that my assemblage point had moved beyond the place of no pity into the place of silent knowledge, but that I still lacked the energy to manipulate it myself. To manipulate it myself meant I would have to have enough energy to move between reason and silent knowledge at will. He added that if a sorcerer had enough energy—or even if he did not have sufficient energy but needed to shift because it was a matter of life and death—he could fluctuate between reason and silent knowledge.

His conclusions about me were that because of the seriousness of our situation, I had let the spirit move my assemblage point. The result had been my entering into silent knowledge. Naturally, the scope of my perception had increased, which gave me the feeling of height, of looming over the bushes.

At that time, because of my academic training, I was passionately interested in validation by consensus. I asked him my standard question of those days.

"If someone from UCLA's Anthropology Department had been watching me, would he have seen me as a giant thrashing through the chaparral?''

"I really don't know," don Juan said. "The way to find out would be to move your assemblage point when you are in the Department of Anthropology.''

"I have tried," I said. "But nothing ever happens. I must need to have you around for anything to take place.''

"It was not a matter of life and death for you then," he said. "If it had been, you would have moved your assemblage point all by yourself.''

"But would people see what I see when my assemblage point moves?" I insisted.

"No, because their assemblage points won't be in the same place as yours," he replied.

"Then, don Juan, did I dream the jaguar?" I asked. "Did all of it happen only in my mind?''

"Not quite," he said. "That big cat is real. You have moved miles and you are not even tired. If you are in doubt, look at your shoes. They are full of cactus spines. So you did move, looming over the shrubs. And at the same time you didn't. It depends on whether one's assemblage point is on the place of reason or on the place of silent knowledge.''

I understood everything he was saying while he said it, but could not repeat any part of it at will. Nor could I determine what it was I knew, or why he was making so much sense to me.

The growl of the jaguar brought me back to the reality of the immediate danger. I caught sight of the jaguar's dark mass as he swiftly moved uphill about thirty yards to our right.

"What are we going to do, don Juan?" I asked, knowing that he had also seen the animal moving ahead of us.

"Keep climbing to the very top and seek shelter there," he said calmly.

Then he added, as if he had not a single worry in the world, that I had wasted valuable time indulging in my pleasure at looming over the bushes. Instead of heading for the safety of the hills he had pointed out, I had taken off toward the easterly higher mountains.

"We must reach that scarp before the jaguar or we don't have a chance," he said, pointing to the nearly vertical face at the very top of the mountain.

I turned right and saw the jaguar leaping from rock to rock. He was definitely working his way over to cut us off.

"Let's go, don Juan!" I yelled out of nervousness.

Don Juan smiled. He seemed to be enjoying my fear and impatience. We moved as fast as we could and climbed steadily. I tried not to pay attention to the dark form of the jaguar as it appeared from time to time a bit ahead of us and always to our right.

The three of us reached the base of the escarpment at the same time. The jaguar was about twenty yards to our right. He jumped and tried to climb the face of the cliff, but failed. The rock wall was too steep.

Don Juan yelled that I should not waste time watching the jaguar, because he would charge as soon as he gave up trying to climb. No sooner had don Juan spoken than the animal charged.

There was no time for further urging. I scrambled up the rock wall followed by don Juan. The shrill scream of the frustrated beast sounded right by the heel of my right foot. The propelling force of fear sent me up the slick scarp as if I were a fly.

I reached the top before don Juan, who had stopped to laugh.

Safe at the top of the cliff, I had more time to think about what had happened. Don Juan did not want to discuss anything. He argued that at this stage in my development, any movement of my assemblage point would still be a mystery. My challenge at the beginning of my apprenticeship was, he said, maintaining my gains, rather than reasoning them out—and that at some point everything would make sense to me.

I told him everything made sense to me at that moment. But he was adamant that I had to be able to explain knowledge to myself before I could claim that it made sense to me. He insisted that for a movement of my assemblage point to make sense, I would need to have energy to fluctuate from the place of reason to the place of silent knowledge.

He stayed quiet for a while, sweeping my entire body with his stare. Then he seemed to make up his mind and smiled and began to speak again.

"Today you reached the place of silent knowledge," he said with finality.

He explained that that afternoon, my assemblage point had moved by itself, without his intervention. I had *intended* the movement by manipulating my feeling of being gigantic, and in so doing my assemblage point had reached the position of silent knowledge.

I was very curious to hear how don Juan interpreted my experience. He said that one way to talk about the perception attained in the place of silent knowledge was to call it "here and here." He explained that when I had told him I had felt myself looming over the desert chaparral, I should have added that I was *seeing* the desert floor and the top of the shrubs at the same time. Or that I had been at the place where I stood and at the same time at the place where the jaguar was. Thus I had been able to notice how carefully he stepped to avoid the cactus spines. In other words, instead of perceiving the normal here and there, I had perceived "here and here."

His comments frightened me. He was right. I had not mentioned that to him, nor had I admitted even to myself that I had been in two places at once. I would not have dared to think in those terms had it not been for his comments.

He repeated that I needed more time and more energy to make sense of everything. I was too new; I still required a great deal of supervision. For instance, while I was looming over the shrubs, he had to make his assemblage point fluctuate rapidly between the places of reason and silent knowledge to take care of me. And that had exhausted him.

"Tell me one thing," I said, testing his reasonableness. "That jaguar was stranger than you want to admit, wasn't it? Jaguars are not part of the fauna of this area. Pumas, yes, but not jaguars. How do you explain that?"

Before answering, he puckered his face. He was suddenly very serious.

"I think that this particular jaguar confirms your anthropological theories," he said in a solemn tone. "Obviously, the jaguar was following this famous trade route connecting Chihuahua with Central America."

Don Juan laughed so hard that the sound of his laughter echoed in the mountains. That echo disturbed me as much as the jaguar had. Yet it was not the echo itself which disturbed me, but the fact that I had never heard an echo at night. Echoes were, in my mind, associated only with the daytime.

It had taken me several hours to recall all the details of my experience with the jaguar. During that time, don Juan had not talked to me. He had simply propped himself against a rock and gone to sleep in a sitting position. After a while I no longer noticed that he was there, and finally I fell asleep.

I was awakened by a pain in my jaw. I had been sleeping with the side of my face pressed against a rock. The moment I opened my eyes, I tried to slide down off the boulder on which I had been lying, but lost my balance and fell noisily on my seat. Don Juan appeared from behind some bushes just in time to laugh.

It was getting late and I wondered aloud if we had enough time to get to the valley before nightfall. Don Juan shrugged his shoulders and did not seem concerned. He sat down beside me.

I asked him if he wanted to hear the details of my recollection. He indicated that it was fine with him, yet he did not ask me any questions. I thought he was leaving it up to me to start, so I told him there were three points I remembered which were of great importance to me. One was that he had talked about silent knowledge; another was that I had moved my assemblage point using *intent;* and the final point was that I had entered into heightened awareness without requiring a blow between my shoulder blades.

"*Intending* the movement of your assemblage point was your greatest accomplishment," don Juan said. "But accomplishment is something personal. It's necessary, but it's not the important part. It is not the residue sorcerers look forward to."

I thought I knew what he wanted. I told him that I hadn't totally forgotten the event. What had remained with me in my normal state of awareness was that a mountain lion—since I could not accept the idea of a jaguar—had chased us up a mountain, and that don Juan had asked me if I had felt offended by the big cat's onslaught. I had assured him that it was absurd that I could feel offended, and he had told me I should feel the same way about the onslaughts of my fellow men. I should protect myself, or get out of their way, but without feeling morally wronged.

"That is not the residue I am talking about," he said, laughing. "The idea of the abstract, the spirit, is the only residue that is important. The idea of the personal self has no value whatsoever. You still put yourself and your own feelings first. Every time I've had the chance, I have made you aware of the need to abstract. You have always believed that I meant to think abstractly. No. To abstract means to make yourself available to the spirit by being aware of it."

He said that one of the most dramatic things about the human condition was the macabre connection between stupidity and self-reflection.

It was stupidity that forced us to discard anything that did not conform with our self-reflective expectations. For example, as average men, we were blind to the most crucial piece of knowledge available to a human being: the existence of the assemblage point and the fact that it could move.

"For a rational man it's unthinkable that there should be an invisible point where perception is assembled," he went on. "And yet more unthinkable, that such a point is not in the brain, as he might vaguely expect if he were given to entertaining the thought of its existence."

He added that for the rational man to hold steadfastly to his self-image insured his abysmal ignorance. He ignored, for instance, the fact that sorcery was not incantations and hocus-pocus, but the freedom to perceive not only the world taken for granted, but everything else that was humanly possible.

"Here is where the average man's stupidity is most dangerous," he continued. "He is afraid of sorcery. He trembles at the possibility of freedom. And freedom is at his fingertips. It's called the third point. And it can be reached as easily as the assemblage point can be made to move."

"But you yourself told me that moving the assemblage point is so difficult that it is a true accomplishment," I protested.

"It is," he assured me. "This is another of the sorcerers' contradictions: it's very difficult and yet it's the simplest thing in the world. I've told you already that a high fever could move the assemblage point. Hunger or fear or love or hate could do it; mysticism too, and also *unbending intent*, which is the preferred method of sorcerers."

I asked him to explain again what *unbending intent* was. He said that it was a sort of single-mindedness human beings exhibit; an extremely well-defined purpose not countermanded by any conflicting interests or desires; *unbending intent* was also the force engendered when the assemblage point was maintained fixed in a position which was not the usual one.

Don Juan then made a meaningful distinction—which had eluded me all these years—between a movement and a shift of the assemblage point. A movement, he said, was a profound change of position, so extreme that the assemblage point might even reach other bands of energy within our total luminous mass of energy fields. Each band of energy represented a completely different universe to be perceived. A shift, however, was a small movement within the band of energy fields we perceived as the world of everyday life.

He went on to say that sorcerers saw *unbending intent* as the catalyst to trigger their unchangeable decisions, or as the converse: their unchangeable decisions were the catalyst that propelled their assemblage points to new positions, positions which in turn generated *unbending intent*.

I must have looked dumbfounded. Don Juan laughed and said that trying to reason out the sorcerers' metaphorical descriptions was as useless as trying to reason out silent knowledge. He added that the problem with words was that any attempt to clarify the sorcerers' description only made them more confusing.

I urged him to try to clarify this in any way he could. I argued that anything he could say, for instance, about the third point could only clarify it, for although I knew everything about it, it was still very confusing.

"The world of daily life consists of two points of reference," he said. "We have for example, here and there, in and out, up and down, good and evil, and so on and so forth. So, properly speaking, our perception of our lives is two-dimensional. None of what we perceive ourselves doing has depth."

I protested that he was mixing levels. I told him that I could accept his definition of perception as the capacity of living beings to apprehend with their senses fields of energy selected by their assemblage points— a very farfetched definition by my academic standards, but one that, at the moment, seemed cogent. However, I could not imagine what the depth of what we did might be. I argued that it was possible he was talking about interpretations—elaborations of our basic perceptions.

"A sorcerer perceives his actions with depth," he said. "His actions are tri-dimensional for him. They have a third point of reference."

"How could a third point of reference exist?" I asked with a tinge of annoyance.

"Our points of reference are obtained primarily from our sense perception," he said. "Our senses perceive and differentiate what is immediate to us from what is not. Using that basic distinction we derive the rest.

"In order to reach the third point of reference one must perceive two places at once."

My recollecting had put me in a strange mood—it was as if I had lived the experience just a few minutes earlier. I was suddenly aware of something I had completely missed before. Under don Juan's supervision, I had twice before experienced that divided perception, but this was the first time I had accomplished it all by myself.

Thinking about my recollection, I also realized that my sensory experience was more complex than I had at first thought. During the time I had loomed over the bushes, I had been aware—without words or even thoughts—that being in two places, or being "here and here" as don Juan had called it, rendered my perception immediate and complete at both places. But I had also been aware that my double perception lacked the total clarity of normal perception.

Don Juan explained that normal perception had an axis. "Here and there" were the perimeters of that axis, and we were partial to the clarity of "here." He said that in normal perception, only "here" was perceived completely, instantaneously, and directly. Its twin referent, "there," lacked immediacy. It was inferred, deduced, expected, even assumed, but it was not apprehended directly with all the senses. When we perceived two places at once, total clarity was lost, but the immediate perception of "there" was gained.

"But then, don Juan, I was right in describing my perception as the important part of my experience," I said.

"No, you were not," he said. "What you experienced was vital to you, because it opened the road to silent knowledge, but the important thing was the jaguar. That jaguar was indeed a manifestation of the spirit.

"That big cat came unnoticed out of nowhere. And he could have finished us off as surely as I am talking to you. That jaguar was an expression of magic. Without him you would have had no elation, no lesson, no realizations."

"But was he a real jaguar?" I asked.

"You bet he was real!"

Don Juan observed that for an average man that big cat would have been a frightening oddity. An average man would have been hard put to explain in reasonable terms what that jaguar was doing in Chihuahua, so far from a tropical jungle. But a sorcerer, because he had a connecting link with *intent,* saw that jaguar as a vehicle to perceiving—not an oddity, but a source of awe.

There were a lot of questions I wanted to ask, and yet I knew the answers before I could articulate the questions. I followed the course of my own questions and answers for a while, until finally I realized it did not matter that I silently knew the answers; answers had to be verbalized to be of any value.

I voiced the first question that came to mind. I asked don Juan to explain what seemed to be a contradiction. He had asserted that only the spirit could move the assemblage point. But then he had said that my feelings, processed into *intent,* had moved my assemblage point.

"Only sorcerers can turn their feelings into *intent,*" he said. "*Intent* is the spirit, so it is the spirit which moves their assemblage points.

"The misleading part of all this," he went on, "is that I am saying only sorcerers know about the spirit, that *intent* is the exclusive domain of sorcerers. This is not true at all, but it is the situation in the realm of practicality. The real condition is that sorcerers are more aware of their connection with the spirit than the average man and strive to manipulate it. That's all. I've already told you, the connecting link with *intent* is the universal feature shared by everything there is."

Two or three times, don Juan seemed about to start to add something. He vacillated, apparently trying to choose his words. Finally he said that being in two

223

places at once was a milestone sorcerers used to mark the moment the assemblage point reached the place of silent knowledge. Split perception, if accomplished by one's own means, was called the free movement of the assemblage point.

He assured me that every nagual consistently did everything within his power to encourage the free movement of his apprentices' assemblage points. This all-out effort was cryptically called "reaching out for the third point."

"The most difficult aspect of the nagual's knowledge," don Juan went on, "and certainly the most crucial part of his task is that of reaching out for the third point—the nagual *intends* that free movement, and the spirit channels to the nagual the means to accomplish it. I had never *intended* anything of that sort until you came along. Therefore, I had never fully appreciated my benefactor's gigantic effort to *intend* it for me.

"Difficult as it is for a nagual to *intend* that free movement for his disciples," don Juan went on, "it's nothing compared with the difficulty his disciples have in understanding what the nagual is doing. Look at the way you yourself struggle! The same thing happened to me. Most of the time, I ended up believing the trickery of the spirit was simply the trickery of the nagual Julian.

"Later on, I realized I owed him my life and well-being," don Juan continued. "Now I know I owe him infinitely more. Since I can't begin to describe what I really owe him, I prefer to say he cajoled me into having a third point of reference.

"The third point of reference is freedom of perception; it is *intent;* it is the spirit; the somersault of thought into the miraculous; the act of reaching beyond our boundaries and touching the inconceivable."

THE TWO ONE-WAY BRIDGES

Don Juan and I were sitting at the table in his kitchen. It was early morning. We had just returned from the mountains, where we had spent the night after I had recalled my experience with the jaguar. Recollecting my split perception had put me in a state of euphoria, which don Juan had employed, as usual, to plunge me into more sensory experiences that I was now unable to recall. My euphoria, however, had not waned.

"To discover the possibility of being in two places at once is very exciting to the mind," he said. "Since our minds are our rationality, and our rationality is our self-reflection, anything beyond our self-reflection either appalls us or attracts us, depending on what kind of persons we are."

He looked at me fixedly and then smiled as if he had just found out something new.

"Or it appalls and attracts us in the same measure," he said, "which seems to be the case with both of us."

I told him that with me it was not a matter of being appalled or attracted by my experience, but a matter of being frightened by the immensity of the possibility of split perception.

"I can't say that I don't believe I was in two places at once," I said. "I can't deny my experience, and yet I think I am so frightened by it that my mind refuses to accept it as a fact."

"You and I are the type of people who become obsessed by things like that, and then forget all about them," he remarked and laughed. "You and I are very much alike."

It was my turn to laugh. I knew he was making fun

of me. Yet he projected such sincerity that I wanted to believe he was being truthful.

I told him that among his apprentices, I was the only one who had learned not to take his statements of equality with us too seriously. I said that I had seen him in action, hearing him tell each of his apprentices, in the most sincere tone, "You and I are such fools. We are so alike!" And I had been horrified, time and time again, to realize that they believed him.

"You are not like any one of us, don Juan," I said. "You are a mirror that doesn't reflect our images. You are already beyond our reach."

"What you're witnessing is the result of a lifelong struggle," he said. "What you see is a sorcerer who has finally learned to follow the designs of the spirit, but that's all.

"I have described to you, in many ways, the different stages a warrior passes through along the path of knowledge," he went on. "In terms of his connection with *intent,* a warrior goes through four stages. The first is when he has a rusty, untrustworthy link with *intent.* The second is when he succeeds in cleaning it. The third is when he learns to manipulate it. And the fourth is when he learns to accept the designs of the abstract."

Don Juan maintained that his attainment did not make him intrinsically different. It only made him more resourceful; thus he was not being facetious when he said to me or to his other apprentices that he was just like us.

"I understand exactly what you are going through," he continued. "When I laugh at you, I really laugh at the memory of myself in your shoes. I, too, held on to the world of everyday life. I held on to it by my fingernails. Everything told me to let go, but I couldn't. Just like you, I trusted my mind implicitly, and I had no reason to do so. I was no longer an average man.

"My problem then is your problem today. The momentum of the daily world carried me, and I kept acting like an average man. I held on desperately to my flimsy rational structures. Don't you do the same."

"I don't hold onto any structures; they hold onto me," I said, and that made him laugh.

I told him I understood him to perfection, but that no matter how hard I tried I was unable to carry on as a sorcerer should.

He said my disadvantage in the sorcerers' world was my lack of familiarity with it. In that world I had to relate myself to everything in a new way, which was infinitely more difficult, because it had very little to do with my everyday life continuity.

He described the specific problem of sorcerers as twofold. One is the impossibility of restoring a shattered continuity; the other is the impossibility of using the continuity dictated by the new position of their assemblage points. That new continuity is always too tenuous, too unstable, and does not offer sorcerers the assuredness they need to function as if they were in the world of everyday life.

"How do sorcerers resolve this problem?" I asked.

"None of us resolves anything," he replied. "The spirit either resolves it for us or it doesn't. If it does, a sorcerer finds himself acting in the sorcerers' world, but without knowing how. This is the reason why I have insisted from the day I found you that impeccability is all that counts. A sorcerer lives an impeccable life, and that seems to beckon the solution. Why? No one knows."

Don Juan remained quiet for a moment. And then, as if I had voiced it, he commented on a thought I was having. I was thinking that impeccability always made me think of religious morality.

"Impeccability, as I have told you so many times, is not morality," he said. "It only resembles morality.

Impeccability is simply the best use of our energy level. Naturally, it calls for frugality, thoughtfulness, simplicity, innocence; and above all, it calls for lack of self-reflection. All this makes it sound like a manual for monastic life, but it isn't.

"Sorcerers say that in order to command the spirit, and by that they mean to command the movement of the assemblage point, one needs energy. The only thing that stores energy for us is our impeccability."

Don Juan remarked that we do not have to be students of sorcery to move our assemblage point. Sometimes, due to natural although dramatic circumstances, such as war, deprivation, stress, fatigue, sorrow, helplessness, men's assemblage points undergo profound movements. If the men who found themselves in such circumstances were able to adopt a sorcerer's ideology, don Juan said, they would be able to maximize that natural movement with no trouble. And they would seek and find extraordinary things instead of doing what men do in such circumstances: craving the return to normalcy.

"When a movement of the assemblage point is maximized," he went on, "both the average man or the apprentice in sorcery becomes a sorcerer, because by maximizing that movement, continuity is shattered beyond repair."

"How do you maximize that movement?" I asked.

"By curtailing self-reflection," he replied. "Moving the assemblage point or breaking one's continuity is not the real difficulty. The real difficulty is having energy. If one has energy, once the assemblage point moves, inconceivable things are there for the asking."

Don Juan explained that man's predicament is that he intuits his hidden resources, but he does not dare use them. This is why sorcerers say that man's plight is the counterpoint between his stupidity and his ignorance. He said that man needs now, more so than ever, to be taught new ideas that have to do exclusively with his inner world—sorcerers' ideas, not social ideas, ideas pertaining to man facing the unknown, facing his personal death. Now, more than anything else, he needs to be taught the secrets of the assemblage point.

With no preliminaries, and without stopping to think, don Juan then began to tell me a sorcery story. He said that for an entire year he had been the only young person in the nagual Julian's house. He was so completely self-centered he had not even noticed when at the beginning of the second year his benefactor brought three young men and four young women to live in the house. As far as don Juan was concerned, those seven persons who arrived one at a time over two or three months were simply servants and of no importance. One of the young men was even made his assistant.

Don Juan was convinced the nagual Julian had lured and cajoled them into coming to work for him without wages. And he would have felt sorry for them had it not been for their blind trust in the nagual Julian and their sickening attachment to everyone and everything in the household.

His feeling was that they were born slaves and that he had nothing to say to them. Yet he was obliged to make friends with them and give them advice, not because he wanted to, but because the nagual demanded it as part of his work. As they sought his counseling, he was horrified by the poignancy and drama of their life stories.

He secretly congratulated himself for being better off than they. He sincerely felt he was smarter than all of them put together. He boasted to them that he could see through the nagual's maneuvers, although he could not claim to understand them. And he laughed at their ridiculous attempts to be helpful. He considered them servile and told them to their faces that they were being mercilessly exploited by a professional tyrant.

But what enraged him was that the four young women had crushes on the nagual Julian and would do anything to please him. Don Juan sought solace in his work and plunged into it to forget his anger, or for hours on end he would read the books that the nagual Julian had in the house. Reading became his passion. When he was reading, everyone knew not to bother him, except the nagual Julian, who took pleasure in never leaving him in peace. He was always after don Juan to be friends with the young men and women. He told him repeatedly that all of them, don Juan included, were his sorcery apprentices. Don Juan was convinced the nagual Julian knew nothing about sorcery, but he humored him, listening to him without ever believing.

The nagual Julian was unfazed by don Juan's lack of trust. He simply proceeded as if don Juan believed him, and gathered all the apprentices together to give them instruction. Periodically he took all of them on all-night excursions into the local mountains. On most of these excursions the nagual would leave them by themselves, stranded in those rugged mountains, with don Juan in charge.

The rationale given for the trips was that in solitude, in the wilderness, they would discover the spirit. But they never did. At least, not in any way don Juan could understand. However, the nagual Julian insisted so strongly on the importance of knowing the spirit that don Juan became obsessed with knowing what the spirit was.

During one of those nighttime excursions, the nagual Julian urged don Juan to go after the spirit, even if he didn't understand it.

"Of course, he meant the only thing a nagual could

mean: the movement of the assemblage point,'' don Juan said. ''But he worded it in a way he believed would make sense to me: go after the spirit.

''I thought he was talking nonsense. At that time I had already formed my own opinions and beliefs and was convinced that the spirit was what is known as character, volition, guts, strength. And I believed I didn't have to go after them. I had them all.

''The nagual Julian insisted that the spirit was indefinable, that one could not even feel it, much less talk about it. One could only beckon it, he said, by acknowledging its existence. My retort was very much the same as yours: one cannot beckon something that does not exist.''

Don Juan told me he had argued so much with the nagual that the nagual finally promised him, in front of his entire household, that in one single stroke he was going to show him not only what the spirit was, but how to define it. He also promised to throw an enormous party, even inviting the neighbors, to celebrate don Juan's lesson.

Don Juan remarked that in those days, before the Mexican Revolution, the nagual Julian and the seven women of his group passed themselves off as the wealthy owners of a large hacienda. Nobody ever doubted their image, especially the nagual Julian's, a rich and handsome landholder who had set aside his earnest desire to pursue an ecclesiastical career in order to care for his seven unmarried sisters.

One day, during the rainy season, the nagual Julian announced that as soon as the rains stopped, he would hold the enormous party he had promised don Juan. And one Sunday afternoon he took his entire household to the banks of the river, which was in flood because of the heavy rains. The nagual Julian rode his horse while don Juan trotted respectfully behind, as was their custom in case they met any of their neighbors; as far as the neighbors knew, don Juan was the landlord's personal servant.

The nagual chose for their picnic a site on high ground by the edge of the river. The women had prepared food and drink. The nagual had even brought a group of musicians from the town. It was a big party which included the peons of the hacienda, neighbors, and even passing strangers that had meandered over to join the fun.

Everybody ate and drank to his heart's content. The nagual danced with all the women, sang, and recited poetry. He told jokes and, with the help of some of the women, staged skits to the delight of all.

At a given moment, the nagual Julian asked if any of those present, especially the apprentices, wanted to share don Juan's lesson. They all declined. All of them were keenly aware of the nagual's hard tactics. Then he asked don Juan if he was sure he wanted to find out what the spirit was.

Don Juan could not say no. He simply could not back out. He announced that he was as ready as he could ever be. The nagual guided him to the edge of the raging river and made him kneel. The nagual began a long incantation in which he invoked the power of the wind and the mountains and asked the power of the river to advise don Juan.

His incantation, meaningful as it might have been, was worded so irreverently that everyone had to laugh. When he finished, he asked don Juan to stand up with his eyes closed. Then he took the apprentice in his arms, as he would a child, and threw him into the rushing waters, shouting, "Don't hate the river, for heaven's sake!"

Relating this incident sent don Juan into fits of laughter. Perhaps under other circumstances I, too, might have found it hilarious. This time, however, the story upset me tremendously.

"You should have seen those people's faces," don Juan continued. "I caught a glimpse of their dismay as I flew through the air on my way to the river. No one had anticipated that that devilish nagual would do a thing like that."

Don Juan said he had thought it was the end of his life. He was not a good swimmer, and as he sank to the bottom of the river he cursed himself for allowing this to happen to him. He was so angry he did not have time to panic. All he could think about was his resolve that he was not going to die in that frigging river, at the hands of that frigging man.

His feet touched bottom and he propelled himself up. It was not a deep river, but the flood waters had widened it a great deal. The current was swift, and it pulled him along as he dog-paddled, trying not to let the rushing waters tumble him around.

The current dragged him a long distance. And while he was being dragged and trying his best not to succumb, he entered into a strange frame of mind. He knew his flaw. He was a very angry man and his pent-up anger made him hate and fight with everyone around. But he could not hate or fight the river, or be impatient with it, or fret, which were the ways he normally behaved with everything and everybody in his life. All he could do with the river was follow its flow.

Don Juan contended that that simple realization and the acquiescence it engendered tipped the scales, so to speak, and he experienced a free movement of his assemblage point. Suddenly, without being in any way aware of what was happening, instead of being pulled by the rushing water, don Juan felt himself running along the riverbank. He was running so fast that he had no time to think. A tremendous force was pulling him, making him race over boulders and fallen trees, as if they were not there.

After he had run in that desperate fashion for quite a while, don Juan braved a quick look at the reddish, rushing water. And he saw himself being roughly tumbled by the current. Nothing in his experience had prepared him for such a moment. He knew then, without involving his thought processes, that he was in two places at once. And in one of them, in the rushing river, he was helpless.

All his energy went into trying to save himself.

Without thinking about it, he began angling away from the riverbank. It took all his strength and determination to edge an inch at a time. He felt as if he were dragging a tree. He moved so slowly that it took him an eternity to gain a few yards.

The strain was too much for him. Suddenly he was no longer running; he was falling down a deep well. When he hit the water, the coldness of it made him scream. And then he was back in the river, being dragged by the current. His fright upon finding himself back in the rushing water was so intense that all he could do was to wish with all his might to be safe and sound on the riverbank. And immediately he was there again, running at breakneck speed parallel to, but a distance from, the river.

As he ran, he looked at the rushing water and saw himself struggling to stay afloat. He wanted to yell a command; he wanted to order himself to swim at an angle, but he had no voice. His anguish for the part of him that was in the water was overwhelming. It served as a bridge between the two Juan Matuses. He was instantly back in the water, swimming at an angle toward the bank.

The incredible sensation of alternating between two places was enough to eradicate his fear. He no longer cared about his fate. He alternated freely between swimming in the river and racing on the bank. But whichever he was doing, he consistently moved toward his left, racing away from the river or paddling to the left shore.

He came out on the left side of the river about five miles downstream. He had to wait there, sheltering in the shrubs, for over a week. He was waiting for the waters to subside so he could wade across, but he was also waiting until his fright wore off and he was whole again.

Don Juan said that what had happened was that the strong, sustained emotion of fighting for his life had caused his assemblage point to move squarely to the place of silent knowledge. Because he had never paid any attention to what the nagual Julian told him about the assemblage point, he had no idea what was happening to him. He was frightened at the thought that he might never be normal again. But as he explored his split perception, he discovered its practical side and found he liked it. He was double for days. He could be thoroughly one or the other. Or he could be both at the same time. When he was both, things became fuzzy and neither being was effective, so he abandoned that alternative. But being one or the other opened up inconceivable possibilities for him.

While he recuperated in the bushes, he established that one of his beings was more flexible than the other and could cover distances in the blink of an eye and find food or the best place to hide. It was this being that once went to the nagual's house to see if they were worrying about him.

He heard the young people crying for him, and that was certainly a surprise. He would have gone on watching them indefinitely, since he adored the idea of finding out what they thought of him, but the nagual Julian caught him and put an end to it.

That was the only time he had been truly afraid of the nagual. Don Juan heard the nagual telling him to stop his nonsense. He appeared suddenly, a jet black, bell-shaped object of immense weight and strength. He grabbed don Juan. Don Juan did not know how the nagual was grabbing him, but it hurt in a most unsettling way. It was a sharp nervous pain he felt in his stomach and groin.

"I was instantly back on the riverbank," don Juan said, laughing. "I got up, waded the recently subsided river, and started to walk home."

He paused then asked me what I thought of his story. And I told him that it had appalled me.

"You could have drowned in that river," I said, almost shouting. "What a brutal thing to do to you. The nagual Julian must have been crazy!"

"Wait a minute," don Juan protested. "The nagual Julian was devilish, but not crazy. He did what he had to do in his role as nagual and teacher. It's true that I could have died. But that's a risk we all have to take. You yourself could have been easily eaten by the jaguar, or could have died from any of the things I have made you do. The nagual Julian was bold and commanding and tackled everything directly. No beating around the bush with him, no mincing words."

I insisted that valuable as the lesson might have been, it still appeared to me that the nagual Julian's methods were bizarre and excessive. I admitted to don Juan that everything I had heard about the nagual Julian had bothered me so much I had formed a most negative picture of him.

"I think you're afraid that one of these days I'm going to throw you into the river or make you wear women's clothes," he said and began to laugh. "That's why you don't approve of the nagual Julian."

I admitted that he was right, and he assured me that he had no intentions of imitating his benefactor's methods, because they did not work for him. He was, he said, as ruthless but not as practical as the nagual Julian.

"At that time," don Juan continued, "I didn't appreciate his art, and I certainly didn't like what he did to me, but now, whenever I think about it, I admire him all the more for his superb and direct way of placing me in the position of silent knowledge."

Don Juan said that because of the enormity of his experience, he had totally forgotten the monstrous man. He walked unescorted almost to the door of the nagual Julián's house, then changed his mind and went instead to the nagual Elías's place, seeking solace. And the nagual Elías explained to him the deep consistency of the nagual Julián's actions.

The nagual Elías could hardly contain his excitement when he heard don Juan's story. In a fervent tone he explained to don Juan that his benefactor was a supreme *stalker,* always after practicalities. His endless quest was for pragmatic views and solutions. His behavior that day at the river had been a masterpiece of *stalking*. He had manipulated and affected everyone. Even the river seemed to be at his command.

The nagual Elías maintained that while don Juan was being carried by the current, fighting for his life, the river helped him understand what the spirit was. And thanks to that understanding, don Juan had the opportunity to enter directly into silent knowledge.

Don Juan said that because he was a callow youth he listened to the nagual Elías without understanding a word, but was moved with sincere admiration for the nagual's intensity.

First, the nagual Elías explained to don Juan that sound and the meaning of words were of supreme importance to *stalkers*. Words were used by them as keys to open anything that was closed. *Stalkers*, therefore, had to state their aim before attempting to achieve it. But they could not reveal their true aim at the outset, so they had to word things carefully to conceal the main thrust.

The nagual Elías called this act waking up *intent*. He explained to don Juan that the nagual Julian woke up *intent* by affirming emphatically in front of his entire household that he was going to show don Juan, in one stroke, what the spirit was and how to define it. This was completely nonsensical because the nagual Julian knew there was no way to define the spirit. What he was really trying to do was, of course, to place don Juan in the position of silent knowledge.

After making the statement which concealed his true aim, the nagual Julian gathered as many people as he could, thus making them both his witting and unwitting accomplices. All of them knew about his stated goal, but not a single one knew what he really had in mind.

The nagual Elías's belief that his explanation would shake don Juan out of his impossible stand of total rebelliousness and indifference was completely wrong. Yet the nagual patiently continued to explain to him that while he had been fighting the current in the river he had reached the third point.

The old nagual explained that the position of silent knowledge was called the third point because in order to get to it one had to pass the second point, the place of no pity.

He said that don Juan's assemblage point had acquired sufficient fluidity for him to be double, which had allowed him to be in both the place of reason and in the place of silent knowledge, either alternately or at the same time.

The nagual told don Juan that his accomplishment was magnificent. He even hugged don Juan as if he were a child. And he could not stop talking about how don Juan, in spite of not knowing anything—or maybe because of not knowing anything—had transferred his total energy from one place to the other. Which meant to the nagual that don Juan's assemblage point had a most propitious, natural fluidity.

He said to don Juan that every human being had a capacity for that fluidity. For most of us, however, it was stored away and we never used it, except on rare occasions which were brought about by sorcerers, such as the experience he had just had, or by dramatic natural circumstances, such as a life-or-death struggle.

Don Juan listened, mesmerized by the sound of the old nagual's voice. When he paid attention, he could follow anything the man said, which was something he had never been able to do with the nagual Julian.

The old nagual went on to explain that humanity was on the first point, reason, but that not every human being's assemblage point was squarely on the position of reason. Those who were on the spot itself were the true leaders of mankind. Most of the time they were unknown people whose genius was the exercising of their reason.

The nagual said there had been another time, when mankind had been on the third point, which, of course, had been the first point then. But after that, mankind moved to the place of reason.

When silent knowledge was the first point the same condition prevailed. Not every human being's assemblage point was squarely on that position either. This meant that the true leaders of mankind had always been the few human beings whose assemblage points happened to be either on the exact point of reason or of silent knowledge. The rest of humanity, the old nagual told don Juan, was merely the audience. In our day, they were the lovers of reason. In the past, they had been the lovers of silent knowledge. They were the ones who had admired and sung odes to the heroes of either position.

The nagual stated that mankind had spent the longer

part of its history in the position of silent knowledge, and that this explained our great longing for it.

Don Juan asked the old nagual what exactly the nagual Julian was doing to him. His question sounded more mature and intelligent than what he really meant. The nagual Elías answered it in terms totally unintelligible to don Juan at that time. He said that the nagual Julian was coaching don Juan, enticing his assemblage point to the position of reason, so he could be a thinker rather than merely part of an unsophisticated but emotionally charged audience that loved the orderly works of reason. At the same time, the nagual was coaching don Juan to be a true abstract sorcerer instead of merely part of a morbid and ignorant audience of lovers of the unknown.

The nagual Elías assured don Juan that only a human being who was a paragon of reason could move his assemblage point easily and be a paragon of silent knowledge. He said that only those who were squarely in either position could see the other position clearly, and that that had been the way the age of reason came to being. The position of reason was clearly seen from the position of silent knowledge.

The old nagual told don Juan that the one-way bridge from silent knowledge to reason was called "concern." That is, the concern that true men of silent knowledge had about the source of what they knew. And the other one-way bridge, from reason to silent knowledge, was called "pure understanding." That is, the recognition that told the man of reason that reason was only one island in an endless sea of islands.

The nagual added that a human being who had both one-way bridges working was a sorcerer in direct contact with the spirit, the vital force that made both positions possible. He pointed out to don Juan that everything the nagual Julian had done that day at the river had been a show, not for a human audience, but for the spirit, the force that was watching him. He pranced and frolicked with abandon and entertained everybody, especially the power he was addressing.

Don Juan said that the nagual Elías assured him that the spirit only listened when the speaker speaks in gestures. And gestures do not mean signs or body movements, but acts of true abandon, acts of largesse, of humor. As a gesture for the spirit, sorcerers bring out the best of themselves and silently offer it to the abstract.

INTENDING APPEARANCES

Don Juan wanted us to make one more trip to the mountains before I went home, but we never made it. Instead, he asked me to drive him to the city. He needed to see some people there.

On the way he talked about every subject but *intent*. It was a welcome respite.

In the afternoon, after he had taken care of his business, we sat on his favorite bench in the plaza. The place was deserted. I was very tired and sleepy. But then, quite unexpectedly, I perked up. My mind became crystal clear.

Don Juan immediately noticed the change and laughed at my gesture of surprise. He picked a thought right out of my mind; or perhaps it was I who picked that thought out of his.

"If you think about life in terms of hours instead of

years, our lives are immensely long," he said. "Even if you think in terms of days, life is still interminable."

That was exactly what I had been thinking.

He told me that sorcerers counted their lives in hours, and that in one hour it was possible for a sorcerer to live the equivalent in intensity of a normal life. This intensity is an advantage when it comes to storing information in the movement of the assemblage point.

I demanded that he explain this to me in more detail. A long time before, because it was so cumbersome to take notes on conversations, he had recommended that I keep all the information I obtained about the sorcerers' world neatly arranged, not on paper nor in my mind, but in the movement of my assemblage point.

"The assemblage point, with even the most minute shifting, creates totally isolated islands of perception," don Juan said. "Information, in the form of experiences in the complexity of awareness, can be stored there."

"But how can information be stored in something so vague?" I asked.

"The mind is equally vague, and still you trust it because you are familiar with it," he retorted. "You don't yet have the same familiarity with the movement of the assemblage point, but it is just about the same."

"What I mean is, how is information stored?" I insisted.

"The information is stored in the experience itself," he explained. "Later, when a sorcerer moves his assemblage point to the exact spot where it was, he relives the total experience. This sorcerers' recollection is the way to get back all the information stored in the movement of the assemblage point.

"Intensity is an automatic result of the movement of the assemblage point," he continued. "For instance, you are living these moments more intensely than you ordinarily would, so, properly speaking, you are storing intensity. Some day you'll relive this moment by making your assemblage point return to the precise spot where it is now. That is the way sorcerers store information."

I told don Juan that the intense recollections I had had in the past few days had just happened to me, without any special mental process I was aware of.

"How can one deliberately manage to recollect?" I asked.

"Intensity, being an aspect of *intent*, is connected naturally to the shine of the sorcerers' eyes," he explained. "In order to recall those isolated islands of perception sorcerers need only *intend* the particular shine of their eyes associated with whichever spot they want to return to. But I have already explained that."

I must have looked perplexed. Don Juan regarded me with a serious expression. I opened my mouth two or three times to ask him questions, but could not formulate my thoughts.

"Because his intensity rate is greater than normal," don Juan said, "in a few hours a sorcerer can live the equivalent of a normal lifetime. His assemblage point, by shifting to an unfamiliar position, takes in more energy than usual. That extra flow of energy is called intensity."

I understood what he was saying with perfect clarity, and my rationality staggered under the impact of the tremendous implication.

Don Juan fixed me with his stare and then warned me to beware of a reaction which typically afflicted sorcerers—a frustrating desire to explain the sorcery experience in cogent, well-reasoned terms.

"The sorcerers' experience is so outlandish," don Juan went on, "that sorcerers consider it an intellectual exercise, and use it to *stalk* themselves with. Their trump card as *stalkers*, though, is that they remain keenly aware that we are perceivers and that perception has more possibilities than the mind can conceive."

As my only comment I voiced my apprehension about the outlandish possibilities of human awareness.

"In order to protect themselves from that immensity," don Juan said, "sorcerers learn to maintain a perfect blend of ruthlessness, cunning, patience, and sweetness. These four bases are inextricably bound together. Sorcerers cultivate them by *intending* them. These bases are, naturally, positions of the assemblage point."

He went on to say that every act performed by any sorcerer was by definition governed by these four principles. So, properly speaking, every sorcerer's every action is deliberate in thought and realization, and has the specific blend of the four foundations of *stalking*.

"Sorcerers use the four moods of *stalking* as guides," he continued. "These are four different frames of mind, four different brands of intensity that sorcerers can use to induce their assemblage points to move to specific positions."

He seemed suddenly annoyed. I asked if it was my insistence on speculating that was bothering him.

"I am just considering how our rationality puts us between a rock and a hard place," he said. "Our tendency is to ponder, to question, to find out. And there is no way to do that from within the discipline of sorcery. Sorcery is the act of reaching the place of silent knowledge, and silent knowledge can't be reasoned out. It can only be experienced."

He smiled, his eyes shining like two spots of light. He said that sorcerers, in an effort to protect themselves from the overwhelming effect of silent knowledge, developed the art of *stalking*. *Stalking* moves the assemblage point minutely but steadily, thus giving sorcerers time and therefore the possibility of buttressing themselves.

"Within the art of *stalking*," don Juan continued, "there is a technique which sorcerers use a great deal: controlled folly. Sorcerers claim that controlled folly is the only way they have of dealing with themselves —in their state of expanded awareness and perception —and with everybody and everything in the world of daily affairs."

Don Juan had explained controlled folly as the art of controlled deception or the art of pretending to be thoroughly immersed in the action at hand—pretending so well no one could tell it from the real thing. Controlled folly is not an outright deception, he had told me, but a sophisticated, artistic way of being separated from everything while remaining an integral part of everything.

"Controlled folly is an art," don Juan continued. "A very bothersome art, and a difficult one to learn. Many sorcerers don't have the stomach for it, not because there is anything inherently wrong with the art, but because it takes a lot of energy to exercise it."

Don Juan admitted that he practiced it conscientiously, although he was not particularly fond of doing so, perhaps because his benefactor had been so adept at it. Or, perhaps it was because his personality— which he said was basically devious and petty— simply did not have the agility needed to practice controlled folly.

I looked at him with surprise. He stopped talking and fixed me with his mischievous eyes.

"By the time we come to sorcery, our personality is already formed," he said, and shrugged his shoulders to signify resignation, "and all we can do is practice controlled folly and laugh at ourselves."

I had a surge of empathy and assured him that to me he was not in any way petty or devious.

"But that's my basic personality," he insisted.

And I insisted that it was not.

"*Stalkers* who practice controlled folly believe that, in matters of personality, the entire human race falls into three categories," he said, and smiled the way he always did when he was setting me up.

"That's absurd," I protested. "Human behavior is too complex to be categorized so simply."

"*Stalkers* say that we are not so complex as we think we are," he said, "and that we all belong to one of three categories."

I laughed out of nervousness. Ordinarily I would have taken such a statement as a joke, but this time, because my mind was extremely clear and my thoughts were poignant, I felt he was indeed serious.

"Are you serious?" I asked, as politely as I could.

"Completely serious," he replied, and began to laugh.

His laughter relaxed me a little. And he continued explaining the *stalkers'* system of classification. He said that people in the first class are the perfect secretaries, assistants, companions. They have a very fluid personality, but their fluidity is not nourishing. They are, however, serviceable, concerned, totally domestic, resourceful within limits, humorous, well-mannered, sweet, delicate. In other words, they are the nicest people one could find, but they have one huge flaw: they can't function alone. They are always in need of someone to direct them. With direction, no matter how strained or antagonistic that direction might be, they are stupendous. By themselves, they perish.

People in the second class are not nice at all. They are petty, vindictive, envious, jealous, self-centered. They talk exclusively about themselves and usually demand that people conform to their standards. They always take the initiative even though they are not comfortable with it. They are thoroughly ill at ease in every situation and never relax. They are insecure and are never pleased; the more insecure they become the nastier they are. Their fatal flaw is that they would kill to be leaders.

In the third category are people who are neither nice nor nasty. They serve no one, nor do they impose themselves on anyone. Rather they are indifferent. They have an exalted idea about themselves derived solely from daydreams and wishful thinking. If they are extraordinary at anything, it is at waiting for things to happen. They are waiting to be discovered and conquered and have a marvelous facility for creating the illusion that they have great things in abeyance, which they always promise to deliver but never do because, in fact, they do not have such resources.

Don Juan said that he himself definitely belonged to the second class. He then asked me to classify myself and I became rattled. Don Juan was practically on the ground, bent over with laughter.

He urged me again to classify myself, and reluctantly I suggested I might be a combination of the three.

"Don't give me that combination nonsense," he said, still laughing. "We are simple beings, each of us is one of the three types. And as far as I am concerned, you belong to the second class. *Stalkers* call them farts."

I began to protest that his scheme of classification was demeaning. But I stopped myself just as I was about to go into a long tirade. Instead I commented that if it were true that there are only three types of personalities, all of us are trapped in one of those three categories for life with no hope of change or redemption.

He agreed that that was exactly the case. Except that one avenue for redemption remained. Sorcerers had long ago learned that only our personal self-reflection fell into one of the categories.

"The trouble with us is that we take ourselves seriously," he said. "Whichever category our self-image falls into only matters because of our self-importance. If we weren't self-important, it wouldn't matter at all which category we fell into.

"I'll always be a fart," he continued, his body shaking with laughter. "And so will you. But now I am a fart who doesn't take himself seriously, while you still do."

I was indignant. I wanted to argue with him, but could not muster the energy for it.

In the empty plaza, the reverberation of his laughter was eerie.

He changed the subject then and reeled off the basic cores he had discussed with me: the manifestations of the spirit, the knock of the spirit, the trickery of the spirit, the descent of the spirit, the requirement of *intent*, and handling *intent*. He repeated them as if he were giving my memory a chance to retain them fully. And then, he succinctly highlighted everything he had told me about them. It was as if he were deliberately making me store all that information in the intensity of that moment.

I remarked that the basic cores were still a mystery to me. I felt very apprehensive about my ability to understand them. He was giving me the impression that he was about to dismiss the topic, and I had not grasped its meaning at all.

I insisted that I had to ask him more questions about the abstract cores.

He seemed to assess what I was saying, then he quietly nodded his head.

"This topic was also very difficult for me," he said.

"And I, too, asked many questions. I was perhaps a tinge more self-centered than you. And very nasty. Nagging was the only way I knew of asking questions. You yourself are rather a belligerent inquisitor. At the end, of course, you and I are equally annoying, but for different reasons."

There was only one more thing don Juan added to our discussion of the basic cores before he changed the subject: that they revealed themselves extremely slowly, erratically advancing and retreating.

"I can't repeat often enough that every man whose assemblage point moves can move it further," he began. "And the only reason we need a teacher is to spur us on mercilessly. Otherwise our natural reaction is to stop to congratulate ourselves for having covered so much ground."

He said that we were both good examples of our odious tendency to go easy on ourselves. His benefactor, fortunately, being the stupendous *stalker* he was, had not spared him.

Don Juan said that in the course of their nighttime journeys in the wilderness, the nagual Julian had lectured him extensively on the nature of self-importance and the movement of the assemblage point. For the nagual Julian, self-importance was a monster that had three thousand heads. And one could face up to it and destroy it in any of three ways. The first way was to sever each head one at a time; the second was to reach that mysterious state of being called the place of no pity, which destroyed self-importance by slowly starving it; and the third was to pay for the instantaneous annihilation of the three-thousand-headed monster with one's symbolic death.

The nagual Julian recommended the third alternative. But he told don Juan that he could consider himself fortunate if he got the chance to choose. For it was the spirit that usually determined which way the sorcerer was to go, and it was the duty of the sorcerer to follow.

Don Juan said that, as he had guided me, his benefactor guided him to cut off the three thousand heads of self-importance, one by one, but that the results had been quite different. While I had responded very well, he had not responded at all.

"Mine was a peculiar condition," he went on. "From the moment my benefactor *saw* me lying on the road with a bullet hole in my chest, he knew I was the new nagual. He acted accordingly and moved my assemblage point as soon as my health permitted it. And I saw with great ease a field of energy in the form of that monstrous man. But this accomplishment, instead of helping as it was supposed to, hindered any further movement of my assemblage point. And while the assemblage points of the other apprentices moved steadily, mine remained fixed at the level of being able to *see* the monster."

"But didn't your benefactor tell you what was going on?" I asked, truly baffled by the unnecessary complication.

"My benefactor didn't believe in handing down knowledge," don Juan said. "He thought that knowledge imparted that way lacked effectiveness. It was never there when one needed it. On the other hand, if knowledge was only insinuated, the person who was interested would devise ways to claim that knowledge."

Don Juan said that the difference between his method of teaching and his benefactor's was that he himself believed one should have the freedom to choose. His benefactor did not.

"Didn't your benefactor's teacher, the nagual Elías, tell you what was happening?" I insisted.

"He tried," don Juan said, and sighed, "but I was truly impossible. I knew everything. I just let the two men talk my ear off and never listened to a thing they were saying.''

In order to deal with that impasse, the nagual Julian decided to force don Juan to accomplish once again, but in a different way, a free movement of his assemblage point.

I interrupted him to ask whether this had happened before or after his experience at the river. Don Juan's stories did not have the chronological order I would have liked.

''This happened several months afterward,'' he replied. ''And don't you think for an instant that because I experienced that split perception I was really changed; that I was wiser or more sober. Nothing of the sort.

''Consider what happens to you,'' he went on. ''I have not only broken your continuity time and time again, I have ripped it to shreds, and look at you; you still act as if you were intact. That is a supreme accomplishment of magic, of *intending*.

''I was the same. For a while, I would reel under the impact of what I was experiencing and then I would forget and tie up the severed ends as if nothing had happened. That was why my benefactor believed that we can only really change if we die.''

Returning to his story, don Juan said that the nagual used Tulio, the unsociable member of his household, to deliver a new shattering blow to his psychological continuity.

Don Juan said that all the apprentices, including himself, had never been in total agreement about anything except that Tulio was a contemptibly arrogant little man. They hated Tulio because he either avoided them or snubbed them. He treated them all with such disdain that they felt like dirt. They were all convinced that Tulio never spoke to them because he had nothing to say; and that his most salient feature, his arrogant aloofness, was a cover for his timidity.

Yet in spite of his unpleasant personality, to the chagrin of all the apprentices, Tulio had undue influence on the household—especially on the nagual Julian, who seemed to dote on him.

One morning the nagual Julian sent all the apprentices on a day-long errand to the city. The only person left in the house, besides the older members of the household, was don Juan.

Around midday the nagual Julian headed for his study to do his daily bookkeeping. As he was going in, he casually asked don Juan to help him with the accounts.

Don Juan began to look through the receipts and soon realized that to continue he needed some information that Tulio, the overseer of the property, had, and had forgotten to note down.

The nagual Julian was definitely angry at Tulio's oversight, which pleased don Juan. The nagual impatiently ordered don Juan to find Tulio, who was out in the fields supervising the workers, and ask him to come to the study.

Don Juan, gloating at the idea of annoying Tulio, ran half a mile to the fields, accompanied, of course, by a field hand to protect him from the monstrous man. He found Tulio supervising the workers from a distance, as always. Don Juan had noticed that Tulio hated to come into direct contact with people and always watched them from afar.

In a harsh voice and with an exaggeratedly imperious manner, don Juan demanded that Tulio accompany him to the house because the nagual required his services. Tulio, his voice barely audible, replied that he was too busy at the moment, but that in about an hour he would be free to come.

Don Juan insisted, knowing that Tulio would not

bother to argue with him and would simply dismiss him with a turn of his head. He was shocked when Tulio began to yell obscenities at him. The scene was so out of character for Tulio that even the farm workers stopped their labor and looked at one another questioningly. Don Juan was sure they had never heard Tulio raise his voice, much less yell improprieties. His own surprise was so great that he laughed nervously, which made Tulio extremely angry. He even hurled a rock at the frightened don Juan, who fled.

Don Juan and his bodyguard immediately ran back to the house. At the front door they found Tulio. He was quietly talking and laughing with some of the women. As was his custom, he turned his head away, ignoring don Juan. Don Juan began angrily to chastise him for socializing there when the nagual wanted him in his study. Tulio and the women looked at don Juan as if he had gone mad.

But Tulio was not his usual self that day. Instantly he yelled at don Juan to shut his damned mouth and mind his own damned business. He blatantly accused don Juan of trying to put him in a bad light with the nagual Julian.

The women showed their dismay by gasping loudly and looking disapprovingly at don Juan. They tried to calm Tulio. Don Juan ordered Tulio to go to the nagual's study and explain the accounts. Tulio told him to go to hell.

Don Juan was shaking with anger. The simple task of asking for the accounts had turned into a nightmare. He controlled his temper. The women were watching him intently, which angered him all over again. In a silent rage he ran to the nagual's study. Tulio and the women went back to talking and laughing quietly as though they were celebrating a private joke.

Don Juan's surprise was total when he entered the

study and found Tulio sitting at the nagual's desk absorbed in his bookkeeping. Don Juan made a supreme effort and controlled his anger. He smiled at Tulio. He no longer had the need to confront Tulio. He had suddenly understood that the nagual Julian was using Tulio to test him, to see if he would lose his temper. He would not give him that satisfaction.

Without looking up from his accounts, Tulio said that if don Juan was looking for the nagual, he would probably find him at the other end of the house.

Don Juan raced to the other end of the house to find the nagual Julian walking slowly around the patio with Tulio at his side. The nagual appeared to be engrossed in his conversation with Tulio. Tulio gently nudged the nagual's sleeve and said in a low voice that his assistant was there.

The nagual matter-of-factly explained to don Juan everything about the account they had been working on. It was a long, detailed, and thorough explanation. He said then that all don Juan had to do was to bring the account book from the study so that they could make the entry and have Tulio sign it.

Don Juan could not understand what was happening. The detailed explanation and the nagual's matter-of-fact tone had brought everything into the realm of mundane affairs. Tulio impatiently ordered don Juan to hurry up and fetch the book, because he was busy. He was needed somewhere else.

By now don Juan had resigned himself to being a clown. He knew that the nagual was up to something; he had that strange look in his eyes which don Juan always associated with his beastly jokes. Besides, Tulio had talked more that day than he had in the entire two years don Juan had been in the house.

Without uttering a word, don Juan went back to the study. And as he had expected, Tulio had gotten there first. He was sitting on the corner of the desk, waiting for don Juan, impatiently tapping the floor with the hard heel of his boot. He held out the ledger don Juan was after, gave it to him, and told him to be on his way.

Despite being prepared, don Juan was astonished. He stared at the man, who became angry and abusive. Don Juan had to struggle not to explode. He kept saying to himself that all this was merely a test of his attitude. He had visions of being thrown out of the house if he failed the test.

In the midst of his turmoil, he was still able to wonder about the speed with which Tulio managed always to be one jump ahead of him.

Don Juan certainly anticipated that Tulio would be waiting with the nagual. Still, when he saw him there, although he was not surprised, he was incredulous. He had raced through the house, following the shortest route. There was no way that Tulio could run faster than he. Furthermore, if Tulio had run, he would have had to run right alongside don Juan.

The nagual Julian took the account book from don Juan with an air of indifference. He made the entry; Tulio signed it. Then they continued talking about the account, disregarding don Juan, whose eyes were fixed on Tulio. Don Juan wanted to figure out what kind of test they were putting him through. It had to be a test of his attitude, he thought. After all, in that house, his attitude had always been the issue.

The nagual dismissed don Juan, saying he wanted to be alone with Tulio to discuss business. Don Juan immediately went looking for the women to find out what they would say about this strange situation. He had gone ten feet when he encountered two of the women and Tulio. The three of them were caught up in a most animated conversation. He saw them before they had seen him, so he ran back to the nagual. Tulio was there, talking with the nagual.

An incredible suspicion entered don Juan's mind. He ran to the study; Tulio was immersed in his book-keeping and did not even acknowledge don Juan. Don Juan asked him what was going on. Tulio was his usual self this time: he did not answer or look at don Juan.

Don Juan had at that moment another inconceivable thought. He ran to the stable, saddled two horses and asked his morning bodyguard to accompany him again. They galloped to the place where they had seen Tulio earlier. He was exactly where they had left him. He did not speak to don Juan. He shrugged his shoulders and turned his head when don Juan questioned him.

Don Juan and his companion galloped back to the house. He left the man to care for the horses and rushed into the house. Tulio was lunching with the women. And Tulio was also talking to the nagual. And Tulio was also working on the books.

Don Juan sat down and felt the cold sweat of fear. He knew that the nagual Julian was testing him with one of his horrible jokes. He reasoned that he had three courses of action. He could behave as if nothing out of the ordinary was happening; he could figure out the test himself; or, since the nagual had engraved in his mind that he was there to explain anything don Juan wanted, he could confront the nagual and ask for clarification.

He decided to ask. He went to the nagual and asked him to explain what was being done to him. The nagual was alone then, still working on his accounts. He put the ledger aside and smiled at don Juan. He said that the twenty-one not-doings he had taught don Juan to perform were the tools that could sever the three thousand heads of self-importance, but that those tools had not been effective with don Juan at all. Thus, he was trying the second method for destroying self-importance which meant putting don Juan into the state of being called the place of no pity.

Don Juan was convinced then that the nagual Julian was utterly mad. Hearing him talk about not-doings or about monsters with three thousand heads or about places of no pity, don Juan felt almost sorry for him.

The nagual Julian very calmly asked don Juan to go to the storage shed in the back of the house and ask Tulio to come out.

Don Juan sighed and did his best not to burst out laughing. The nagual's methods were too obvious. Don Juan knew that the nagual wanted to continue the test, using Tulio.

Don Juan stopped his narration and asked me what I thought about Tulio's behavior. I said that, guided by what I knew about the sorcerers' world, I would say that Tulio was a sorcerer and somehow he was moving his own assemblage point in a very sophisticated manner to give don Juan the impression that he was in four places at the same time.

"So what do you think I found in the shed?" don Juan asked with a big grin.

"I would say either you found Tulio or you didn't find anybody," I replied.

"But if either of these had happened, there would have been no shock to my continuity," don Juan said.

I tried to imagine bizarre things and I proposed that perhaps he found Tulio's *dreaming body*. I reminded don Juan that he himself had done something similar to me with one of the members of his party of sorcerers.

"No," don Juan retorted. "What I found was a joke that has no equivalent in reality. And yet it was not bizarre; it was not out of this world. What do you think it was?"

I told don Juan I hated riddles. I said that with all the bizarre things he had made me experience, the only things I could conceive would be more bizarreness, and since that was ruled out, I gave up guessing.

"When I went into that shed I was prepared to find that Tulio was hiding," don Juan said. "I was sure that the next part of the test was going to be an infuriating game of hide-and-seek. Tulio was going to drive me crazy hiding inside that shed.

"But nothing I had prepared myself for happened. I walked into that shed and found four Tulios."

"What do you mean, four Tulios?" I asked.

"There were four men in that shed," don Juan replied. "And all of them were Tulio. Can you imagine my surprise? All of them were sitting in the same position, their legs crossed and pressed tightly together. They were waiting for me. I looked at them and ran away screaming.

"My benefactor held me down on the ground outside the door. And then, truly horrified, I saw how the four Tulios came out of the shed and advanced toward me. I screamed and screamed while the Tulios pecked me with their hard fingers, like huge birds attacking. I screamed until I felt something give in me and I entered a state of superb indifference. Never in all my life had I felt something so extraordinary. I brushed off the Tulios and got up. They had just been tickling me. I went directly to the nagual and asked him to explain the four men to me."

What the nagual Julian explained to don Juan was that those four men were the paragons of *stalking*. Their names had been invented by their teacher, the nagual Elías, who, as an exercise in controlled folly, had taken the Spanish numerals *uno, dos, tres, cuatro*, added them to the name of Tulio, and obtained in that manner the names Tuliúno, Tulíodo, Tulítre, and Tulícuatro.

The nagual Julian introduced each in turn to don Juan. The four men were standing in a row. Don Juan faced each of them and nodded, and each nodded to him. The nagual said the four men were *stalkers* of such extraordinary talent, as don Juan had just corroborated, that praise was meaningless. The Tulios were the nagual Elías's triumph; they were the essence of unobtrusiveness. They were such magnificent *stalkers* that, for all practical purposes, only one of them existed. Although people saw and dealt with them daily, nobody outside the members of the household knew that there were four Tulios.

Don Juan understood with perfect clarity everything the nagual Julian was saying about the men. Because of his unusual clarity, he knew he had reached the place of no pity. And he understood, all by himself, that the place of no pity was a position of the assemblage point, a position which rendered self-pity inoperative. But don Juan also knew that his insight and wisdom were extremely transitory. Unavoidably, his assemblage point would return to its point of departure.

When the nagual asked don Juan if he had any questions, he realized that he would be better off paying close attention to the nagual's explanation than speculating about his own foresightedness.

Don Juan wanted to know how the Tulios created the impression that there was only one person. He was extremely curious, because observing them together he realized they were not really that alike. They wore the same clothes. They were about the same size, age, and configuration. But that was the extent of their similarity. And yet, even as he watched them he could have sworn that there was only one Tulio.

The nagual Julian explained that the human eye was trained to focus only on the most salient features of anything, and that those salient features were known beforehand. Thus, the *stalkers'* art was to create an impression by presenting the features they chose, features they knew the eyes of the onlooker were bound to notice. By artfully reinforcing certain impressions, *stalkers* were able to create on the part of the onlooker an unchallengeable conviction as to what their eyes had perceived.

The nagual Julian said that when don Juan first arrived dressed in his woman's clothes, the women of his party were delighted and laughed openly. But the man with them, who happened to be Tulítre, immediately provided don Juan with the first Tulio impression. He half turned away to hide his face, shrugged his shoulders disdainfully, as if all of it was boring to him, and walked away—to laugh his head off in private—while the women helped to consolidate that first impression by acting apprehensive, almost annoyed, at the unsociability of the man.

From that moment on, any Tulio who was around don Juan reinforced that impression and further perfected it until don Juan's eye could not catch anything except what was being fed to him.

Tuliúno spoke then and said that it had taken them about three months of very careful and consistent actions to have don Juan blind to anything except what he was guided to expect. After three months, his blindness was so pronounced that the Tulios were no longer even careful. They acted normal in the house. They even ceased wearing identical clothes, and don Juan did not notice the difference.

When other apprentices were brought into the house, however, the Tulios had to start all over again. This time the challenge was hard, because there were many apprentices and they were sharp.

Don Juan asked Tuliúno about Tulio's appearance. Tuliúno answered that the nagual Elías maintained appearance was the essence of controlled folly, and *stalkers* created appearance by *intending* them, rather than by producing them with the aid of props. Props created artificial appearances that looked false to the eye. In this respect, *intending* appearances was exclusively an exercise for *stalkers*.

Tulítre spoke next. He said appearances were solicited from the spirit. Appearances were asked, were forcefully called on; they were never invented rationally. Tulio's appearance had to be called from the spirit. And to facilitate that the nagual Elías put all four of them together into a very small, out-of-the-way storage room, and there the spirit spoke to them. The spirit told them that first they had to *intend* their homogeneity. After four weeks of total isolation, homogeneity came to them.

The nagual Elías said that *intent* had fused them together and that they had acquired the certainty that their individuality would go undetected. Now they had to call up the appearance that would be perceived by the onlooker. And they got busy, calling *intent* for the Tulios' appearance don Juan had seen. They had to work very hard to perfect it. They focused, under the direction of their teacher, on all the details that would make it perfect.

The four Tulios gave don Juan a demonstration of Tulio's most salient features. These were: very forceful gestures of disdain and arrogance; abrupt turns of the face to the right as if in anger; twists of their upper bodies as if to hide part of the face with the left shoulder; angry sweeps of a hand over the eyes as if to brush hair off the forehead; and the gait of an agile but impatient person who is too nervous to decide which way to go.

Don Juan said that those details of behavior and dozens of others had made Tulio an unforgettable character. In fact, he was so unforgettable that in order to project Tulio on don Juan and the other apprentices as if on a screen, any of the four men needed only to insinuate a feature, and don Juan and the apprentices would automatically supply the rest.

Don Juan said that because of the tremendous consistency of the input, Tulio was for him and the others the essence of a disgusting man. But at the same time, if they searched deep inside themselves, they would have acknowledged that Tulio was haunting. He was nimble, mysterious, and gave, wittingly or unwittingly, the impression of being a shadow.

Don Juan asked Tuliúno how they had called *intent*. Tuliúno explained that *stalkers* called *intent* loudly. Usually *intent* was called from within a small, dark, isolated room. A candle was placed on a black table with the flame just a few inches before the eyes; then the word *intent* was voiced slowly, enunciated clearly and deliberately as many times as one felt was needed. The pitch of the voice rose or fell without any thought.

Tuliúno stressed that the indispensable part of the act of calling *intent* was a total concentration on what was *intended*. In their case, the concentration was on their homogeneity and on Tulio's appearance. After they had been fused by *intent*, it still took them a couple of years to build up the certainty that their homogeneity and Tulio's appearance would be realities to the onlookers.

I asked don Juan what he thought of their way of calling *intent*. And he said that his benefactor, like the nagual Elías, was a bit more given to ritual than he himself was, therefore, they preferred paraphernalia such as candles, dark closets, and black tables.

I casually remarked that I was terribly attracted to ritual behavior, myself. Ritual seemed to me essential in focusing one's attention. Don Juan took my remark seriously. He said he had *seen* that my body, as an energy field, had a feature which he knew all the sorcerers of ancient times had had and avidly sought in others: a bright area in the lower right side of the luminous cocoon. That brightness was associated with resourcefulness and a bent toward morbidity. The dark sorcerers of those times took pleasure in harnessing that coveted feature and attaching it to man's dark side.

"Then there is an evil side to man," I said jubilantly. "You always deny it. You always say that evil doesn't exist, that only power exists."

I surprised myself with this outburst. In one instant, all my Catholic background was brought to bear on me and the Prince of Darkness loomed larger than life.

Don Juan laughed until he was coughing.

"Of course, there is a dark side to us," he said. "We kill wantonly, don't we? We burn people in the name of God. We destroy ourselves; we obliterate life on this planet; we destroy the earth. And then we dress in robes and the Lord speaks directly to us. And what does the Lord tell us? He says that we should be good boys or he is going to punish us. The Lord has been threatening us for centuries and it doesn't make any difference. Not because we are evil, but because we are dumb. Man has a dark side, yes, and it's called stupidity."

I did not say anything else, but silently I applauded and thought with pleasure that don Juan was a masterful debater. Once again he was turning my words back on me.

After a moment's pause, don Juan explained that in the same measure that ritual forced the average man to construct huge churches that were monuments to self-importance, ritual also forced sorcerers to construct edifices of morbidity and obsession. As a result, it was the duty of every nagual to guide awareness so it would fly toward the abstract, free of liens and mortgages.

"What do you mean, don Juan, by liens and mortgages?" I asked.

"Ritual can trap our attention better than anything I can think of," he said, "but it also demands a very high price. That high price is morbidity; and morbidity could have the heaviest liens and mortgages on our awareness."

Don Juan said that human awareness was like an immense haunted house. The awareness of everyday life was like being sealed in one room of that immense house for life. We entered the room through a magical opening: birth. And we exited through another such magical opening: death.

Sorcerers, however, were capable of finding still another opening and could leave that sealed room while still alive. A superb attainment. But their astounding accomplishment was that when they escaped from that sealed room they chose freedom. They chose to leave that immense, haunted house entirely instead of getting lost in other parts of it.

Morbidity was the antithesis of the surge of energy awareness needed to reach freedom. Morbidity made sorcerers lose their way and become trapped in the intricate, dark byways of the unknown.

I asked don Juan if there was any morbidity in the Tulios.

"Strangeness is not morbidity," he replied. "The Tulios were performers who were being coached by the spirit itself."

"What was the nagual Elías's reason for training the Tulios as he did?" I asked.

Don Juan peered at me and laughed loudly. At that instant the lights of the plaza were turned on. He got up from his favorite bench and rubbed it with the palm of his hand, as if it were a pet.

"Freedom," he said. "He wanted their freedom from perceptual convention. And he taught them to be artists. *Stalking* is an art. For a sorcerer, since he's not a patron or a seller of art, the only thing of importance about a work of art is that it can be accomplished.''

We stood by the bench, watching the evening strollers milling around. The story of the four Tulios had left me with a sense of foreboding. Don Juan suggested that I return home; the long drive to L.A., he said, would give my assemblage point a respite from all the moving it had done in the past few days.

"The nagual's company is very tiring," he went on. "It produces a strange fatigue; it could even be injurious."

I assured him that I was not tired at all, and that his company was anything but injurious to me. In fact, his company affected me like a narcotic—I couldn't do without it. This sounded as if I were flattering him, but I really meant what I said.

We strolled around the plaza three or four times in complete silence.

"Go home and think about the basic cores of the sorcery stories," don Juan said with a note of finality in his voice. "Or rather, don't think about them, but make your assemblage point move toward the place of silent knowledge. Moving the assemblage point is everything, but it means nothing if it's not a sober, controlled movement. So, close the door of self-reflection. Be impeccable and you'll have the energy to reach the place of silent knowledge."